BUILDING
SOCIAL
PROBLEM-SOLVING
SKILLS

Maurice J. Elias
John F. Clabby

BUILDING SOCIAL PROBLEM-SOLVING SKILLS

Guidelines from a School-Based Program

Jossey-Bass Publishers · San Francisco

Copyright © 1992 by Jossey-Bass Inc., Publishers, 350 Sansome Street,
San Francisco, California 94104. Copyright under International, Pan
American, and Universal Copyright Conventions. All rights reserved.
No part of this book may be reproduced in any form—except for brief
quotation (not to exceed 1,000 words) in a review or professional
work—without permission in writing from the publishers.

Library of Congress Cataloging-in-Publication Data

Elias, Maurice J.
    Building social problem-solving skills : guidelines from a school-
based program / Maurice J. Elias, John F. Clabby.
      p.   cm.—(Jossey-Bass social and behavioral science series)
(Jossey-Bass education series)
    Includes bibliographical references and index.
    ISBN 1-55542-433-3
    1. Problem solving—Study and teaching. 2. Decision-making—Study
and teaching.   3. Social skills—Study and teaching.   4. Social
adjustment—Study and teaching.   I. Clabby, John F., date.
LB1062.5.E43   1992
370.11'5—dc 20   91-41080
                                                  CIP

FIRST EDITION
HB Printing   10 9 8 7 6 5 4 3 2   *Code 9231*

A joint publication in the
Jossey-Bass
Social and Behavioral Science Series
and the
Jossey-Bass Education Series

Psychoeducational Interventions: Guidebooks for School Practitioners

Consulting Editors

Charles A. Maher
Rutgers University

Joseph E. Zins
University of Cincinnati

Contents

ix

Contents

Preface

In 1990, the United States set forth a formal set of national goals for education. In 1991, the government put forth its completed health objectives for the year 2000. Both of the policy statements emphasize the necessity of socializing our youth to become responsible citizens and thoughtful, healthy, drug-free, productive members of society. To turn these policies into realities—realities accessible to all segments of the population, regardless of race, cultural background, or socioeconomic status—requires sound, proven models. In this book, we present one such model.

Our approach seeks to bolster what we believe to be the most basic of social competencies: social problem-solving skills, which refer to the areas of self-control, social awareness, group participation, and interpersonal decision making, particularly of the kind that occur in everyday contexts or under stressful circumstances. It has been field tested over a number of years through the Improving Social Awareness–Social Problem Solving (ISA-SPS) Project, which we began in 1979 with Tom Schuyler, then a school principal in Middlesex Borough, New Jersey. Using action research, we have developed specific approaches for enhancing students' social problem solving; however, we have gone beyond this and extracted the principles that allow these approaches to work in the schools. Thus, we have been able to combine principles and practices in a way that we believe is unique in a book of this kind.

In writing this book, we decided to make maximum use of our individual roles within the ISA-SPS Project, to allow us to speak most clearly to readers whose identity may be that of researcher, practitioner, or policy maker in a broad range of fields, including education; human services; mental health; social work; counseling; or school, community, clinical, or preventive psychology. National goals for education, health, and mental health cannot be attained without multidisciplinary collaboration. We have authored separately the five parts of this book to bring forward most vividly the perspectives that have fueled our lively partnership and flourishing project, and to better allow these perspectives to be shared and bridged so that common action can be taken.

Over the life of the project, Maurice J. Elias has taken the primary role of conceptualizing and directing the research, application, and public policy areas of the project. Therefore, he has authored the parts of the book most germane to those areas, Parts One, Two, and Five. Part One provides a conceptual and pragmatic linkage of decision making and problem solving with the social competencies needed to manage healthily, happily, and productively in today's society and the society in which current and future generations of children will become adults. In Part Two, a "user-friendly" action-research framework is used to describe procedures for developing, implementing, monitoring, evaluating, and institutionalizing an SPS or related program. Illustrations are drawn from the history of the ISA-SPS Project, selected to emphasize the confluence of forces that determine the progress and success of *any* research or action project, whether it involves one classroom or multiple school districts. The specific empirical underpinnings of the ISA-SPS Project are illustrated in Chapter Four through a review of the project's empirical findings over a decade. Part Five takes a look at the cutting edge of our work. The action-research framework is presented as a means by which we have been able to shape the social decision-making approach to circumstances in schools requiring new adaptations and applications. These illustrations are provided to guide readers in making the inevitable modifications that implementation in local school contexts will require.

The final chapter provides an overview of key areas that school-based professionals will need to address as they work to enhance the social competence of children and adolescents.

Throughout the life of the project, John F. Clabby has taken the primary role of directing the administrative, training, and classroom consultation areas of the project. He has authored the parts pertaining to these areas and has endeavored to speak "practitioner to practitioner." Part Three is organized around a practical set of key elements that comprise the structure of effective, enduring, school-based interventions. Chapter Five describes the process of getting started, which involves matching one's program ideas to setting needs and conducting initial planning. Subsequent chapters address the selection of appropriate materials and describe the social decision-making and social problem-solving curriculum that has formed the core of the ISA-SPS Project's curriculum-based approach. The focus is on grades K–12, featuring samples of SPS lessons at elementary, middle, and high school levels that teach the foundations of SPS thinking as well as applications of SPS to a specific need of older students: preparation for the world of work. Part Four is aimed at preparing school-based professionals for their roles as leaders and developers of workshops, program consultants, and counselors in the area of social decision making and problem solving. Samples are provided of professional development and parent education workshop procedures used successfully in school settings.

As we thought about organizing this book, we were driven by an overall question: what do we wish we had had as a guide when we began our work in 1979, and what can give impetus to the work that needs to be done now and over the next decade? We both recognized the need for a conceptual and empirical base *and* a practical procedural guide. Neither a historical accounting, a "cookbook" manual, nor a research summary would alone suffice to move the field toward systematically promoting students' social problem-solving abilities. This book is designed to provide current and future professionals in all disciplines relating to the schools with stimulation and inspiration for sustained action. As such, it becomes part of a growing effort to bridge the gap between ideas and implementation.

We envision this book as being used in graduate coursework in school, community, and preventive psychology; education; and school counseling. Further, we see it as valuable for researchers and practitioners in those fields and to policy makers on school boards, governmental agencies, and the legislature. We say this with confidence because of the responses we have received as our work has been read and used in all of those arenas.

Acknowledgments

Numerous individuals have contributed to this work since 1979, more than we ever could hope to thank explicitly. We single out for special acknowledgment our closest colleagues, Thomas Schuyler, Linda Bruene, Charlotte Hett, Maryellen Taylor, Louise Krikorian, Maureen Papke, Michael Gara, Virginia Brinson, Gary Lamson, Howard Rubinstein, Leslie Branden-Muller, Bill Commins, Pat Dooley, Barbara Zak, and Margo Hunter. Also, this book never would have come to fruition without the tireless editorial work of Joseph Zins, the inspiring vision of Gracia Alkema, and the production talents at Jossey-Bass. We are grateful for their help.

We would like to express personal thanks to other very important people.

Maurice Elias would like to thank the hundreds of undergraduates and many graduate students who have contributed to the intellectual vigor and practical appeal of the ISA-SPS Project's work. Similarly, many teachers and principals have shared their suggestions with us and thereby have joined us in building a curricular approach we can all share proudly. Among many sources of professional support, five deserve special acknowledgment for their contributions of action-research acumen and much-appreciated collegiality and friendship: Barry Barbarasch, Ed Dunkelblau, Brian Friedlander, Steven Tobias, and Roger Weissberg. Finally, he is especially grateful for the love, nurturance, confidence, and encouragement provided by Ellen Elias and the discursive duo, Sara and Samara. It is to the three of them that he dedicates his work.

John Clabby would like to thank Terry Brennan, Richard Flamini, Neal Geminder, Joseph Kovaleski, and Stefani Sheppa for their early comments on the ASPIRE lessons and Dan Davenport,

John Kazmark, Howard Rubinstein, and Lisa Webster for their more recent comments. Appreciation is also extended to Jane Carroll and Kathie Marcinkiewicz for their skillful preparation of portions of the manuscript. Finally, appreciation is expressed to his children, Lauren, Jack, Sheila, and Patrick, and their mother and his wife, Wendy, who is the source of his inspiration and the person to whom he dedicates his work.

February 1992   Maurice J. Elias
                                                   Highland Park, New Jersey

                                                   John F. Clabby
                                                   Red Bank, New Jersey

The Authors

Maurice J. Elias is associate professor of psychology and coordinator of the Internship Program in Applied, School, and Community Psychology at Rutgers University. He received his B.A. degree (1974) in psychology from Queens College of the City University of New York and his M.A. (1977) and Ph.D. (1980) degrees in clinical-community psychology from the University of Connecticut.

Elias's main research activities have been in the area of preventive mental health and social competence promotion. Most recently, he has been studying the long-term impact of implementing so-called "model" prevention programs in public schools. Since 1985, he has served as cochair of the William T. Grant Foundation-supported action-research Consortium on the School-Based Promotion of Social Competence. He also consults at numerous school and mental health settings to help develop enduring programs to enhance the competence of children and adolescents. In 1986, he received an award from the American Psychological Association and the American Psychological Foundation for excellence in psychology in the media, for his book *Teach Your Child Decision Making* (1986, with J. F. Clabby). In 1988, he received honorable mention for his ongoing newspaper column "Parenting Matters" (*Central New Jersey Home News*). Elias received the prestigious Lela Rowland Prevention Award (with T. Schuyler and J. F. Clabby) from the National Mental Health Association in 1988.

In the following year, his work in social decision making and problem solving was approved by the U.S. Department of Education's Program Effectiveness Panel as a national program for excellence in education, and dissemination funding has been provided by the National Diffusion Network. In 1990, Elias received from the American Psychological Association Division of Consulting Psychology the National Psychological Consultants to Management Award (with J. F. Clabby) for his approach to the development, implementation, evaluation, and maintenance of school-based programs.

Other books by Elias include *Social Decision-Making Skills: A Curriculum Guide for the Elementary Grades* (1989, with J. F. Clabby), *Problem Solving/Decision Making for Social and Academic Success: A School-Based Approach* (1990, with S. Tobias), *Social Decision Making in the Middle School: Models for Excellence* (in press), and *Parenting with Pride: Raising Your Children with Thoughtfulness and Self-Respect* (in preparation, with J. F. Clabby and C. Hett).

John F. Clabby is the chief psychologist for the University of Medicine and Dentistry of New Jersey–Community Mental Health Center (UMDNJ-CMHC) at Piscataway, where he is also the director of the Social Problem Solving Program. Clabby is also an assistant clinical professor of psychiatry at UMDNJ–Robert Wood Johnson Medical School. He received his B.A. degree (1972) from Fordham University in sociology, his M.A. degree (1975) from Montclair State College in psychology, and his Ph.D. degree (1977) from the University of Southern Mississippi in school psychology.

Clabby's main professional activities have focused on training others in the development and implementation of social problem-solving/decision-making programs, and the use of this approach in psychotherapy and consultation practice. Clabby is a certified school psychologist in Connecticut and New Jersey and is also a licensed psychologist in those states, maintaining a private practice in the Monmouth County, New Jersey, area. In 1986, he received the National Psychology Award for Excellence in the Media (book category) from the American Psychological Association and American Psychological Foundation for *Teach Your Child Decision Making* (1986, with M. J. Elias). In 1988, Clabby was a co-recipient (with T. Schuyler and M. J. Elias) of the Lela Rowland Prevention Award from the National Mental Health Association, for outstanding work in the area of prevention. In 1989, his work (with M. J. Elias) in social decision making and problem solving was approved by the U.S. Department of Education's Program Effectiveness Panel as a national program for excellence in education, and dissemination funding has been provided by that agency's National Diffusion Network. In 1990, he was given (with M. J. Elias) the National Psychological Consultants to Management Award for excellence in consulting psychology, awarded by the American Psychological Association Division of Consulting Psychology.

Clabby is also coauthor of *Social Decision-Making Skills: A Curriculum Guide for the Elementary Grades* (1989, with M. J. Elias).

BUILDING
SOCIAL
PROBLEM-SOLVING
SKILLS

PART ONE

Conceptual Foundations
of
Social Problem Solving

The area of social decision making and problem solving has societal and conceptual roots that make it highly suitable to serve as an intervention model and research focus for the 1990s and beyond. Our work in this area has been operationalized through a longitudinal, interdisciplinary action-research project, the Improving Social Awareness–Social Problem Solving (ISA-SPS) Project. Part One will examine the *social context* that defines the competencies that children need both to cope in the present and to manage successfully in their future roles. A second focus is the *conceptual background* undergirding our emphasis on social competence and prevention and the specific influences on our social decision-making approach. It is important for researchers, practitioners, and policy makers to have a clear sense of the importance of enhancing the social competence of children and adolescents and its links to the goals of education, citizenship, and the workplace. By the conclusion of Part One, the reader should understand the perspectives that guide our work and fuel our continued enthusiasm for the social decision-making and problem-solving approach as a viable and essential aspect of building children's social competence.

Part One serves as a springboard to Part Two, which uses an action-research framework to "take apart" our work from a historical-developmental perspective. This allows readers to trace

1

the action-research principles that have forged the major emphases and structures of the ISA-SPS Project and guided the elaboration and extension of the project's curriculum-based approach. Through the use of the ISA-SPS Project as an example, it is intended that practitioners and researchers will be able to begin to use an action-research model in their own settings, to plan, manage, evaluate, and document the work being done in prevention and social competence enhancement. The area of documentation is essential, for without it, there is little way to capture the implementation and contextual details needed for the replication and dissemination of sound research and practice. Part Two concludes with a presentation of the specific empirical evidence gathered over a decade of action-research inquiry into the workings of the ISA-SPS Project. This is provided both to establish the research base for the interventions to be described in Parts Three and Four and to illustrate how diverse sources of action-research evidence can be combined to document a curriculum-based, school-centered social decision-making and problem-solving approach to enhancing social competence.

Chapter One

Enabling Students to Meet Future Challenges: Essential Social Problem-Solving Skills

If children are to experience healthy relationships and occupy meaningful and productive roles in society as adults, they must be competent at communicating and working cooperatively with others. They need to be able to express their own opinions and beliefs, to understand and appreciate the perspective of others who differ from them in background, needs, or experiences, and to become skilled at reasoned disagreement, negotiation, and compromise as methods of solving problems when their own needs or interests conflict with those of others. Indeed, in the face of decreasing resources and increasing global interdependence, it can be argued that such qualities are essential to our survival. The question, then, is not *whether* we must enhance children's social competencies, but rather *how* to accomplish this goal. (Battistich, Elias, & Branden-Muller, in press)

There is a need to act in a forceful way to ensure that current and future generations of children possess the skills they will require to be healthy, productive, and satisfied members of adult society. This need is a major impetus for educational reform and school restructuring, and schools will be at the center of efforts directed at providing the requisite skills. Leaders in many fields are recognizing that among the skills that all children will need are those that enable them to think clearly, make thoughtful decisions, and resolve in a satisfactory manner the many problems and challenges they will face in and out of school. This book describes work that has been done to help provide children with these needed skills.

That these skills are necessary and as important as what previous generations labeled as "basic" academic skills is no longer open to dispute, and evidence for this view will be presented in this chapter and the one that follows. Further, skills necessary for sound social decision making and problem solving have a role in closing the gaps among students, especially those who are within the special education system and those from low socioeconomic circumstances and cultural or ethnic backgrounds different from those of the mainstream in their communities. Keen social observers have decried the growing distance among students in our schools, a distance that is intellectual, social, economic, and political (Crabbe, 1989; London, 1987). Professionals and citizens working in and with the schools must recognize that it is unlikely that this distance will diminish spontaneously.

The Urgent Need for Action

In a society that seems so closely tied to mass media images of the present, messages about future calamities often are perceived only dimly. Yet history is replete with examples of civilizations and cultures that paid a heavy price for failing to heed available warnings. The staggering events in Eastern Europe and the Soviet Union beginning in 1989 show that dramatic change is possible but also frightening in its uncertainty. Are we strong enough to trade a known present for an unclear future?

On a lesser scale, this dilemma confronts American education and is played out in each state and local education authority, in both the public and private sectors. Do we dare to embark on change? Would it not be acceptable to let the "next" set of administrators deal with the difficulties on the horizon? After all, it is argued by some, the horizon is so far away.

There are many who believe that the horizon is almost within reach. Indeed, some hold that for minority and impoverished children and adolescents, there is no more time. Significant reports have been issued that reflect the growing sense of urgency in their topics: *A Nation at Risk* (National Commission on Excellence in Education, 1983), *Turning Points* (Carnegie Council on Adolescent Development, 1989), *Before It's Too Late* (Center for Early Adolescence, 1988), *Dealing with Dropouts* (Office of Educational Research and Improvement, 1987), *Within Our Reach* (Schorr, 1988), and *The Forgotten Half* (William T. Grant Commission on Work, Family, & Citizenship, 1988). Each report goes beyond decrying the present trends and offers feasible solutions toward which efforts can be initiated in the present. First, however, there must be a tangible "feel" for the reasons impelling action.

Beyond Statistics

Certainly, data show that large segments of our teenage-and-younger population are exposed to conditions that are likely to harm their psychosocial growth. Family disruptions seem to head everyone's list, because of both the specific turmoil caused by the process of separation and divorce and the harsh realities faced by upward of eight million "latchkey" children and the over one-half million teenagers who have become parents each year since 1982. These children—and their children—face significant risks of alcohol and other drug abuse and a variety of behavioral and emotional problems that may lead them to mental health services or into the correctional system (Carnegie Council on Adolescent Development, 1989; London, 1987; William T. Grant Commission on Work, Family, and Citizenship, 1988).

These numbers, however, do not reveal several important facets of the problem. Schorr (1988) and Ramsey & Patterson (1989) have made clear, recent statements about the cyclic nature of what happens to children. Each has pointed out that children who "come through the system" do so with scars, even if they have not had difficulties "severe" enough to lead them to societal assistance or rehabilitative agents. They are impaired in their ability to form and sustain relationships, to parent, to become stable, productive members of the workforce, and to participate as planful, forward-thinking members of a democracy. Professionals, overwhelmed by demands for their services, have adopted a threshold that allows far too many children to "slip through the cracks." The often-verbalized notion that it is also "the parents' responsibility," while true, implies that parents can act as a form of safety net for their children. Unfortunately, the safety net is itself frayed and riddled with holes. When one is highly engaged in attempting to survive by meeting only visible and pressing demands, the tendency is to avoid taking on additional tasks. So until those who hit the net and fall through are able to cry out and call attention to their plight, other needs will assume the bulk of the attention and resources.

A Paradox with a Lit Fuse

The paradox of expecting the afflicted to rise up and make themselves heard is not without precedent. All of the statistical trends noted above fall more heavily on members of ethnic and cultural minorities, particularly to the extent to which they are impoverished and lack education (Gibbs, Huang, & Associates, 1989; London, 1987; William T. Grant Commission on Work, Family, & Citizenship, 1988). In our society, this refers most prominently to citizens of black or Hispanic ethnic and cultural heritage. Yet as fewer adolescents enter the work force in a manner that employers find to be satisfactory, it is clear that the problems are no longer those of "the minorities." The disaffection of the urban underclass can be found in middle- and upper-class adolescents in white America. They experience confusion about their identities, their future social roles, and the amount to which they will have to work to carve out their dreams (Irwin, 1987).

Much of this confusion is stirred by the power of our media, particularly television, in shaping both our images and our thought processes. In a public television series on the media, Bill Moyers showed how children are identifying more with "images" and less with close adults; these images are conveyed by the mass media and picked up and reinforced within peer groups. Television portrays life as a fast-paced succession of images to be bought, sold, copied, and moved around, and it is images of consumption, physical attractiveness, and power that seem to be most prominent (Perry, 1991). Where are the images that portray health, work, learning, sustained effort, and thoughtfulness? And how will they become salient in a mass media culture with a relatively short attention span?

The lit fuse can be seen in the alienation of children (and, sadly, many parents) from schooling and learning. School failure and dropout rates are themselves images—images of generations of children who do not see school as a bridge to their future. However, there is no doubt that the cycle potentiated by school disaffection is insidious and harmful; it will greatly increase the gaps among youth in our society and threaten our society's ability to reach its economic and social potential (Center for Early Adolescence, 1988; William T. Grant Commission on Work, Family, & Citizenship, 1988). The lit fuse is also reflected in the difficulty that various sectors of our society—notably business and government—are experiencing in filling the roles they have to offer. For the sake of our collective future, children need to be guided by positive images and to learn the skills required to actualize and participate in the roles these images describe.

The Role of the Schools

The continuing undercurrent of emphasis on basic academic skills is probably driven more by economic and workplace forces—both domestic and international—than by a genuine concern with the well-being of our nation's children and youth. For if the latter were the case, compelling statements about the inextricable bond linking personal, social, affective, and cognitive development would be more in the forefront. Arguments have been made that "placing an overlay of strong academic demands on the current educational climate is likely to result in few increases in learning and instead exacerbate current stress-related problems and lead to further alienation among our student population" (Elias, 1989, pp. 393–394). There have been calls for including "character education" as part of schooling to help counter the mass media imagery and restore to children and adolescents a sense of focus, stability, and history; this, in turn, would allow them to see that competitive, individualistic capitalism is not the only metaphor that can be used to understand the business world or family life (Baumrind, 1987; Gilligan, 1987; London, 1987). Finally, specific visions of schools as engaging places of learning and growth have been articulated, and in specific terms (see, for example, Carnegie Council on Adolescent Development, 1989; Center for Early Adolescence, 1988; *Educational Leadership*, 1988).

Such considerations multiply in importance as our schools become more culturally diverse and have to address noncollege and college youth with equal seriousness (Gibbs, Huang, and Associates, 1989; William T. Grant Commission on Work, Family, & Citizenship, 1988). It is necessary to explicate pathways toward accomplishment for all students in school, perhaps by borrowing from special education and having an individualized educational program (IEP) for all students, in which a segment is devoted to a long-term perspective on how the child is being prepared for one or more adult roles (Elias, 1989). Although many enrichments result from diversity, we have a responsibility to step back for a moment and study its effects. It can be helpful to attempt to take a task-analytic perspective on what many children and parents are experiencing as they work their way through our educational system.

Mirman, Swartz, and Barell (1988) have identified some of the experiences of "at-risk" children in the schools. They sit in the classroom and have difficulty making cognitive connections across subject areas and between classroom learning and their lives outside the school; they do not feel skilled at many academic tasks; their learning goals are set for them and they neither identify with them or understand their immediate or broad purposes; they often are directed in how to learn, and it is not always in ways that are best suited for them; and they have a difficult time taking advantage of any extracurricular offerings. Children are at risk to the extent to which they fit this profile, regardless of their cultural or socioeconomic background.

Figure 1.1 contains a representation of a school and its programs, showing the many specialized areas that are now addressed by programs or curricula; many of these are, individually, excellent. Both the American Psychological Association and the National Association of School Psychologists have identified prevention pro-

Figure 1.1. Prevention Programs Without a Common Framework.

Source: Improving Social Awareness-Social Problem Solving Project, Rutgers University and the University of Medicine and Dentistry of New Jersey.

grams that have shown themselves to be of value in many of the areas listed in the figure (Price, Cowen, Lorion, & Ramos-McKay, 1988; Zins & Forman, 1988). But what happens when they are combined in the course of the school day? Over the course of a year? Over the course of three years? From preschool through grade 12? The answer also is implied in the representation: a jumbled confusion. Certainly, there are students who are capable enough to integrate the diverse elements of each program into some coherent whole, and there are school districts that place a high value on curricular integration. But Figure 1.1 portrays the predominant situation.

Part of the solution involves intervention at the levels of both the person and the environment (Elias, 1987, 1989). Specifically, children require the confidence and competence (1) to feel invested in learning what the programs are conveying and (2) to have the skills to learn from the various programs and carry their learnings into their everyday lives. However, it is important for the environment to provide integration and coordination to the diverse efforts that are being made and thereby to reduce the confusion. Mirman et al.'s (1988) prescription for at-risk children is appropriate for all children: "We believe that by teaching at-risk children to think carefully and independently through decisions and problems, we will help them see that they have choices, that they have some control over their lives. . . . The extent to which at-risk students are afforded opportunities to engage in collaborative problem solving may determine whether or not they become less disaffected with the school" (pp. 138–139, 145). Empowerment and engagement relate to choice and control; these, in turn, relate to a basic sense of confidence and the social competence skills required to interact effectively in the school, family, and neighborhood. To better define the competencies in question, it will be valuable to consider briefly what is meant by "social competence" and its relevance for all students.

Social Competence as a Life Skill
for Adaptation to Diverse Environments

Anyone attempting to discuss the topic of social competence would be well advised to read Burton White's (1988) treatment of the area. He believes that such discussions must be delimited and pragmatic. First, he notes that "social competence should address factors that differ from intelligence and language or, at the very least, do not overlap with them any more than is necessary" (p. 34). He then reviews the efforts of the federal Office of Child Development, the RAND Corporation, and the Educational Testing Service to develop a definition of social competence during the late 1960s and early 1970s. A "panel of experts" generated a list of twenty-nine component areas, ranging from "fine motor dexterity to general knowledge to quantitative and relational concepts to appropriate regulation of antisocial behavior" (White, 1988, pp. 36–37). He describes as far-fetched the idea that functioning programs could be developed to implement all the facets of the definition.

Waters and Sroufe (1983), essentially agreeing with White, urge that greater attention be paid to key processes relating to social interaction and to their development over time and under different environmental conditions. A first step in following their suggestion is to determine the extent to which there is a consensus with regard to the attributes of a socially competent individual. Evidence from a variety of sources suggests a high level of agreement concerning the domains that reflect social competence (Commission on the Prevention of Mental-Emotional Disabilities, 1986; Consortium on the School Based Promotion of Social Competence, in press; Westchester County Social Competence in the Schools Task Force, 1990). Socially competent children, at least as defined in mainstream American culture, are those who

- Possess a positive sense of self-worth
- Feel capable as they interact with others and take on new developmental tasks and challenges
- Behave ethically and act responsibly toward others
- Appreciate the benefits of a multiracial society and respect the values of others
- Are skilled in interpersonal encounters and communication, get along with others, and develop long-term interpersonal relationships
- Develop sound work habits, motivation, and values
- Engage in health-enhancing and health-protective behaviors
- Are motivated to become productive citizens by serving as positive, contributing members of their peer group, family, school, and community
- Avoid engaging in behavior that may lead to negative consequences such as substance abuse, unwanted teen pregnancy, AIDS, social isolation, serious physical injury, dropping out of school, depression, suicide, unemployment, or criminal prosecution

Given the realities in Figure 1.1, attaining even this deceptively simple set of outcomes is a major challenge. Nevertheless, wise change agents such as Sarason (1978, 1982), Weick (1984), and Cowen (1980) have argued that a coordinated, determined set of "baby steps" toward programmatic goals pursued by diligent, persistent, committed individuals will lead to a series of local "small wins" that ultimately will fuel momentum toward widespread and lasting change. They urge that those concerned with children and schools define manageable, practical segments of the ecological landscape as the focus for research, intervention, and policy. To do so, a simplification strategy is called for. Two elements of such a strategy in the area of social competence promotion are a cross-cultural, panhistorical perspective and a long-term adaptation perspective.

A Cross-Cultural, Panhistorical Perspective

Jacob Bronowski, in his masterwork *The Ascent of Man* (1973), traced the evolution of humanity and civilization from the origins of life to the present era. Among his observations and reflections, he identified certain "defining qualities" of human beings, or core "skills" that allow the potential for human survival and advancement. These qualities include the ability to think of several ways to reach a goal; forethought, analysis, and planning; the documentation of attempts to solve problems through artistic and linguistic forms; and the ability to recognize and use feelings as information with which to guide decision making, problem solving, and action. Bronowski's perspective allowed him to recognize that *Homo sapiens* survived and thrived because of an ability to master the challenges and realities of social and physical environments. But not all *Homo sapiens* subgroups exercised their competencies—including their social competencies—equally. Assorted norms and differences across subgroups, which we now refer to as cultural and ethnic variations, reflect the range of conditions to which humans could and did adapt. No less significant is the record of adaptational failures and the importance of documenting and learning from them.

From Bronowski's perspective, the ascent of humanity is the trajectory forged by humans who are exercising their basic social competencies by adapting to new and varied environmental circumstances as well as by recognizing noxious environments, and avoiding, changing, or entering them only with extensive preparation. What Bronowski and other philosophers, historians, and chroniclers of human progress do is to unhinge, decouple, and otherwise differentiate social competence and adjustment. One can be socially competent, possessing or even displaying the key "human" qualities noted earlier, without being seen as adjusted. Conversely, one can be viewed as very well adjusted and yet show significant deficiencies in social competence.

From a cross-cultural perspective, the skills that comprise social competence go beyond cultural variation and instead are identified with shared features at the level of humanity. Adjustment, on the other hand, is inextricably bound to cultural, historical, and situational norms and expectations. Some school-related examples include a passive, shy, compliant, dependent child who may be viewed by teachers as adequately adjusted—causing little trouble and succeeding in school, for example—but who may have deficiencies in social competence. Another example is a child who is creative, thoughtful, planful, insightful, and tuned into his or her own feelings and those of others, but who is seen by teachers and peers as poorly adjusted. More complex is the example of an inner-city teenager who turns to selling drugs for his or her livelihood; such a child could be seen as adjusted or as lacking in social competence. But from Bronowski's perspective, perhaps it would be most sensible to consider the environment with which the teenager is being forced to cope as being noxious, and to focus upon change at that level.

The consensus on the attributes of socially competent children reflects the need to view competence in a way that befits the increasing complexity of our society. Bronowski has attempted to define the enduring skills that have allowed social groups to participate in the "ascent" most vigorously. A more recent and equally useful perspective is found in the emerging construct of "practical intelligence" (Sternberg & Wagner, 1986). Mercer, Gomez-Palacio, and Padilla (1986) point out that practical intelligence is linked to social roles. They identify several roles as being present across family, community, peer, school, nonacademic school, earner/consumer, and self-maintenance cultures. The skills needed to successfully perform these roles are indicators of social competence. From another perspective, social competence can be examined by determining the extent to which the distinctive skills described by Bronowski are enacted within and across roles. Another way to define risk would be in terms of deficiencies in both skills and the preparation neces-

sary to apply those skills across roles, and perhaps across environments as well.

A Long-Term Adaptation Perspective

The cross-cultural, panhistorical perspective attempts to focus on
the characteristics of both individuals and environments. The long-
term perspective focuses more heavily on individuals. It represents
an extension and further explication of Bronowski's set of basic
human skills. Rutter (1987) reviewed adaptation difficulties and the
specific socialization factors that seemed to assist children and adolescents in overcoming those difficulties. He concluded that there
is a set of "mechanisms" that serve a protective function to individuals even when they are in circumstances that most would find to
be harmful. These mechanisms combine with the skills described in
Bronowski (1973); the processes defined by Waters and Sroufe
(1983), Dodge, Pettit, McClaskey, and Brown (1986), and Lewis &
Saarni (1984); emerging work in the field of practical intelligence
(Sternberg & Wagner, 1986); and a long tradition of findings in
preventive mental health (Commission on the Prevention of
Mental-Emotional Disabilities, 1986; Elias & Branden, 1988; Price
et al., 1988) to suggest what Elias (1990) refers to as an outline of
"protective factors." These protective factors ask to what extent the
child is able to

1. Articulate goals of his or her actions
2. Think of more than one way to reach a goal
3. Plan a sequence of goal-directed actions
4. Realistically anticipate the consequences of, and potential ob-
    stacles to, actions
5. Express a positive sense of self-efficacy (a sense of "I can" and
    a general optimism about the outcomes of her or his person-
    ally initiated actions)
6. Express a positive connection and relationship to at least one
    significant, accessible adult
7. Describe participation in and a positive connection to one
    social group experience (school, club, hobby, peer group;
    music or art-related instruction; sports)

8. Show sensitivity to his or her own feelings and those of others
9. Approach and converse with peers, showing appropriate eye contact, using an appropriate tone of voice, displaying proper posture, and using appropriate language
10. Approach and converse with adults, showing appropriate eye contact, using an appropriate tone of voice, displaying proper posture, and using appropriate language
11. Manage stressful situations adequately
12. Recognize when she or he needs help and effectively seek out that help
13. Begin, follow through on, and complete tasks and projects
14. Live with parents or primary caretakers who provide adequate shelter and basic living resources, do not engage in extremes of permissiveness or punitiveness, and have the capacity to contain their own conflict, discord, and disagreements concerning childrearing

The protective factors can be thought of as a core set of skills that is made up of the social competencies necessary for long-term human adaptation. They encompass several areas: self-control and self-regulation, self-efficacy expectancies, skills for prosocial group participation and interaction, skills to promote social decision making and problem solving, and skills to extend and enrich one's social networks and social awareness. There also is an acknowledgment of the influence, but not the determining force (cf. Belsky, 1980), of considerations related to the child's primary socialization environment.

These skills are close to White's (1988) sense of what would provide a workable perspective concerning social competence. They represent aspects of functioning that

- Are reasonably distinct but clearly interrelated
- Are presented in practical terms that lend themselves to observation and lay discussion
- Can be translated into areas for intervention and training at levels of both the person and the environment (that is, efforts can be directed toward creating environments that will encour-

age the development, nurturance, and continuing, broad expression of the skills across various role contexts)
- Are interrelated with other competencies that are not explicitly identified (which means that efforts to build the competencies in the above list of protective factors will have a radiating effect, without the need to address each skill separately)
- Are likely to be associated with positive "adjustment," although cultural variations and developmental norms and expectations concerning the nature and degree of expression of these skills may require the continued use of such terms as "appropriate," "adequate," and "realistic" in any overall listing of competencies

The Social Decision-Making and Problem-Solving Approach of the ISA-SPS Project

In 1979, we cofounded the Improving Social Awareness–Social Problem Solving Project to allow us to work within the reality of school-based contexts such as those depicted in Figure 1.1. Our goal was to operationalize the protective factors and incorporate them into a family of interventions that was designed to promote social competence at the individual, dyadic, small-group, classroom, school, and district levels. In addition, we felt that it was necessary to generate a simplified skills array that would reflect panhistorical, cross-cultural, and long-term adaptation *and* be feasibly implementable with high quality in diverse school settings.

Through an action-research process that occurred over a period of a decade, the skills in Exhibit 1.1 have been identified as the focus of intervention. Overall, they are referred to most often as social decision-making and problem-solving skills. However, they reflect three main areas:

A. Self-control skills: These are skills necessary to accurately process social information, delay behavior long enough to thoughtfully access one's social decision-making abilities, and approach others in a way that avoids provoking their anger or annoyance.

B. Social awareness and group participation skills: These are skills that underlie the exercise of social responsibility and positive interactions in groups. They include learning how to recognize

Exhibit 1.1. Focal Skills for ISA-SPS Project Interventions.

A. Self-control skills
   1. Listen carefully and accurately
   2. Remember and follow directions
   3. Concentrate and follow through on tasks
   4. Calm oneself down
   5. Carry on a conversation without upsetting or provoking others
B. Social awareness and group participation skills
   6. Accept praise or approval
   7. Choose praiseworthy and caring friends
   8. Know when help is needed
   9. Ask for help when needed
  10. Work as part of a problem-solving team
C. Social decision-making and problem-solving skills
  11. Recognize signs of feelings in self
  12. Recognize signs of feelings in others
  13. Describe accurately a range of feelings
  14. Put problems clearly into words
  15. State realistic interpersonal goals
  16. Think of several ways to solve a problem or reach a goal
  17. Think of different types of solutions
  18. Do skills 16 and 17 for different types of problems
  19. Differentiate short- *and* long-term consequences
  20. Look at effects of choices on self *and* others
  21. Keep positive *and* negative possibilities in mind
  22. Select solutions that can reach goals
  23. Make choices that do not harm self or others
  24. Consider details before carrying out a solution (who, when, where, with whom, and so on)
  25. Anticipate obstacles to plans
  26. Respond appropriately when plans are thwarted
  27. Try out one's own ideas
  28. Learn from experiences or from seeking out input from adults, friends
  29. Use previous experience to help "next time"

and elicit trust, help, and praise from others; recognize others' perspectives; choose friends; and share, wait, and participate in groups.

C. Social decision-making skills and problem-solving skills: These skills, which represent the cornerstone of our approach, are incorporated into a sequential strategy that is used to understand, analyze, and react to stressful and problematic situations and situations that involve meaningful choices or decisions. The strategy has been identified as involving eight "steps," listed here in the language in which they have been presented in many of our curricular programs in the schools:

1. Look for signs of different feelings.
2. Tell yourself what the problem is.
3. Decide on your goal.
4. Stop and think of as many solutions to the problem as you can.
5. For each solution, think of all the things that might happen next.
6. Choose your best solution.
7. Plan it and make a final check.
8. Try it and rethink it.

The following chapter explicates the ways in which these skills operate to facilitate positive adaptation, with a focus on the social decision-making strategy. A detailed rationale, conceptual foundation, and evidentiary base for the choice of these specific skills will be presented, along with the associated curricular and instructional foundations needed to operationalize these ideas effectively. Chapter Three illuminates the action-research processes that led to the development of the specific forms our work has taken, and Chapter Four outlines the results of over a decade of empirical study. The remaining parts of the book show how these principles and findings have been incorporated into a variety of interventions for children at all grade levels.

A Guiding Vision

Our guiding vision in this work can be seen in Figure 1.2. In this vision of a schoolhouse, there is a common framework (denoted as "SPS"), which allows diversity to become synergy. It reflects what can happen when the social competencies of self-control, social awareness and group participation, and social decision making and problem solving are taught to individuals and adopted by the environment of children as an organizing principle.

We recognize that the confusion portrayed in Figure 1.1 persists in part because "instruction . . . typically places little emphasis on the development of thinking and other higher order skills"

Figure 1.2. A Common Framework Provides Synergy.

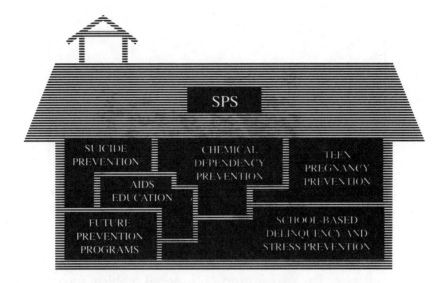

Source: Improving Social Awareness–Social Problem Solving Project, Rutgers University of Medicine and Dentistry of New Jersey.

(Levine, 1988, p. 118) and because the slow pace of change in the schools is linked to the history and structure of education, unions, teacher and administrator training, national and state policies concerning education, and an inadequately shared vision of the need for urgent action that was outlined earlier. Too often, the problem can be so large that change is discouraged. Nevertheless, inspired by Sarason (1978, 1982), Cowen (1980), and Weick (1984), it is possible for each school-based professional in every setting to define "baby steps" and "small wins" that can contribute to reaching the goal of preventing harmful outcomes and promoting the social competencies needed to meet the challenges of the twenty-first century and beyond.

Chapter Two

Designing School-Based Intervention Programs: Theoretical Perspectives

A substantial body of longitudinal research implies that explicit early instruction in social problem solving (social decision making) averts subsequent problem behaviors. . . . The hypothesized process is that problem-solving skills contribute to the development of an internal locus of control. That, in turn, builds a sense of self-efficacy and self-esteem, which ultimately strengthens resistance to substance abuse, among other problem behaviors. (Benard, Fafoglia, & Perone, 1987, pp. 5-6)

The skills needed for effective decision making and problem solving in social contexts are, of course, numerous. Self-control, group participation, and social awareness are among the most necessary ingredients. Without skills in paying attention, self-regulation, interpersonal understanding, and communication, an individual will possess neither the accurate and complete information needed for problem solving nor the patience and time needed to access and use whatever decision-making skills he or she possesses (Elias, Branden-Muller, & Sayette, 1991). Implicit in the above quotation from Benard et al. (1987) is that there is a process by which social decision-making and problem-solving competencies prevent psychosocial dysfunction and promote adaptive functioning. The elaboration of such a process is necessary if one is to understand the way in which building social competencies can be structured into school-based intervention programs. Incorporating these perspectives, we may define social decision-making and problem-solving skills for an individual as involving

1. Expectations concerning the outcome of a situation (positive or negative)
2. Expectations concerning the extent to which personal initiative can lead to problem resolution
3. The ability to understand the meaning of social situations and the feelings, motives, and perspectives of the different persons involved (including oneself)
4. The ability to define goals in a given situation
5. The ability to consider multiple options and envision their consequences, and to develop a detailed plan to reach a chosen goal
6. The ability to react to obstacles, or roadblocks, that are encountered
7. Preferred qualitative styles of resolving problems and handling decisions
8. The ability to monitor experiences and use that information to refine future performance in problem-solving and decision-making situations

These definitions have been proposed by Allen, Chinsky, Larcen, Lochman, and Selinger (1976); Bransford, Sherwood, Vye, and Rieser (1986); Dewey (1933); Duncker (1945); D'Zurilla and Goldfried (1971); Elardo and Cooper (1977); Elias et al (1991); Ford (1982); Goldfried and Davison (1976); Houtz and Feldhusen (1975); Osborn (1963); Parnes (1962); Rotter (1978); Spivack, Platt, and Shure (1976); and Weissberg, Gesten, Liebenstein, Schmid, & Hutton (1980).

This listing hints at the process by which these skills serve to promote competence. Consider a child who is observed calmly approaching a group of peers. After a moment of conversation, she turns and walks away, seemingly dejected. Among the phenomena one might wish to understand are the child's decision to approach the group and her eventual departure from the situation. This child potentially is faced with a problematic situation. How she feels in the situation and understands the event (skill area 3), the extent to which she would like to join (skill area 4), and the way in which she thinks about possible ways to join (skill area 5) are the social decision-making building blocks of action. But powerful mediating influences are exerted by skill areas 1 and 2, and these expectancies can either short-circuit or promote further thoughtful social decision making. Further interactive effects are provided by the strength and flexibility of the goal (skill area 4), the match of qualitative behavioral style (skill area 7) to particular circumstances, the extent to which the situation undergoes changes over time (skill area 6), and the degree of integration of prior experiences into current responses (skill area 8).

An additional layer of mediators can be identified as the *social environment* and *social relationship* contexts. The former refers to the location of the behavior (schoolyard, neighborhood street) and the norms that exist in that context. The latter refers to the nature of the interactions that take place in the setting, the typical and historical patterns of interaction between the individual and others in the setting, and the causes that individuals typically attribute to the behaviors of others observed in the situation.

In summary, it can be said that the cognitive and behavioral capacities required for resolving problematic situations are developmentally formed in the individual's continuous interaction with the physical, interpersonal, and sociocultural environment. Social adaptation seems to embody a complex systems process; therefore we should expect the relationship between social decision-making cognitions and behaviors to be indirect and mediated by a variety of factors. At a molar level are individuals' experiences within key socialization systems such as health care services during pregnancy, birth, and early infancy; families; schools; and neighborhoods. Experiences within these systems form general cognitive and affective capabilities, qualitative behavioral styles and competencies, and interpersonal expectancies (Bower, 1972; Bronfenbrenner, 1979; Rotter, 1954; Rutter, 1975). At a molecular level, mediational processes may be explained by the metacognitive mechanisms that integrate specific social-cognitive skills and govern their operation (Flavell, 1979; Loper, 1980).

Many areas are relevant to understanding behavioral performance. Social environment and interrelationship factors form cognitive expectancies, social decision-making and problem-solving competencies, and standards for behavioral performance. Feedback from behavioral performance influences an individual's social decision-making skills and expectancies and may also have an impact on relevant social environments and on the individual's relationships with persons in them. And the considerations raised thus far constitute only a partial model. In the following section, the focus will be on social decision-making processes. This will be followed by a consideration of social decision-making instruction and training, which ultimately incorporate both molecular and molar factors into the fabric of sound interventions. For although social decision-making and problem-solving skills seem to be central mediators of adaptive behavioral performance, translation of social decision-making competencies into appropriate behavioral performance requires that a number of other factors be in proper alignment.

The Operation of Social Decision-Making and Problem-Solving Skills in Individuals

It is relevant to consider mechanisms through which social decision-making skills combine to exercise an important influence on adaptive human functioning. Our ability to *anticipate* allows us to *plan* and exert control over events that move too swiftly for us to be able to cope with them by reacting directly (Flavell, 1979; Kaplan, 1975). We are able to plan because we can cognitively represent events and the pathways to goals contained in those events; we also generate rules to apply to variants of situations that have been directly or indirectly experienced (Miller, Galanter, & Pribram, 1960; Mischel, 1979; Schank & Abelson, 1977). In addition to an adaptive and flexible rule- and plan-making ability, humans also seem to possess the ability to organize their experiences into *scripts*, sequences of actions that define the structure (or schema) of well-known situations from the point of view of all participants (Harre, 1974; Mischel, 1979; Schank & Abelson, 1977). Scripts can be thought of as complex, overlearned behavior sequences that we automatically invoke for the appropriate situation, such as a classroom or religious setting. As these scripts and their developmental precursors are invoked in interpersonal situations, behavioral routines become further organized and integrated into the individual's cognitive, affective, and behavioral repertoire.

Children seem to develop many in-school scripts that may differ as a function of the setting and the children or adults who are present. For example, there is a script for interacting with substitute teachers that would be inappropriate to invoke with one's regular teacher or the principal. One perspective on maladjustment is that it involves children's improper use of scripts or the application of poorly formed or incomplete scripts to situations. What might have gone wrong? Did some cognitive deficit lead to incomplete script formation? Are important cues not being attended to? Are experiences not being monitored and processed for subsequent consideration? A moment's reflection should be sufficient to allow one to find examples of children whose scripts seem predominantly maladaptive or competent. Social decision-making and problem-solving skills can be thought of as building blocks of scripts, and interventions designed to build these skills should foster the growth and application of well-formed scripts that are linked to appropriate contexts of use.

Among current models describing the organization of knowledge for solving problems, the procedural network seems most appropriate (Greeno, 1980). Procedural networks encompass specific skills, such as those outlined earlier, and relate cognitive and behavioral decision points not only to prior conditions but to the consequences associated with a pattern of possible actions. This "feed-forward" capability is a critical dimension of adaptive problem resolution. For the child who wants to join a group of peers, the feed-forward capability allows a modification of strategies based on past experiences to reflect current expectation levels and the idiosyncratic features of the present situation. This provides great potential adaptive flexibility and emphasizes the subtle factors (for example, attention to the particular details of a situation) that mediate social adjustment. Complex script and procedural networks in the social-cognitive domain continue to be in the formative stages, as are perspectives on the nature of their acquisition and development. Thus, it should be of little surprise that the empirical relationships of social-cognitive problem-solving skills to behavioral adjustment have been far from isomorphic, and that the success of intervention programs has been positive but not as consistent as might be expected (Denham & Almeida, 1987).

Streams of Influence on the Development of the ISA-SPS Approach

The specific skill base used in the ISA-SPS Project derives from a variety of influences. Some of the more theoretical and configural influences were elaborated on or alluded to in previous sections. However, traditions derived from intervention-oriented inquiry have also shaped our views and contributed much of pragmatic value. While many such influences are excluded from the summary that follows, it should be noted that the streams of influence that will be identified are those that have had a significant, tangible influence in developing the focal skills identified by the ISA-SPS Project. Figure 2.1 portrays the major streams of influence as they have served to inform the social decision-making and problem-solving content of our program.

Dewey and Piaget

Although not interventionists per se, Jean Piaget and John Dewey conceptualized their work as ultimately directed toward promoting positive change and growth in children. Piaget provides more than a cognitive developmental framework for understanding children's social decision making and problem solving. In his writing, he describes humans as being motivated to adapt to and master their environments. This orientation toward mastery and adaptation is highly consistent with a problem-solving perspective. Indeed, Piaget viewed development as the outcome of a series of encounters with disequilibrating forces. From moment to moment and at each major stage of development, children bring to bear their various cognitive, affective, and behavioral capacities to resolve the disequilibration and increase their ability to adapt to and master their

Figure 2.1. Streams of Influence in the Development of the ISA-SPS Social Decision-Making Approach.

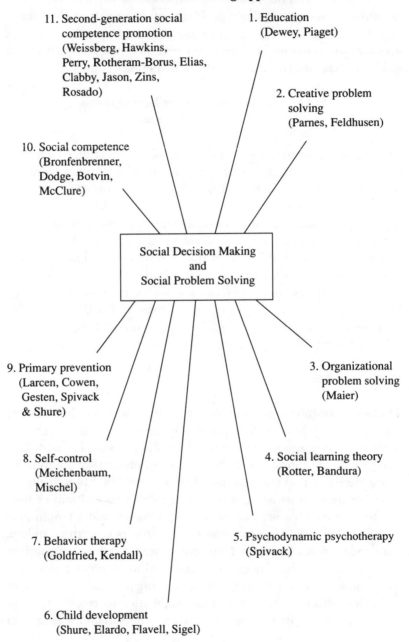

11. Second-generation social
    competence promotion
    (Weissberg, Hawkins,
    Perry, Rotheram-Borus, Elias,
    Clabby, Jason, Zins,
    Rosado)

1. Education
   (Dewey, Piaget)

2. Creative problem
   solving
   (Parnes, Feldhusen)

10. Social competence
    (Bronfenbrenner,
    Dodge, Botvin,
    McClure)

Social Decision Making
and
Social Problem Solving

9. Primary prevention
   (Larcen, Cowen,
   Gesten, Spivack
   & Shure)

3. Organizational
   problem solving
   (Maier)

8. Self-control
   (Meichenbaum,
   Mischel)

4. Social learning theory
   (Rotter, Bandura)

7. Behavior therapy
   (Goldfried, Kendall)

5. Psychodynamic psychotherapy
   (Spivack)

6. Child development
   (Shure, Elardo, Flavell, Sigel)

environment. In more current terms, we think of disequilibration as consisting of stressful events, stressors, critical life transitions, conflicts, frustrations, and problematic situations. Piaget realized that from early infancy, when children are attempting to solve the problem of how to maintain caregiver attachment and prompt feeding, hugging, and changing of diapers, they are continually solving the problems with which their environment confronts them. John Dewey, the seminal philosopher and educator, spent much of his time observing what it was that successful children did to adapt to the demands of schooling. In his 1933 book *How We Think,* Dewey summarized his many observations of children and listed what we now think of as the basic steps for problem solving and decision making. While Dewey's enumeration of steps was not as comprehensive as the one we have incorporated into our work, it represents, nevertheless, a significant influence on our thinking, in that our work is consistent with his observations.

The Creative Problem Solvers

Sidney Parnes (1962) and John Feldhusen (1975) represent individuals who emphasized the human capacity for creativity. Their studies of the things we do that rigidify and narrow our ability to solve problems as well as those that enhance our ability to solve problems have been instrumental in demonstrating that creative problem-solving techniques, often reserved for gifted and talented students, are both accessible to and necessary for *all* students. The pragmatic importance of creative problem solving is brought home poignantly by N.R.S. Maier's work (1970) in organizational problem solving. Maier assisted industries that confronted tremendous demands for the production of munitions and equipment during World War II to support our war effort on the European continent. It became clear that existing methods of increasing production had their limits. Maier was among a handful of industrial/organizational psychologists who pioneered the concept of allowing work groups to brainstorm methods of increasing their own productivity. Once they were allowed to be creative and find their own solutions, groups of workers ultimately generated novel ideas that greatly spurred productivity and allowed our nation's industries to meet their obligations to the military and to our allies overseas.

Social Learning Theorists

Both Julian Rotter and Albert Bandura emphasized the influence of expectancies on behavior. The concept of internal and external loci of control was simply one of many expectancies that Rotter identified and wrote about, and only one of many with relevance for children's decision making and problem solving. Indeed, problem-solving abilities must be affected by the extent to which one believes that he or she, as opposed to the external environment, is the locus of finding effective ways of acting. Rotter also identified expectancies for outcome—that is, expectancies developed by individuals that their own actions or the actions of others affecting their problems would result in a successful or unsuccessful outcome. Bandura incorporated both of these notions into the construct of self-efficacy and has helped make it abundantly clear that one should not expect to see problem-solving effort and activity in children who do not believe that they are agents of their own problem resolution or who believe that problem resolution is unlikely to be positive. This contribution helped to shift the emphasis away from teaching isolated sets of behavioral or cognitive skills and began to shift the focus toward the context of these actions in which problem-solving and decision-making skills actually would be used by children.

Everyday Interpersonal-Cognitive Problem Solvers

George Spivack was trained in traditional psychodynamic therapy and was a skillful practitioner of this art at the Devereaux Child Development Center in Pennsylvania. He found that, although he was able to assist children in reaching insights about difficulties in their lives, their own emotional functioning, and the ways in which they interacted with other people, when they returned from home visits, many of them would report stories reflective of extreme personal and interactional difficulty. Even when their insights were examined and found to be intact, it became apparent that they lacked the fundamental skills needed to manage day-to-day, moment-to-moment interactions. Through further research, Spivack identified some of the missing skills as "interpersonal-cognitive problem solving skills" (ICPS). ICPS skills are similar to the skills that we identify in steps 4–7 of our social decision-making program. Basically, they represent an emphasis on generating alternative solutions to a problem, considering a variety of consequences, and elaborating a planful way of moving from means to ends. Realizing that by the time many youngsters reach adolescence, deficiencies in ICPS skills will already have led them into numerous difficulties, Spivack began to focus his work on building skills early for the purpose of preventing later difficulties. This eventuated in his seminal work with preschool populations (Spivak & Shure, 1974).

Child Development Specialists

While social decision-making skills are identified as being important from very early in life, they do undergo certain forms of development. These developmental transformations will be discussed later in this chapter; however, it is essential to point out here that the work of colleagues such as Myrna Shure, Phyllis Elardo, John Flavell, and Irv Sigel emphasized that it is children that we are talking about, not adults in miniature. Shure always has kept a focus on the playfulness, inconsistency, honesty, concern for adult approval, and eagerness with which many children face the world before sometimes having their hopeful expectancies turned negative. One cannot engage in interaction with children for a very long period of time without discovering that they are not as cognitively oriented or sophisticated as some of them appear to be or as some of their parents and teachers wish to see them. Children are strongly emotional in their reactions to problems, choices, and difficult situations, more so at some stages of development than at others; this emotionality is an element that our team has found deeply important and that we have acknowledged in our approach to teaching social decision-making skills (Elias et al., 1991).

Self-Control Theorists, Therapists, and Researchers

The rise of a cognitive-behavioral perspective in therapy and research led to an emphasis on the importance of self-control skills for children. Through the work of Marvin Goldfried, Phil Kendall, Walter Mischel, and Don Meichenbaum, it became very clear that children's impulsive responses functionally preclude their use of whatever decision-making and problem-solving capabilities they actually possess. Mischel, in particular, studied the predictive significance of poor skills in dealing with delay of gratification and found that lack of such skills in early childhood was a precursor of later social and behavioral difficulties. From a clinical perspective, Kendall, Meichenbaum, and others recognized the need to help children deal with strong feelings—particularly stressful feelings—when they face difficult situations in real life. From their work, we became convinced of the necessity of helping children make the linkage from practicing problem solving in protective or hypothetical situations to carrying out these skills in the complicated and affect-laden reality of the schoolyard, the street, and the home.

Preventive Interventionists

A major influence on our work was the movement in the 1970s toward school-based preventive interventions. It was a movement that gained force as part of the larger community mental health and psychology rebellions against the orthodoxy and treatment-centered focus of traditional clinical models. It was reasoned by many that building children's skills in social and affective areas would serve to prevent a variety of psychological disorders and negative social conditions, and prevention programs were instituted with that goal in mind. However, programs ran into difficulty because researchers, funders, and policy makers often asked the question, "What are you preventing?" At the stage of knowledge existing at that time, and indeed, at present, there is little means to frame a precise answer to that question. Prevention is, by its very nature, nontargeted, reflecting multifactorial causality. The skills needed for preventing depression overlap with those needed for preventing social withdrawal, identity disorders, and even disorders such as attention deficit disorder and antisocial behavior. Nevertheless, despite being unable to link interventions directly to clinically unambiguous preventive outcomes, researchers and practitioners who collaborated on programs, such as Spivack and Shure, Steve Larcen, and others, developed excellent intervention models and began to show how ideas from research and clinical practice could be translated into school-based, curriculum-centered programs that could be taught by teachers and other school personnel and woven into the fabric of children's everyday lives. There appeared to be less need for children who received these programs to find their way to alternate care. Nevertheless, it was difficult to document precisely what was being prevented and to what extent a preventive effect was taking place.

Social Competence Promotion Program Developers: The First and Second Generations

Emerging in full force in the 1980s and poised to meet the challenges of the schools in the 1990s and beyond are programs designed to develop children's social competencies. These programs claim to build social decision-making and problem-solving skills, foster self-control, assist with stress management, and provide instruction in affective awareness and development. The goal of these programs is not to prevent some specific disorder, but rather to impart skills known to be necessary for sound adjustment in the future. If a preventive effect accrues, this is highly desirable, of course.

The first generation of these programs is embodied in the work of Steve Larcen, Emory Cowen, Ellis Gesten, Larry McClure, and Gilbert Botvin, among others. The focus is the development of curricular "modules" designed to be inserted into school programs for a circumscribed period of time. These programs have been successful in generating skill acquisition and behavior change but less so in demonstrating long-term retention and generalization once a program has been concluded.

Learnings from the social competence promotion programs have led to a second generation of such programs, of which the ISA-SPS Project is one (see Figure 2.1). These programs are characterized by an intense focus on the process of implementation, not only while the research team is present in the schools to provide consultation, but also when the team is no longer there to watch what is going on. There is also more extensive instructional time, generalization training, a multiyear focus, and an intention to have an

impact on organizational functioning. These considerations become critical when a program is disseminated into new settings. For
the practitioner and researcher, there is little substitute for knowing
precisely what is being carried out in a program. The study of
implementation processes, over both the long and short term, and
the more general interfacing of school-based competence promotion
programs with larger issues of educational reform and with initiatives in the schools concerning massive problems such as AIDS and
substance abuse are both part of the purview of the second generation of social competence promotion programs.

Conceptual Foundations of ISA-SPS Approaches
to Intervention and Implementation

The previous discussion about second-generation social competence promotion programs introduces a fuller consideration of the
ISA-SPS perspective on questions such as "What does it mean to say
that one is conducting an intervention," and especially a 'curricular
intervention'?" and "What is involved when one says that one has
'implemented' a program?" In reviews of social decision-making
and problem-solving interventions (see, for example, Denham &
Almeida, 1987; Urbain & Kendall, 1980), distinctions rarely are
made between programs with short- and long-term goals. It is as if
outcome were uncorrelated with intervention intensity, duration,
and fidelity. Of course, research into health education curricula has
shown that these variables are highly relevant to outcome (King,
1986; Walberg, 1986).

Interventions from a traditional research perspective seem
focused primarily on demonstrating short-term skill gains that will
persist over time. This implicitly follows an "inoculation" model
that ultimately is an inappropriate paradigm for social-cognitive
and behavioral skill training, especially with children (Cartledge &
Milburn, 1986; Ladd & Mize, 1983; Lipsitz, 1977). Parameters to
maximize integration of skills and transfer, generalization, and continuity of use of skills must be built into the design of an intervention. Therefore, a curricular intervention in actuality operates at
individual, dyadic, small group, organizational, and community
levels.

The curriculum is the part of the intervention in which key concepts and skills are introduced, and their components, practice, and link to other relevant skills made explicit. It is through the interactions, prompts, and reinforcement occurring during the non-formal lesson time that the key skills and concepts are practiced, clarified, extended, and made truly relevant to intervention recipients. The occurrence of these nonformal events should be observable from the intervention plan—that is, it should include features of the "curricular" intervention with the discernable purpose of fostering skill use, integration, transfer, and generalizations—and this should occur over time.

An additional feature of a curricular intervention, from the ISA-SPS perspective, is relevance. Learning and behavior change will not occur unless the instructional process is perceived by the learner as relevant (Rotter, 1954). In heterogeneous classes and especially with children of ethnic and cultural minorities or those with high-risk status, special steps often must be taken to ensure the relevance of the curriculum, the lesson activities, the concepts, and the skills being taught (Mirman et al., 1988). Therefore, it is useful to explicate further the principles that guide the structure of the ISA-SPS social decision-making interventions, because they constitute features one would expect to find in curricular and other interventions.

Provide a Cognitive Strategy

Traditional approaches to prevention and social and affective skill building too often are organized around *content:* a unit on alcohol, a unit on stereotypes and group differences, a unit on self-esteem, a unit on family living, and so on. Much more promising is the use of a common framework that unifies many of these content areas and provides a strategy that can be employed across content areas to meet a variety of mandates. The framework of decision making and the strategy of critical problem-solving thinking skills have been used with much success by the ISA-SPS Project in a number of schools. This framework is summarized in the list of social decision-making steps:

1.   Look for signs of different feelings.
2.   Tell yourself what the problem is.
3.   Decide on your goal.
4.   Stop and think of as many solutions to the problem as you can.
5.   For each solution, think of all the things that might happen next.
6.   Choose your best solution.
7.   Plan it and make a final check.
8.   Try it and rethink it.

The list is presented in the language used in elementary, middle, and high school classrooms. These steps are taught carefully to students as a social decision-making strategy through a structured curriculum. For instructional purposes, the curriculum includes specific applications to the variety of decision-making situations that occur in an everyday school context. However, teachers are provided with guidelines for flexible application to topics of particular local concern.

This approach capitalizes on the utility of providing children with realistic thinking frames as organizers. It reinforces learning and use of the strategy by preparing students to use decision-making skills to responsibly handle a variety of important life areas (Jones, 1986; Perkins, 1986). Perhaps most significantly, the approach helps children to come to an understanding and an acceptance of social decisions for which there are no healthy alternatives, such as those concerning drug and alcohol use and smoking. The eight steps also serve as a basis for discussing the benefits of resisting pressures to engage in high-risk and unlawful behaviors and for deriving constructive, responsible means of coping with those pressures.

Focus on Decision-Making Situations

Many difficulties from which children suffer are the outcome of concrete decision-making situations that often occur outside of adult supervision: "Who are you going to hang out with on the schoolyard?" "C'mon, let's spray-paint the school." "I can't believe you're worried about schoolwork. Forget it and forget class. Come with us." "You gotta smoke—everyone else is." "Are you going to listen to what they tell you in those assemblies?" Such everyday situations place a child at social crossroads. A child's pathway on the road to higher risk or greater competence will be strongly influenced by the *decisions* she or he makes when confronting these and related personal and interpersonal situations. The social decision-making steps and strategy are taught to children precisely so that they can have a reliable guide to help them in such circumstances.

Make the Framework and Strategy Usable by Educators and Parents

The decision-making framework and the problem-solving strategy provide educators and parents with the tools they need if they are to have a sustained impact in the face of the constant stressors experienced by so many children today and in the foreseeable future. The framework and strategy are effective because they are grounded in the steps presented above and in related skills that can be used consistently across developmental periods. As children grow older, their understanding of situations and their cognitive abilities become more sophisticated. However, the decision-making strategy taught in elementary school can be used through high school. Educators and parents can keep pace with developmental changes by building on a sound and growing foundation of skills and experiences. Learning to read and learning to drive a car both provide excellent analogies to the benefits that can accrue from a guided, continuous application of a set of strategies over time and varying situations. We are not taught to read each book, or even each type of book, separately. Nor is there a separate learning process to prepare us to drive on one-way streets, dirt roads, or four-lane toll roads. We are given strategies for reading and driving that eventually become internalized and generalized. Similarly, the social decision-making and problem-solving approach uses the eight steps as building blocks to help children develop a strategy for generalized use in interpersonal and decision-making situations.

Use a Curriculum-Based Procedure

To most effectively build the set of skills outlined, a school-based, curriculum-based approach is advisable. Such an approach has several important merits: (1) it conveys a sense of commitment to the value of social decision-making skills, (2) it provides a structured, consistent focus of instruction for children who need such a focus, (3) it provides formal lessons as an opportunity to introduce concepts and examples and allows for guided practice and reinforcement of skills throughout the school day, and (4) it sets parameters for a common language to be used with the children in the classroom, in encounters with other school staff, and in the home. The latter point is essential, as the necessity of reinforcing curriculum skills across various school and home activities too often is underemphasized. The unifying elements of this approach help a school district transform its services from resembling those in Figure 1.1 to resembling those in Figure 1.2.

Consider Developmental Expectations
When Planning Instruction

Social decision making and related skills and abilities undergo developmental progression. However, it is valuable to place these skills in the broader domain of psychosocial growth outlined by Erik Erikson (1954). His "psychosocial stages" provide a sense of the developmental trajectory of young people during each major age period. These stages also allow us to understand the direction and context within which specific skills are organized.

Erikson's stages of *trust* and *autonomy* cover the years from birth to the age of two (approximately; the sequence is more reliable than the specific age boundaries). Successful social adaptation is linked to children's receiving physical and emotional security and beginning to recognize their capacity to move about and in other ways have commerce and interaction with the world around them. Rudiments of social decision-making abilities are developing during the first two years. Even infants exhibit precausal, "if-then" motor association as they learn what they must do to have their needs met. Yet from their earliest interactions, the rudiments of *language* are appearing. They learn how to get people to hold, feed, and change their diapers long before they can ask for such things, but their verbal behavior is part of their adaptational success. From these early experiences, children begin to develop a nonverbal sense of expectancy concerning their ability to exert an influence on having their needs met and concerning the nature of outcomes to situations in which they are involved. Later, a sense of self-efficacy will emerge from this early, generalized sense of trust.

The stage of *initiative,* which is linked to the early childhood period (ages two to seven), brings with it new requirements for social adaptation as children encounter day-care, preschool, and school environments. Children must improve their motor and verbal control and begin to show awareness of and accommodation to social rules (in addition to parental rules). In early childhood, growing language and cognitive capabilities fuel advances in social decision making. Children can be expected to identify basic feelings, pick up on a central theme in situations, decenter both in communication and in their sense of space, consider alternative ways to reach a goal, and recognize alternative consequences to their actions. Language and conceptual skills that are prerequisite to mature social decision making evolve at this time. Children acquire terms to help them with integration and differentiation (is–is not; and-or; same-different; all-some), divergent production (other; else), causal inferences (if-then; why-because), and qualification or specification (where; with whom; to whom; when; now-later; before-after). Expectancies become more closely linked to perception of ongoing experiences, and children begin to develop an early sense of what Rotter (1978) calls an "expectancy" for the usefulness of being a good problem solver.

When children enter the stage of *industry,* they are in what is usually called middle childhood (ages seven to eleven). In school and in extracurricular activities, successful adaptation requires more focus and continuity than in prior stages. Self-awareness of goals and goal attainment is needed if children are to be able to carry out projects and participate in teams and performances; these attributes are also behind their penchant for collecting things and reading book series during the latter part of this age period. This is preparation for the period of *identity,* which extends from preadolescence into the teen years. Students build on prior experiences to attempt to answer the questions "Who am I?" and "What can I become?"—questions that take on an emotional charge and a sense of reality as children move into formal operational cognitive capabilities.

In middle childhood, key social decision-making abilities include a broadening vocabulary to label a range of feelings in self and others, an improved ability to link sequences of events, a more accurate sense of perspective, an expanded ability to consider alternative solutions and consequences and formulate elaborated plans for means-end linkage, and the beginning of an ability to anticipate obstacles to one's plans. Adolescence requires both more matured expectancies and integrated social decision-making skills. With regard to expectancies, successful adaptation is aided by an appropriate internal locus of control, a realistic sense of which situations will have positive outcomes, and a general tendency to consider multiple alternatives, consequences, and plans before acting. With regard to decision making, advances in reciprocal perspective taking fuel improvements in the identification of emotions, causal inference, and the ability to consider multiple alternatives, consequences, and plans; the formation of contingency plans; and a flexible response to obstacles.

In general, the psychosocial stages are the engines of development, fueled by the emergence of new language and social decision-making skill capabilities at each level. Nevertheless, control is exercised on the engine so that it does not become a runaway. The forces of social adaptation—other people, norms, rules, and structures—force a greater integration of skills, mobilization of expectancies before action, precise use of language, and the capacity for flexible and synergistic use of skills. The most effective curricular and skill-based training programs are sensitive to converging areas of developmental change in children and work "with the flow."

Mobilize an Array of Teaching Methods and Integrative Instructional Strategies

A curriculum lesson is not synonymous with a lecture. Unfortunately, the relative simplicity and clarity (on paper, at least) of lecture-oriented instruction helps to perpetuate its popularity, particularly when program-oriented research is occurring. In contrast, Table 2.1 provides an instructional framework guided by learning theory and developmental considerations (Gagne, 1975). The instructional planning process is considered to have three major elements. Each element has a corresponding set of recommended techniques. Interventions developed by the ISA-SPS Project use stories, cartoons, and videotaped materials with greatest frequency; video has been a key vehicle for engaging students in special education classes. ISA-SPS Project interventions incorporate many teaching methods within each instructional lesson and emphasize cumulative review. Finally, they use all of the integrative mechanisms in Table 2.1 as part of curricular programs. This reflects a commitment to planning explicitly for transfer and generalization of learning. The bottom section of the table summarizes the strategies required to ensure long-term skill gains. Skills must be elicited and external and internal feedback must be encouraged. The effectiveness of doing so is enhanced by continuity of instruction, both across settings within schools, across grade levels, and between school and home.

Foundations of ISA-SPS Approaches to Intervention and Implementation: Conclusion

As the preceding section suggests, a second-generation social competence promotion curricular intervention is highly intensive and extensive. Numerous considerations go into the definition of the key skills, their organization as a set of strategies, and their translation into developmentally sensitive instructional and implementation procedures. From Bronowski's lofty perspective concerning human social competencies to specifying the need for oral and written practice exercises, there are connecting fibers that are designed to mend the safety net beneath our children and adolescents. Gradually, these fibers can be woven into protective garments that can fortify and sustain children so that they will be less likely to fall out of the mainstream and through the safety net.

This detailed perspective on the theory and practice of social competence promotion is not meant to stifle action. Instead, it

**Table 2.1. Techniques and Considerations for the
Design of Social Decision-Making Curricular Activities.**

Elements of Instructional Planning

1. Activate motivation Inform learner of objectives Direct attention	2. Stimulate recall Access prerequisite, preceding skills	3. Enhance retention Promote transfer of learning

Suggested Techniques

1. Stimulus materials Stories Photographs Newspaper, maga- zine articles, cartoons Records, audio- cassettes Filmstrips Video materials	2. Primary teaching methods Discussion (guiding, modeling) Small-group interaction Language concepts, feel- ings games Role playing Puppetry Practice exercises (oral and written) Presentation of novel tasks, situations Video, audio, or filmstrip material with pauses	3. Integrative mechanisms Assign books with rele- vant themes; reports, discussions Use related themes in writ- ing activities; open-ended stories, pictures portraying conflict, open-ended sentences Units on common, prob- lematic situations—preju- dice, new birth, separation and divorce, family rela- tionships, persons with handicaps, making friends Programs for assemblies, parents—songs, skits, plays Prepare video vignettes Life-space interviews; dia- loguing to encourage SPS, especially role-taking, alternatives, consequences

Necessary Components for Reaching Long-Term Goals

1. Elicit performance of skills	2. Provide constructive feedback Promote internal monitoring	3. Promote problem-solving environments in school, home, and other settings

serves as a complement to the seriousness of the problem outlined
in Chapter One. No significant changes will result from poorly
conceived and weakly implemented programs with little continuity.
Serious problems demand serious and comprehensive intervention.
The considerations raised thus far have fueled a family of diverse,
successful, practical, and replicated preventive and remediative in-

terventions, primarily but not solely school based, over the last decade. The ISA-SPS Project has built on the streams of influence
outlined in Figure 2.1; the specific programs and intervention approaches will be presented in some detail in Parts Three and Four,
but first the action-research procedures used to operationalize the
social and conceptual foundations, as well as the results of those
procedures, will be presented in Part Two.

The Social
Problem-Solving
Approach in Action

Much has been written about the process of developing, implementing, evaluating, and sustaining programs or innovations in schools (see, for example, Commins & Elias, in press; Elias, 1987; Elias & Weissberg, 1990; Hord, Rutherford, Huling-Austin, & Hall, 1987; Huberman & Miles, 1984; Sarason, 1982; Stolz, 1984; Weissberg, Caplan, & Sivo, 1989; Zins & Ponti, 1990). Rather than simply providing a review of this extensive literature, we have chosen a more integrative approach, using this rich literature throughout the course of our work. Here we articulate in detail the action-research process that has guided us. We do so with the intention of providing a model that (1) has been valuable to school-oriented practitioners and researchers, (2) allows for systematic documentation and sharing of actions and findings, and (3) has guided flexible and ecologically successful adaptations of the social decision-making and problem-solving approach. Chapter Three contains a decision-oriented history of the growth of the ISA-SPS Project and illustrates the application of our action-research model. Chapter Four presents key empirical findings generated by the Project, as well as some limitations of the data gathered thus far.

Using Action Research as a Framework for Program Development

As has been noted, the ISA-SPS Project focuses on children's social competence as an outcome of the linkages between children's home and school contexts. We have identified a set of key skills that children need to cope with stressors. How do environments support or thwart the growth of these skills? And what special process is needed to enter the school and home environments in a genuine way and determine whether our research findings can be translated into constructive and enduring environmental change? The method we have chosen, *action research,* involves entering a system, studying phenomena of interest, and testing our understanding by attempting planned change in the system. The outcome of such an intervention creates a new context in which to study the original phenomena and continue the cycle of research and action.

As a result of sensitive considerations about the action-research process on the part of Lewin (1951), Sanford (1970), Kelly (1979), Sarason (1978), Price and Smith (1985), Muñoz, Snowden, and Kelly (1979), Billington, Washington, and Trickett (1981), and others, some consensus about common features of that process has been developed. We have further refined these views in light of our own experiences; Exhibit 3.1 presents an outline of what we see as the primary facets of the action-research cycle. There is a clear bias in our view toward detailed, early planning and cautious expansion.

Exhibit 3.1. Outline of Facets of the Action-Research Cycle.

Facet	Brief Description
I.	Identify setting need/program idea
II.	Formulate program/early planning
	A. Consider goals, targets, measures
	B. Identify and obtain relevant research, practice models
	C. Determine a vehicle for turning idea into practice
	D. Consider initial balance of action and research goals
III.	Search for suitable setting
	A. Assess systems' readiness (use resiliency-resistances balance, Table 3.1)
	B. Anticipate entry hurdles, measures needed to build trust
	C. Identify compatible, nonidentical incentive systems
IV.	Conduct initial negotiations
	A. Identify gatekeepers, power within system, constituents for the program
	B. Specify a process of defining priority areas, control over conduct of implementation and research in focal setting
	C. Specify resources, mutual expectations/benefits (for example, time, personnel, funding, space, materials, direct and indirect outcomes)
V.	Secure commitment/build team
	A. Assemble resources
	B. Design pilot project
VI.	Implement pilot project
VII.	Evaluate pilot project
	A. Design formative component: implementation process, formal and informal utilization, satisfaction of consumers and constituents
	B. Design summative component: outcomes on recipients, impact on environment, differential effects
	C. Determine "fit" of research program and host environment (values, vested interests, objectivity)
	D. Determine how evaluation information is likely to be used and how it should be provided
	E. Consider how to manage system tensions and define balance of research and action goals
	F. Decide next step (move to next facet, recycle to preceding facet)
VIII.	Develop project
	A. Incorporate evaluation information
	B. Expand resources
	C. Identify methods for formal capacity building
	D. Identify and build social support system of researchers, host participants
	E. Determine research design/program structure

Exhibit 3.1. Outline of Facets of the Action-Research Cycle, Cont'd.

Facet	Brief Description
IX.	Implement project
X.	Monitoring, evaluation, feedback/modification (MEF/MOD)
	A. Determine when, how, what to measure
	B. Design formative component
	C. Design summative component
	D. Identify how monitoring and evaluation information is to be provided and used
	E. Identify contributions to theory and practice
	F. Reconsider "fit" with host environment
	G. Identify procedure, resources to document and ensure ongoing occurrence of MEF/MOD process
XI.	Processes for program maintenance, extension, termination
	A. Specify short- and long-term goals
	B. Specify responsibilities for monitoring resources, commitments, system pressures
	C. Build a program committee or team
XII.	Dissemination
	A. Determine scope of dissemination—within system, outside
	B. Decide how to "broadcast" and "market" program
	C. Make training arrangements
	D. Put in place a MEF/MOD process
	E. Recycle to other facets as needed

Early miscalculations, such as choosing an inappropriate or "unready" setting, failing to clarify mutual expectations, or allowing deficiencies in resources that will ultimately prevent adequate program implementation, extract a heavy toll later in the process. Table 3.1 presents indicators that can be used to assess the likelihood that a school setting can successfully host a program like social decision making and problem solving. By determining the balance of factors suggesting resiliency with those that are harbingers of resistance, decisions about selecting host settings can be clarified (see Elias & Clabby, 1984a, for a more detailed discussion of the initial action-research facets).

An essential feature of action research is that it creates numerous, explicit decision points. The pilot project becomes a critical checkpoint to avert a major commitment of resources in pursuit of an elusive goal. During the pilot study evaluation and subsequent program development process, investigators must clarify in-

**Table 3.1. Critical Indicators of the Resiliency-Resistances Balance
Across Organizational Domains.**

Domain	Signs of Resiliency	Signs of Resistance
1. Planning and decision making	School mission, goals openly discussed in explicit, complex, proactive terms Planning for workshop, in-service times Willingness to grant released time Interested in feedback—positive or negative; learning oriented	Reactive, crisis oriented Outcome oriented
2. Organizational processes a. Internal cohesion	Homogeneity across schools, within and between levels Identifiable and acknowledged coalitions Special Services with a non-negative relationship to administrators and regular education staff	Poor follow-through across schools[a] High turnover, low stability Power concentrated in relatively closed cliques Rebelliousness versus administration; litigiousness[b]
b. Personal growth orientation	Minimally defensive interpersonal relationships Concerned with incentives for all persons involved in the schools Oriented toward collaborative, facilitative relationships[c] Professional development of staff encouraged	Defensive, suspicious Apathetic[c]
c. Participation	Broad participation, job enlargement encouraged Coordinators utilized for grade levels, curriculum projects	Opposed to job enlargement, role expansion Structure of school routine discourages participation
d. Conflict management, managerial style	Conflicts confronted, managed openly A demonstrated capacity to manage different values, ideologies[a]	Conflicts avoided, subtly smoothed Conservative, highly structured, formal style, low flexibility

**Table 3.1. Critical Indicators of the Resiliency-Resistances Balance
Across Organizational Domains, Cont'd.**

Domain	Signs of Resiliency	Signs of Resistance
	Blend of administrators with longevity in system and new people with new ideas	Authoritarian management style
3. External boundary relationships	Volunteers welcome Generally good fit with wider community, constituencies Outside consultants regularly used[a]	Poor relationship with external systems; few outside consultants, poor relationships with parents; impermeable boundaries Boundaries not "managed" at all— excessively permeable Strong orientation toward satisfying external constituencies
4. History	Prior history of involvement in extended, programmatic efforts Positive accomplishments or attitudes in the social and affective domain	Key decision makers are new to the system

[a]This is also a sign in the history domain (no. 4). [b]This is also a sign in the personal growth area (no. 2b). [c]This is also a sign in the participation area (no. 2c).

tentions and resources before moving into implementation. The final three facets are later steps in the cycle but not afterthoughts. *Monitoring, evaluation, feedback/program modification* (MEF/ MOD); consideration of program maintenance; and dissemination activities must occur throughout the life of the project. Indeed, it is MEF/MOD that filters and channels information for decision making at each of the many action-research decision points.

During the course of our project, a number of different procedures have been used to measure the impact of training on recipients, the fidelity of implementation of program-related practices, skill acquisition, and the extent of generalization to a variety of social and academic domains. (Many of these measures are described in Chapter Four and can be found in Elias & Clabby, 1989.) Perhaps the ISA-SPS Project's most practical tools for MEF/MOD have been curriculum feedback sheets, "consumer satisfaction" surveys, a profile of social decision-making strengths, and existing school records, such as report card achievement and effort grades, areas designated as needing improvement, mid-marking-period notices, and discipline records. School records are especially useful when baseline data are gathered on cohorts prior to training, when equivalent groups receiving no program or various levels or types of programs are compared with a group receiving a focal program, and, ideally, when the staff members who keep the records are unaware that their data will be used to evaluate a particular program.

Many improvements in ISA-SPS Project intervention procedures have developed from having teachers and members of the ISA-SPS team complete curriculum feedback sheets after each lesson or topic in order to outline the group or class activities, indicate students for whom the activities were most or least effective, describe the most and least effective or favorable aspects of the session, note points to follow up in the next meeting, and specify suggested changes in the activities for the future. Global ratings (1 = low, 5 = high) are given in the areas of children's attentiveness, effectiveness of lessons and activities, and overall quality of the session. These sheets are used both as an aid in supervision of instruction and as a stimulus for curricular improvement and modification.

Consumer satisfaction surveys are administered at the end of the academic year or following a major curricular unit. A common format is used with students, teachers, and administrators. First, general attitudes and preferences are surveyed; then feedback concerning the elements of the program that were liked most and least are elicited through open-ended questions. Next, components of curricular lessons are outlined in detail and perspectives about each component are elicited with a yes-no format (for example, "Did you like 'Keep Calm'?" or "Did you feel that the decision-making steps were helpful?"). Finally, questions probe ways in which the program has been helpful, and individuals are asked to share anecdotes about applications of the program that they can recall making

(Elias & Clabby, 1989). The use of MEF/MOD procedures such as these have been essential both for fine-tuning programs and for making adaptations to children's special needs and to special instructional circumstances (examples will be provided in Chapter Eleven).

We view the twelve facets of action research shown in Exhibit 3.1 as an integral part of our project. They have provided powerful concepts for planning our work and understanding the results. However, listings of facets, or even more complex flow charts or path diagrams, fail to convey the dynamic process of interdependence, interplay, and recycling among components of a model. Further, the dimension of time often is underemphasized. Therefore, an action-research case history is presented next to add these configural dimensions. What follows below is an illustration of how the ISA-SPS Project has used the action-research process to carry out its work.

The Cornerstone of Action Research:
The "Fit" Between Idea and Need

A genuine action-research collaboration emerges when a pressing need within a host environment is matched with a viable, tangible program idea that can address that need. A process ensues by which members of separate systems—in our case, school personnel, community mental health center staff, and university-based action researchers—fit together to become an action-research *team*. The strategy for enhancing social competence and improving children's interpersonal coping has already been outlined. Next, the nature of the community needs at the inception of our work will be described. The focus will then center on the process of creating an action-research linkage. How was the search for an appropriate setting and subsequent negotiations accomplished? Findings are drawn from both anecdotal and interview data. The section will close with an overview of two essential ingredients for ensuring maintenance of a good fit between idea and need: a *vehicle* to convey the idea and an *evaluation* component to monitor its impact on the need.

Social Decision-Making and
Problem-Solving Skills: The Idea

Our view of the "idea" was that social decision-making and problem-solving thinking skills possibly were a fourth "R" in the array of so-called basic academic skills. "Basic skills" should also include practical intelligence, a knowledge of how to think and how to solve problems—a belief that educators now are expressing to a much greater degree than they were in 1979 (Sternberg & Wagner, 1986). We felt that improved social competence skills would allow children to devote more school time and energy to academic tasks, another belief that has been confirmed by recent data (George & Oldaker, 1986). In summary, as early as 1979, we believed that social decision-making and problem-solving skills represented a confluence of considerations in cognitive, developmental, school, clinical, and social psychology, providing a framework and a potential technology that awaited an opportunity to be further concretized and tested by an action-research team.

Community-Based, Preventively Oriented Services for Children:
The Need for the Community Mental Health Center

The University of Medicine and Dentistry of New Jersey–Community Mental Health Center (UMDNJ-CMHC) at Piscataway, like most other CMHCs, is mandated to provide consultation and education (C and E) services to the community. One of the thrusts of the mandate is to encourage centers to adopt a proactive stance toward prevention of mental illness. Perhaps because of its development out of a medical school heritage, the UMDNJ-CMHC at Piscataway has had a special interest in community education and training. In fact, the CMHC developed the role of center-wide C and E coordinator, with the person occupying that position charged with stimulating effective programming. Additionally, an educator-clinician was added to each of the three community-based outpatient service teams. This person formally was designated to provide consultation services to children and educators in the schools.

Special problems of management and effectiveness accompany CMHC consultation programs. For example, most C and E efforts consist of telephone contacts and occasional in-person clinical case liaison exchanges. Single-session talks to various groups and, in rare cases, a more continuous and systematic service such as four- or six-session training programs for paraprofessionals are also offered. Designing and carrying out even these short-term community interventions takes a significant amount of legwork and preparation. More importantly, while a well-executed C and E presentation can gather positive public relations for the CMHC, it is questionable how much real impact such time-limited interventions actually have on the mental health of the community.

Thus, a dilemma confronts educator-clinicians. They are expected to provide effective, efficient programming for children. To develop an effective program, they must think beyond a six-session training format. However, announcing a planned "stay" in a school for any period of time beyond the several-session format raises the skepticism and critical eye of any experienced and competent principal, as well it should. When educator-clinicians contemplate entry into a system, they must find, adapt, or develop a proposal that is not only sound in terms of research validation, but has sufficient commonsense appeal to withstand the review of a seasoned principal with influence within his or her system. This particular task, embodying the needs of the CMHC for community-based, preventively oriented C and E services for children, was taken on by educator-clinician John Clabby in the fall of 1979.

Restoring Children's Sound Interpersonal Development: The Need of the Community

Middlesex Borough is a multiethnic community of fifteen thousand persons located in central New Jersey. Approximately 60 percent of the population is blue collar, 35 percent skilled white collar, and 5 percent professional. At the start of the project, the borough had four elementary schools (grades K–5), one middle school (grades 6–8), and one high school (grades 9–12). The Middlesex Borough school system is run by a local school board and is also administratively linked to the larger Middlesex County Superintendent of Schools office, which serves as the local representative of the New Jersey State Department of Education. This administrative structure is quite common in the Northeast and in other densely populated areas of the United States.

Prior to 1979, the CMHC focused on cultivating a case liaison relationship with the Middlesex schools: occasionally, there was some limited C and E programming. In fall 1979, however, the CMHC learned, through various channels, that the leadership in the school system was becoming increasingly concerned that a number of its students did not possess satisfactory social and affective coping skills. Much of the attention centered on the children's difficulties in adjusting to middle school and subsequent continuation of these problems. Significantly, many behavioral problems were perceived as contributing to academic underachievement. Through parent conferences, teachers were learning about the stressors in family life, including what appeared to be an above-average incidence of marital disruption and alcoholism. Principals were distressed with having to manage a lengthening parade of youngsters with behavioral problems. The community even sponsored the development of a Youth Aid Bureau to provide counseling for the growing number of juveniles who were having contact with the Middlesex police.

In summary, fall 1979 found key members of the Middlesex Borough school system sensing a problem—children's emotional and behavioral difficulties—that encouraged a visionary look beyond the confines of their own closed system. The need was pressing enough to consider inviting outside resources to provide some assistance.

How the Idea and the Need Came Together

For a variety of reasons, the history of the CMHC's relationship to the Middlesex Borough school system was not an ideal one. The CMHC was plagued by high turnover in school liaison positions. Within the school system, the Department of Special Services, with its staff of school psychologists, social workers, and learning consultants, is typically delegated the role of liaison to outside support agencies. As can happen, Special Services seemed to adopt a competitive stance with the CMHC. This attitude, and resulting actions, served to discourage CMHC outreach efforts to that system—again, a typical reaction to an unfortunately typical situation.

Significantly, once the C and E staff members had "armed" themselves with what was then referred to as the social problem-solving model, the decision was made not to let past issues interfere with pursuing an opportunity to offer a program that seemed to have the potential to help many Middlesex youngsters. Additionally, the program was seen as an opportunity to learn about acquisition of SPS, an important research question, as well as a pilot opportunity for related consultation and education efforts. At this point, several facets of the action-research cycle began to come together. First, some formulation of the program had to be made, then the search for an entry setting had to occur, and finally, a negotiating process had to ensue during which the idea and need could be carefully fit together.

Initial Formulation and Search for a Setting

The educator-clinician developed a one-page proposal, devoid of mental health jargon, that outlined a social problem-solving program for one class of fourth graders. The idea was that the educator-clinician would come in for two thirty-minute sessions each week with one fourth-grade class. The procedure was that the consultant would read interpersonal conflict stories from *AWARE: Activities for Social Development* (Elardo & Cooper, 1977) and then lead a problem-solving discussion with the children. An eventual goal was for the classroom teacher to lead the discussions and work with increasingly specific curricular materials.

A search of past activities in which the two systems had collaborated suggested that an approach might be made to one of the elementary school principals, Tom Schuyler. On his own, he had successfully sponsored some presentations to the Parent-Teacher Organization by CMHC clinicians, as well as a time-limited parents' group. Because he was the senior principal in the district with significant administrative successes, it was felt that he might be both interested and well placed enough to sponsor a preventive project within the district.

Once the contact with the principal was made, the community's need began to emerge more clearly. The primary concern within the school system seemed to center on the students who were already in Von E. Mauger Middle School. Conversations with CMHC staff members had indicated that clinical cases in which the identified client was a middle school student seemed to be the most difficult. It also became apparent that parents were especially anxious about the developmental changes their children were experiencing. The principal noted that at Parent-Teacher Organization meetings, parents of the fifth graders would be seen in informal groups, apprehensively discussing their children going off to the sixth grade.

It was felt that the best way to help children adjust to what appeared to be some significant stressors in the middle school (that is, peer group inclusion-exclusion situations, pressures concerning substance abuse, fears of confrontations with older students, anxieties about clashes with authority figures, and parents anxious about middle school) was to equip them with coping skills before they entered the middle school. Program development thus began to center on a fourth-grade program with the idea that two years of training in critical problem-solving thinking would help to boost these children's resourcefulness, competence, and confidence when they entered the sixth grade. Further, once work began with fourth and then fifth graders, members of the action-research team would become an informal part of the school environment. They would be seen as mental health specialists; within that role, it was likely that they would be asked to help some of the teachers of the children who had been classified by the Special Services staff as emotionally disturbed. These special children also had to make the transition to middle school and were even less skilled at successfully negotiating such a change.

In summary, the idea proposed by the educator-clinician matched several levels of needs within the community, school, and CMHC. By conceptualizing the program not strictly as an intervention, but rather as an opportunity for genuine collaboration with the school system, some significant entry hurdles were surmounted. The key was collaboration and, through negotiation concerning the final form the program would take, the cultivation of a true partnership.

Negotiation and Reformulation

The initial approach to the building principal confirmed many of our assumptions about the need for a social problem-solving program and the appropriateness of selecting him as a gatekeeper within the school system. In his schools, the resiliency-resistances balance, which provides an index of a school system's readiness for change (Elias & Clabby, 1984b), was favorable toward program development (see Table 3.1).

The way the program was prepared and presented to the principal minimized the negotiations that had to occur. First, the proposal was clear and fit well within his general educational philosophy, which took the form of a commonsense approach to educating children for a range of adult experiences, including understanding and getting along with oneself and others. Second, the position of the principal as an "insider" within his system, with many experiences, contacts, and resources at his disposal, was being respected. In the critical issues of selecting personnel to become involved in the training, defining the teacher's role as gradually moving from observer to coleader to leader, and assisting the principal in providing assurances of accountability to the superintendent and board of education, the project staff was responsive to the principal's judgment and concerns. This tangibly conveyed a sense of partnership that facilitated increased trust and furthered mutual involvement. Specifically, the principal wished to have two of his fourth-grade teachers involved in carrying out the program, because they both were skillful in leading class groups, highly motivated, willing to try new methods, and concerned with the affective growth of their students. Although this doubled the anticipated workload of the educator-clinician, it was seen as important to make this reformulation, because it allowed a more adequate experimental design, increased the foothold of the program in the schools, efficiently used available school resources, and conveyed a flexible attitude toward responding to sound suggestions.

Implicit here is a third point: the building principal had previous involvement with research and had generally found these experiences to be favorable. More importantly, however, we came to appreciate his intuitive understanding of the special demands of a research and development program. Finished products and polished presentations do not exist; instead, materials and ideas are in a state of refinement and flux. His grasp of this fact and his work to help make school personnel and parents more comfortable with the situation were essential to allowing a genuinely collaborative spirit to develop on the project team. Members of the ISA-SPS team have refused to take the traditional role of "consultant-experts," and this gradually came to be recognized by project participants. The results of our formative evaluations indicated consistently that members of the project team were perceived as genuinely interested in the school and staff, accessible, and receptive to feedback, as well as knowledgeable about the technical aspects of social problem solving. In concise terms, our approach espoused collaboration and our subsequent actions have been seen as consistent with this orientation.

A final point that seemed to influence the building principal's receptiveness to our initial approach was our commitment to the school beyond the pilot study. Indeed, the term "pilot" was originally used by the principal. Our goal was to have an impact on the middle school. Although we did not explicitly and formally address this during the negotiation process, agreement gradually and naturally unfolded concerning issues such as follow-up of students and supportive work with parents and other school staff members. While a prevailing mode of school consultation seems to involve explicit contracting, our experience has been that a contract cannot substitute for a frequent and honest exchange of views and ideas—if you will, a positive, problem-solving climate. The initial informal, flexible, but clear manner of negotiating entry and program development issues served as a model for subsequent activities and fit the style and preference of the building principal and the educator-clinician.

In summary, the preparation undertaken by the educator-clinician and his genuine commitment to a collaborative partnership short-circuited some potentially difficult entry and negotiation issues. The program was reformulated to involve two teachers, and the eventual transfer of ownership of the program to the school was clarified. More importantly, a tone was set that enabled subsequent steps in the project to appear "workable" by the project leaders and the resources to which they had access. The project next expanded to incorporate an evaluation component and then to refine the curricular materials that would be conveying the program's ideas to the teachers, children, and parents.

The Role of Evaluation in Action-Research Planning

At the time of the initial interview between the educator-clinician and principal, it was agreed informally that it was quite likely that such a program would be actualized during that school year. The educator-clinician, who had a strong background in traditional individual psychometrics, recognized the difficulties inherent in measuring whether the children were making progress in learning social problem-solving skills. He contacted prominent researchers in the problem-solving field in search of some evaluation-research collaboration concerning this problem. A clinical/community psychologist from nearby Rutgers University, Maurice Elias, was nominated as a specialist in social problem-solving measurement. The UMDNJ-CMHC and the Department of Psychology of Rutgers University, although located very close to each other, at that time had relatively little ongoing collaboration concerning service programs or program evaluations. It was a significant step when the educator-clinician and Department of Psychology faculty member successfully met to join action with research.

From the perspective of the school system and CMHC, a monitoring and evaluation system was welcomed as a means of providing accountability for project activities. For the university, systematic data collection and carefully designed interventions are necessary conditions for generating scientifically acceptable knowledge. For all participants, the full cycle of MEF/MOD activities—monitoring, evaluation, feedback, and program modification—summarizes the ongoing nature of action research. Information is needed for informed decision making at two primary levels: (1) ensuring the effectiveness of the program for children at different developmental periods and (2) attending to the broader environment within which the program is embedded to enable adjustments to different environmental presses to be made. For a developmental project like ISA-SPS, a long stay within the host environment is necessary to gather (and ultimately analyze) the data needed to make meaningful conclusions and recommendations.

The Role of a Vehicle in an Action-Research Collaboration

An understanding of the internal demands, language, and incentive structure of the host environment as they relate to an action-research project is critical if the action-research team is to enter into and be part of the system for a reasonable length of time. With specific regard to the school system, the consultants from CMHC and the university began to reframe their ideas in terms of a fit with educational nomenclature and structure so that perception of the ISA-SPS Project as an alien intruder was minimized. In short, the consultants began speaking in "teacher-ese."

What seemed to encourage initial teacher cooperation was that the written materials were focused and concrete and required a minimum amount of teacher preparation. We were not convinced that the Elardo and Cooper (1977) curriculum met our needs for a systematic and cumulative introduction of problem-solving thinking skills. However, we realized that having written materials available minimized both teacher anxiety about leading effective discussions and opposition due to work overload. *A* vehicle was, initially, more important than *the* vehicle. It was through our pilot project experience, as well as by examining the content of the early school system-CMHC-university planning meetings, that it became apparent that successful action research requires a concrete focus, a vehicle around which opportunities for research- and service-related activities can be organized.

Different settings have different vehicles that they respond to: (1) for the community mental health center, it is the *program* or *project*, (2) for the university, it is the *written publication*, (3) for philanthropic private foundations, it is a *proposal*, and (4) for a school system, it is the *curriculum*. Introducing a multifaceted, multiyear curriculum in a systematic way allows for the scientific investigation of many processes, involving children, parents, and teachers in a variety of clusters such as classrooms, families, and schools. Under such circumstances, ISA becomes more than a project title; it becomes a generative concept for exploring linkages among contributors to children's interpersonal development. Significantly, the classroom-based curriculum is the vehicle that allows us to negotiate the many winding roads and occasional dead ends that come between CMHCs, schools, parents, and the university. Also, in the service of keeping the vehicle "tuned up" and working smoothly, we can incorporate into our explorations some measure of experimental rigor in settings that are beset with managing a seemingly endless flow of critical environmental presses. In the following section, we address some specific examples of ways in which we have put our action-research ideas into practice to develop our action-research vehicle.

Development of the Action-Research Vehicle

As we have implied in previous sections, any action-research vehicle must have the capacity for dynamic adaptation to the changing circumstances of the host environment. Creating this capacity, we have found, is a formidable challenge. In our initial conceptualization of the curriculum development process, we focused on monitoring, evaluation, and feedback as the primary determinants of curriculum change. Specifically, we set up a system to provide periodic feedback on the occurrence, content, and instructional techniques of the lessons (formative evaluation), as well as a study of the outcomes of exposure to all, part, or none of the curriculum (summative evaluation). Once our work began, however, we began to identify another very powerful set of factors influencing our action decisions regarding curricular change. We define this set as *environmental press*, which includes school and community factors, community mental health center goals and mandates, and pressures from the university environment and funding sources.

The process through which the curriculum evolved during the first three years of the project can aptly be described as dialectical. Our progress, which is outlined in detail in Appendix A, represented an amalgamation of the various influences on curricular form and structure in effect up to that time. These influences were operationalized within a revised curriculum, which then became the focal point of renewed formative and summative evaluation activity and environmental press. Most revealing is the relative influence of the research and environmental press factors in the decision-making process. Through the first three years of the project, environmental press for project expansion was the most significant shaping force. Between years 1 and 2, parents from nonparticipating schools exerted considerable pressure upon the district superintendent to include their children in the project. Similarly, the CMHC was interested in expanding its contacts beyond the original pilot study population. The favorable impressions generated about the project had several main sources: (1) enthusiastic responses from participating teachers, (2) positive feedback from children to their parents, (3) a deep philosophical commitment to the premises of the project on the part of key administrators, and (4) the visible, supportive presence of CMHC and university project team members (including students).

Implications for School Interventions

What are the implications for those who wish to carry out similar improvements of intervention vehicles introduced into their schools? First of all, the presence of an active monitoring, evaluation, and feedback component heightens participants' sense of accountability and, we believe, awareness of what they are doing and the impact it is having. This creates an environment that is primed for gathering anecdotal information. Second, we see information from both formative and summative research activities as being *supportive* of macrolevel decision making and *essential* to microlevel decision making. Decisions to expand the curriculum often are made before deliberations about evaluation results are completed. However, as Appendix A shows, our findings were consistent with the decisions made—there was good reason to link fourth- and fifth-grade curriculum sequences, to maintain instructional and application phases, and to provide a vehicle for reinforcement of the children's learning in middle school. Where summative and, especially, formative data were essential was in determining the precise manner in which the curriculum needed to be changed.

A critical example is reflected in the research findings from year 1: children seemed to be learning the early problem-solving steps more effectively than later ones. An analysis of lesson-by-lesson feedback revealed that, indeed, children rarely were given a chance to use the later steps, because each discussion would begin with the first steps and many concluded after a cursory study of the later steps. This finding converged with other research and suggested a strategy of teaching problem-solving steps sequentially. The steps would be introduced cumulatively about one per week, and each would be practiced until it was grasped by the class. A basic "unit" of action research is thus highlighted: an action step is followed by both *outcome* and *process* information, which allows *interpretation* of the outcome data and leads to *specific suggestions* for revised action. The new action can be implemented, and the cycle of action research can continue. A second key example was the development of the readiness phase of the curriculum to accommodate the needs of special education students and teachers. (Note that using a cumulative model as a starting point may be found to be inadequate in certain school contexts; Chapter Eleven will describe how other settings made action-research-based adaptations consistent with their needs.)

By examining the flow of action, information, and subsequent action, we can see that the vehicle for action research must be robust in order to adapt to shifting staff demands and environmental presses. Each year's work stimulates the emergence of new concepts, demands, and questions. The diverse and exciting nature of the issues raised (see Appendix A for specific examples) provides ongoing indicators of the power, utility, and scope of a curriculum as a viable intervention vehicle in school settings. Hence, throughout this book, the term *curriculum-based approach* is used to describe the basic SPS intervention format.

Moving from a "Vehicle" to a Service Delivery System

By the fourth year of the project, it became clear that the environmental press would lead to increases in demands for training. This, in turn, necessitated expanded forms of service delivery. Actually, it required a shift from thinking of the educator-clinician as a consultant to several schools to considering him as a program manager and director of a service delivery unit of the CMHC. Gradually, the "catchment area" of the program grew from two towns in central

New Jersey to a county with a population of over one-half million, and then to the State of New Jersey; after a decade, responsibilities included national dissemination. A brief outline of the major steps in the development of the ISA-SPS Project follows, to illustrate both the history of the project and how the form of service delivery of a program must change to adapt to increases in demand.

County Training Unit

In year 4, the ISA-SPS Project was encouraged to provide more equitable services throughout the county. A grant application submitted to the County Mental Health Board, and approved and funded by the County Board of Freeholders, authorized expansion into two large suburban school districts, in addition to the Middlesex and South Plainfield schools located near the CMHC. Exhibit 3.2 shows how the work of the first three years of the project allowed a specification of resources and procedures that became guidelines for building the capacity for a Middlesex county-wide training center. These considerations, moreover, are no different in scope from the planning any school-based practitioner must do when moving an intervention from a pilot site to multiple sites within a school district, or across districts.

UMDNJ-CMHC Social Problem-Solving Unit

Despite the gathering of resources, it was clear that a new structure would be needed to house the ISA-SPS service delivery component and allow for the development of staffing and procedures that were more consonant with a school-based prevention and consultation mission than with the CMHC's more traditional clinical mission. In year 6, UMDNJ established the Social Problem-Solving Unit for the CMHC, housed in its own building. This unit, directed by John Clabby, was one of very few CMHC-based preventive and social competence promotion service units in the country. Through interfacing with the ISA-SPS Project research team at Rutgers and the CMHC's own research and evaluation resources, led by Michael Gara, the SPS program began to evolve a systematic procedure for working with school districts and for providing the required action-

Exhibit 3.2. A Regional Primary Preventive Training Center: Dissemination Components Resulting from Action Research.

Components	Examples from Middlesex ISA-SPS
1. Research findings	1. Yearly evaluation reports, empirical studies
2. Intervention materials	2. Comprehensive critical thinking skills curriculum
3. Intervention technology	3. Twenty-hour workshop/training, follow-up program
4. Implementation principles	4. Project case history, book chapters outlining methods
5. Trained staff	5. CMHC staff, graduate students, teachers
6. Supervisors, master trainers	6. Continuing education workshops, project training
7. MEF/MOD technology	7. Observation checklists, consumer satisfaction, self-report indices, staff ratings
8. Ongoing project sites	8. Middlesex, South Plainfield schools
9. Structure, vehicle through which dissemination activities can occur	9. Continuing education workshops, regional training center

research and MEF/MOD components. The following list outlines the procedures used for engaging and working with school districts that approach the SPS Unit for services:

1. Assemble materials, staff, other components of action research
2. Identify potential school districts, make initial contacts
3. Do organizational preassessment; if adequate, proceed; if not, return to step 2
4. Develop an interdisciplinary core planning team (CPT)
5. Establish goals, parameters; select focus, vehicle for program, training requirements
6. Set up pilot project; implement
7. Supervise implementation, MEF/MOD; evaluate pilot project
   a. *Continue:* Change program or solidify and expand: go to step 8

or

    b.   *Discontinue:* Offer feedback to schools, center staff; go to step 9
8.   Reconvene CPT; begin internal dissemination
    a.   Begin staff development
    b.   Revise materials
    c.   Build support from constituencies
9.   Have center staff and CPT determine the nature of subsequent involvement with the district
    a.   Continue program development
    b.   Continue program consultation
    c.   Continue consultation about quality control
    d.   Use as resource for expansion to other districts
    e.   No further involvement

These procedures can be adapted by school practitioners to organize intervention activities and decision-making processes with their districts. The need for having interventions proceed from a base in a *team*, rather than through the isolated work of one or two individuals, is especially worth noting (Elias & Clabby, 1984a). Appendix B outlines the detailed and specific manner in which action-research arrangements are made with the SPS Unit; this is of particular importance as the volume of intervention work accelerates and it is desirable to maintain coordination and continuity across sites and over time. The concept of a "contracted evaluation plan" has added immeasurably to the organization, management, and follow-through of multisite interventions.

    Recognition of the work of the ISA-SPS Project has served as an environmental press catalyzing further growth. In the first six years of the project, action-research grant funds from the National Institute of Mental Health and the William T. Grant Foundation totaling nearly $600,000 in direct costs allowed for intensive and careful research and action using the framework shown in Exhibit 3.1. Data from this work justified the creation of the CMHC-based service delivery unit. In 1988, further acknowledgment was received from the National Mental Health Association when the ISA-SPS Project received the Lela Rowland Award as the outstanding prevention program in the country. Through leaders in the National

Mental Health Association, the project was encouraged to take on a national constituency.

The project's focus also was broadened and sharpened by being designated in 1988 by the New Jersey Department of Education as a model program for substance abuse prevention at the elementary grades. Among the data relevant to this designation was the follow-up study funded by the Schumann Fund for New Jersey, described in Claim 4 in Chapter Four, in which some long-term prevention of substance abuse was noted. The department created a grant program that allowed four districts to adopt the ISA-SPS program at the elementary grades for the purpose of primary prevention of substance abuse. This coincided with the publication of revised field-tested, "teacher-friendly" curriculum materials (Elias & Clabby, 1989) and recruitment of volunteers, such as those who work with the National Mental Health Association. The ISA-SPS Project now offers a year-round set of continuing education courses and workshops through the Continuing Education Center for the Promotion of Competence in the Schools, sponsored jointly by the Rutgers University Center for Applied Psychology and the CMHC at Piscataway (UMDNJ). Additional training contracted with individual school districts is provided through CMHC's SPS Unit.

Establishment of these service structures was timely because in 1989, the ISA-SPS Project experienced dramatic increases in requests for programs, particularly those concerning alcohol and drug abuse prevention. The service structures shown in the list of procedures above enabled the team to provide more standardized service delivery than ever before. A current action-research focus is integration of the social decision-making approach with districts' existing substance abuse prevention curricula at the elementary and middle school levels.

Rutgers University–UMDNJ Continuing Education Center for the Promotion of Social Competence in the Schools

With the receipt of the Lela Rowland Award, it became clear that the constituency for the social decision-making approach extends beyond schools and parents to other community agencies and groups; this approach successfully passed scientific review by the

Program Effectiveness Panel (PEP) of the National Diffusion Network (NDN) of the U.S. Department of Education. Receiving federal validation allowed the project to apply for developer/demonstrator funds from the NDN. This application was funded in 1990 for four years, with the possibility of renewals, and provided support for bringing the social decision-making approach to targeted states throughout the country. ISA-SPS staff work closely with a network of NDN facilitators for public and private schools, based in each U.S. state and territory, whose role is to bring PEP- and NDN-approved programs into their locations. The dissemination process is being aided by the publication of MEF/MOD-generated procedures for infusing social decision making and problem solving into a range of "niches" in the schools. The procedures are used as a starting point for applications of the approach with diverse populations, ranging from grades K-12 across cultural and ethnic groups, and including children who are considered to be gifted and talented, emotionally disturbed, attention deficit disordered, or required to cope with parental alcoholism (Elias & Tobias, 1990).

Conclusion

As of this writing, the ISA-SPS Project is most visible at the SPS Unit of the UMDNJ-CMHC at Piscataway. The SPS Unit has a full-time, highly trained, multidisciplinary service delivery staff equipped to implement CMHC and NDN charges to disseminate the program to school-based sites across New Jersey and the United States. The SPS Unit gradually has built the capacity to take on all key action research functions and is in the process of acquiring a computer-based capacity for self-sufficient analysis of data, thereby incorporating the procedures outlined in Appendix B.

The ISA-SPS Project focus is moving toward two missions: applied research and professional development. ISA-SPS research projects seek to further illuminate the conditions that contribute to social competence deficits and strengths in varying populations, school and community settings, and family living contexts. As an example, Robinson and Elias (in preparation) are investigating deficits in receptive and expressive nonverbal skills that are evident in urban special education children, many of whom are "crack babies" who have grown up and failed in mainstream public school settings. Information taken from this research will be used to enhance preventive and remediative interventions by the SPS Unit and related service providers in mental health and education. Finally, a major goal is the expansion of the Continuing Education Center for the Promotion of Social Competence in the Schools, so that it can more effectively reach its large constituency and become a focal point for skill building and renewal for diverse groups of professionals, parents, and policy makers.

Researchers and practitioners should note that the evolution of the project as described was not preplanned. It emerged from the mixture of a variety of personalities, forces, and circumstances. However, we have made explicit efforts here to study and document the trajectory of the processes involved and to set down guidelines that can be applied for school-based projects with varied content, scope, duration, and size.

Chapter Four

Examining the Effectiveness of Social Problem-Solving Programs

Interventions derived from the ISA-SPS Project have been subjected to an action-research process encompassing cycles of operation, evaluation, and modification. As noted previously, many environmental and configural factors influence the effectiveness of a program and decisions made about its continuity and directions; however, there should be no doubt that systematic data gathering has a necessary and important place in the program development process. Such data provide the most reliable information for refining a program as well as supplying the kind of documentation needed to secure the funding and other resources needed to keep a program functioning at an acceptable level, if not an optimal one.

This chapter illustrates how the ISA-SPS Project has organized its data around a central set of "claims." Not all settings will use the diverse forms of data collected, analyzed, and reported here. The guidelines to keep in mind are that the data to be gathered must be sensibly related to the questions being asked, and that data gathering must be approached rigorously and systematically. Partnerships with colleges, universities, and educational resource centers or state departments of education often can enhance the research-oriented resources. However, much of what follows requires no highly specialized statistical skills and should serve not only as an empirical warrant for the interventions to be described in Parts

Three through Five of this book, but also as examples to be adapted in one's own work.

Goals and Audiences

School-based programs derived from the ISA-SPS Project have the following major goals, each of which will be addressed in the subsequent section on claims of effectiveness:

1. Following training, teachers will improve in their ability to facilitate children's social decision making and problem solving.
2. Children receiving the program will improve their social decision-making and problem-solving skills relative to controls.
3. Children receiving the program in elementary school will show more prosocial behavior in school and a greater ability to cope with stressors upon transition to middle school than children who are not receiving the program.
4. Children in high school who received the program in elementary school will show greater positive, responsible, prosocial behavior and decreased antisocial, self-destructive, and socially disordered behavior, compared to controls who did not receive the program.

A concluding statement will describe ISA-SPS programs from an organizational, environment-centered perspective.

The primary target audiences for this program are elementary school–aged students, their teachers, school administrators, guidance and child study team staff, and parents. Students with various special education classifications, disaffected youth, and other high-risk populations have been served, as have students in regular education classes. The program also has been modified for use (and linkage with the elementary program) at the pre-K, middle school, and high school levels.

Modality of Intervention

The ISA-SPS Project is based on a curriculum approach that incorporates three phases: a *readiness phase,* which targets self-control and group participation and social awareness skills; an *instructional phase,* which teaches an eight-step social decision-making strategy to students; and an *application phase,* in which the children are taught to use the skills in relevant, "real-life" interpersonal and academic situations and thereby transfer and generalize their classroom learning. These three phases have evolved from our research to create a structure that allows maximal engagement, participation, and carry-over by the broadest range of students. The emphasis and pacing of learner activities is adjusted for classroom or group composition (for example, self-contained special education classes, below-grade-level regular education classes, regular education classes with mainstreamed special education students, or talented and gifted classes), as well as age level (Elias & Clabby, 1989; Elias & Tobias, 1990). Historically, the instructional phase was developed first and served as the basis for our pilot curriculum studies. Next, the application phase was added. The use of an explicit application phase reflects developmental theory, which suggests that it is not until children reach early adolescence and the cognitive stage of formal operations that one can begin to expect cognitive strategies to become more integrated, generalized, and consistent. The application phase is designed from the social learning theory view (Rotter, 1954) that maintenance and generalization of skills are a function of the relevance of the strategy and the extent to which the appropriate use of the strategy is reinforced by the environment. Finally, the readiness phase was added in response to teachers' concerns that students lacked adequate self-control, social awareness, and group participation skills to benefit maximally from the program. This need was especially apparent among students with behavioral, emotional, perceptual, or communication handicaps. (This recaps the detailed discussion of the early development of the curriculum found in Chapter Three.)

Although there are different nuances to teaching lessons in different phases, instruction in all phases shares several common features:

1. The primary objective is to teach children a set of heuristic social decision-making and problem-solving thinking steps.
2. Lessons are given to groups of children and are conducted on

a regular basis by the classroom teacher or other consistent group leader.

3. Extensive guided practice is built into most lessons; videotapes are used to provide skill modeling and hypothetical stories for skill practice.

4. Leaders conduct lessons in a manner that involves facilitative questioning or dialoguing to stimulate integration of learning. The three levels of facilitation are *low* ("Stop banging the ruler on the table!"); *moderate* ("Could you find some other use for the ruler or put it away?"); and *high* ("What else could you be doing now?" or "How do you think others feel about your banging?"). Facilitation is also accomplished through inquiry-oriented worksheets and writing assignments.

5. Classroom activities often involve cooperative, small-group discussion to promote peer-mediated learning.

6. Lessons are designed to be enjoyable to students and not to demand significant preparation time.

7. Leaders and significant others are provided with specific instructions to reinforce or promptly use the social decision-making and problem-solving skills in everyday school and home situations, in order to promote generalization and transfer.

Staff and Training Considerations

The program typically is formally conducted by classroom teachers in regular or special education once or twice per week (twice for special education); it has been integrated into various parts of the school routine in the districts with which we have worked, including health, family life education, social studies, substance abuse prevention, AIDS prevention, language arts, group guidance, club periods, and character education. In special education classes, the program meets IEP areas relating to social-emotional skill development and related behavioral and self-management deficits. It has been used successfully by teachers in classes as large as thirty-five, although smaller ones are desirable. It also has been used by school psychologists, guidance counselors, social workers, learning consultants, health educators, and other school personnel as the basis for running full-class or small groups over the course of a year or for a more delimited time period. Such groups have varied from general problem-solving "rap" sessions to others focused on substance abuse prevention, remediation, or relapse prevention. The data to be presented reflect teacher-led, classroom-based program implementation. (Further descriptions of the ISA-SPS training procedures can be found in Part Four.)

Settings and Participants

The primary development site, for which the data on all claims are presented in this report, is Middlesex Borough, a community of fifteen thousand in central New Jersey. It is a primarily blue collar, multiethnic, predominantly white town, which during the research period had been particularly hard hit by economic recession and familial disruption. There are four elementary schools, one middle school, and one high school in the district, a modal configuration in the Northeast.

In addition to this site, expansion has focused on a variety of districts in New Jersey, including urban districts with significant minority populations, large suburban districts, and rural districts, as well as districts that reflect a full range of socioeconomic circumstances. Some score well above average on standardized academic tests and some are closer to basal-level standards. Finally, special education is the focus of the program in several districts and a shared focus with regular education in others.

The populations on which the data for the claims of effectiveness were based included various cohorts of program recipients in Middlesex Borough. Regular education classes included small numbers of special education students mainstreamed in during program time, as well as some who were brought in for various academic subjects. Follow-up data were collected on trained students when they became sixth graders and high school students in Middlesex Borough. Attrition for the follow-ups was under 10 percent.

Evidence

As noted earlier, the data are organized as evidence for "claims." This format is used by the Program Effectiveness Panel of the U.S.

Department of Education's National Diffusion Network. In granting NDN approval to our program in July 1989, the Program Effectiveness Panel reviewed and accepted the claims presented here.

Claim 1: Following training, teachers will improve in their ability to facilitate children's social decision making and problem solving.

Feedback from consultants, ratings of periodic videotapes, reports of student observers, examination of lesson books, and principals' reports all converge to indicate that teachers have carried out the lessons as scripted and have encouraged social decision-making and problem-solving applications in their classrooms. Where project supervision and ongoing monitoring have been withdrawn, quality control is monitored by building principals and site leaders. Teachers' acquisition of an understanding of the social decision-making approach is shown in a 1980–1981 evaluation study (Elias, 1981). In October 1980, half of the teachers began the instructional phase, with the others serving as a delayed control. In January 1981, the original group began the application phase, while the controls received training and began the instructional phase. At three points during the year—September 1980, December 1980, and June 1981—teachers were given a series of hypothetical school-based problem situations and were asked how they would respond.

Teacher questioning strategies were measured by presenting teachers with a series of short vignettes derived from the work of Irving Sigel and George Spivack and Myrna Shure. Sigel in particular has done extensive research on the role of questioning in facilitating cognitive development, representational competence, and social schema (Copple, Sigel, & Saunders, 1979; Sigel, 1985). In his work with regular and special education students, he has developed a hierarchy of types of teacher (or parent) responses to problematic or decision-making situations faced by students. This hierarchy ranges from responses that are *inhibitory* of children's representational competence, such as authoritarian responses that tell children what to do with little or no explanation ("Don't hit other children because I said so"), those that are *moderately facilitative* of children's cognitive abilities, such as responses that help children see consequences or suggest alternatives from which they can choose

("If you hit other children, then they will not want to play with you" or "When you are angry at other children, you can talk to an adult or you can just walk away"), and those that are *highly facilitative* of children's cognitive representations, such as open-ended questions that encourage the child to think about the situation and reflect on possibilities and options ("What are all the things you can think of doing when you get angry at other children?" or "What do you really want to have happen on the playground?").

Spivack and Shure (1974; Shure & Spivack, 1978) operationalized some of Sigel's work and created a written self-report used to assess parents' questioning strategies. We combined Spivack and Shure's work with Sigel's and developed open-ended vignettes in which teachers' responses can be reliably scored along Sigel's continuum and vignettes in which teachers choose their most likely first and second courses of action from seven possible responses, each structured to reliably and objectively represent a point in Sigel's hierarchy. In addition, we have had observers and program consultants formally and informally observe, audiotape, or videotape lessons and we have developed reliable coding systems to identify the questioning strategies used by teachers.

The data demonstrated that teachers undergoing training in the fall significantly increased their use of the questioning strategies that have been found to be highly facilitative of problem-solving thinking and behavior (Copple et al., 1979). The pattern shown by teachers in our baseline assessment in the study is modal, consistent with existing research. Both the experimental and control groups had approximately 25 percent inhibitory responses and 37 percent moderately or highly facilitative responses at the start of the year (note that a self-report is usually more positive than observed behavior, but the pattern of response distributions and the changes over time are analogous in both modalities). After completing the instructional phase, the experimental group differed significantly in its questioning strategies from the control group. Completing the instructional phase was significantly associated with a 57 percent reduction in the use of inhibitory approaches to helping children resolve problem situations. Teachers who were not trained until January showed a 40 percent increase in their use of styles inhibitory of children's problem solving, compared to those who were trained at the beginning of the school year.

After receiving training, the control teachers' styles shifted markedly, so that by the end of the year, 86 percent of their responses to problematic situations could be considered highly or moderately facilitative of children's problem solving, and only 14 percent were inhibitory. (Rutter and others have found that this sort of balance is characteristic of "effective schools" and point out that inhibitory responses are linked to children's learning boundaries and limits and therefore have an important role to play, but not one that should predominate and shape the cognitive environment in the landscape of learning.) This represented a 61 percent reduction in the use of inhibitory strategies by the control group, following its instructional phase training and implementation. The responses of the experimental and control groups were barely distinguishable when they were compared at year's end; the former group had maintained its gains.

Claim 2: Children receiving the program will improve their social decision-making and problem-solving skills relative to controls.

In the evaluation of the pilot curriculum (Elias, 1980), two experimental fourth-grade classes (thirty-seven children) receiving two thirty-minute lessons per week from mid-January through May 1980 were compared with three fourth-grade classes (fifty-one children) receiving no treatment. The children's social problem-solving skills were measured with the Group Social Problem-Solving Assessment (GSPSA) and the Social Problem Situation Analysis Measure (SPSAM). The GSPSA is a criterion-referenced, developmentally-based, group-administered instrument that assesses three aspects of knowledge of social problem-solving concepts (Elias, Rothbaum, & Gara, 1986): Problem Analysis and Action, Specificity of Planning, and Interpersonal Sensitivity. Scores from the GSPSA have discriminated behaviorally and emotionally disordered middle school children from other subgroups in their school and are not correlated with the children's academic abilities. The SPSAM is individually administered and consists of a semistructured interview, designed according to Piaget's *méthode clinique,* in which children are presented with a series of pictures representing the unfolding action in a problematic situation. The children are questioned to elicit their responses at various points in the sequence, particularly when hypothetical obstacles to their generated solutions are encountered. Scores are derived for Interpersonal Sensitivity, Expectancies for Problem Solving (Locus of Control and Outcome), and Means-Ends Cognitions, under obstacle and nonobstacle conditions. Qualitative indices of strategies for problem resolution (for example, aggressive, prosocial, nonconfrontative) are also provided (Elias, Beier, & Gara, 1989).

While the groups did not differ initially, following training the experimental (E) group showed significantly better knowledge of problem-solving concepts than the control (C) group. Further exploration of this difference showed that the experimental group made particularly meaningful gains in sensitivity to others' feelings and in understanding consequences, and in both cases had significantly higher scores than the control group postassessment. On the SPSAM, which is more sensitive to subtle changes than the group assessment, 50 percent of the experimental group showed meaningful improvement in interpersonal perspective taking (compared to 10 percent of the controls) and 50 percent of the experimental group showed improvement in positive expectancies for problem solving and in means-end thinking (such as considering consequences and planning) when faced with interpersonal obstacles, compared to 24 percent of the controls. Similar differences were found under nonobstacle conditions. Also, half of the experimental group's qualitative problem resolution strategies reflected improvement in the use of realistic, personally initiated, and socially appropriate methods for coping with problems and obstacles, whereas the same was true for only 29 percent of the controls.

The instructional and application phases of the curriculum were evaluated by examining scores on the GSPSA over three time periods. Two groups of fourth and fifth graders were compared, one that received both phases and one that received the instructional phase in the spring only. A multivariate analysis of covariance found an overall experimental-control difference at $p < .001$. Univariate covariance analyses indicated that, from September to December, experimental children made substantial gains in Interpersonal Sensitivity and Problem Analysis and Action (which reflects a child's ability to examine a problem, define it, set goals, and prepare for alternative actions).

Control students, who received no training, showed no significant differences over this period. From December to June, E students received the application phase and C students received the instructional phase. By June, C students had made substantial gains in Interpersonal Sensitivity and Problem Analysis and Action. In Specificity of Planning, however, which is a focus of the application phase, the E group made gains and the C group did not. Thus, the C group responded to the instructional phase much as the E group did and actually "caught up" to the E group in Interpersonal Sensitivity by June (Elias & Clabby, 1989), as can be seen in Table 4.1.

Table 4.1. Experimental-Control Comparisons on the
Group Social Problem-Solving Assessment.

GSPSA Variable	E^a			C^b		
	Sept.	Dec.	June	Sept.	Dec.	June
Interpersonal Sensitivity	9.89 (2.20)[c]	10.23 (1.95)	10.29 (1.54)	9.33 (2.87)	9.57 (2.63)	10.38 (2.01)
Problem Analysis and Action	10.37 (3.62)	11.42 (3.68)	12.47 (3.72)	9.30 (4.14)	9.01 (4.56)	10.55 (4.43)
Specificity of Planning	4.83 (1.63)	5.27 (1.43)	5.51 (1.27)	4.65 (1.82)	5.11 (2.00)	4.96 (2.08)

[a]$n = 120$. [b]$n = 112$. [c]Standard deviations are in parentheses.

As an additional index, students were asked how they would approach a problem they are facing. Raters were given unmarked, standardized protocols with students' responses before and after the instructional phase. The raters consistently identified protocols that were obtained prior to social problem-solving lessons, with approximately 88 percent accuracy. Qualitative analyses suggested that prior to training, children's responses were vague and disorganized, and that they indicated no clear or systematic approach to handling problems. After the instructional phase, children's responses reflected a substantial use of the eight social problem-solving steps, particularly the first four (examining feelings through considering alternatives). Children were also asked about their use of what they learned concerning social problem solving in a variety of settings. Experimental children exceeded controls, with the greatest use of social problem solving reported to take place at home with peers and in class, and the least use reported at lunch (Elias, 1981).

The readiness phase of the curriculum was pilot tested in the third grade at Watchung School during the 1985–86 school year. One teacher conducted weekly forty-minute lessons over an eleven-week period while the other third-grade teacher in the school served as a control. Children were pretested on the concepts covered in the SPS readiness lessons using a criterion-referenced, developmentally based assessment, Getting Along With Others. Interrater reliability across multiple trials consistently exceeded 90 percent. The assessment covered key readiness skills such as paying attention, listening, dealing with being upset, and knowing what to look for in a friend.

Prior to training, children's answers were vague and nonspecific. After training, experimental and control students were tested again. Among the experimental group, 100 percent were able to give specific, acceptable strategies for paying attention, compared to 60 percent in the control group; 63 percent of the experimental group were able to identify two or three ways to tell how they knew they were upset, compared to 27 percent in the control group. In the self-control area, 56 percent of the experimental group were able to use a specific strategy to become less upset, such as Keep Calm, asking for help, or thinking about the problem; 44 percent said to ignore or forget the problem. On the other hand, 44 percent of the control group had no strategy at all to help them become less upset. The remaining answers took the form of ignoring the actual problem or using aggressive behavior. All of the children in the experimental group were able to list four specific qualities desirable in a friend; in contrast, 81 percent of the children in the control group could only name one or zero qualities that were desirable in a friend.

Claim 3: Children receiving the program in elementary school will show more prosocial behavior in school and a greater ability to cope with stressors upon transition to middle school than children who are not receiving the program.

In the pilot curriculum evaluation (Elias, 1980), experimental teachers rated their students as becoming more socially appropriate, adaptive in coping, and self-reliant from January to June. Control teachers, interestingly, saw some deterioration, particularly in self-reliance (35 percent decline and 25 percent improvement versus 14 percent and 65 percent, respectively, for the experimental group). In data analyses focusing on the impact of the program on peer relationships, children who showed significant gains on the GSPSA after receiving the instructional phase of the curriculum were found to show corresponding gains in sociometric scores for socially appropriate and constructive problem solving behaviors, with $p < .05$.

It has been suggested that transfer of social-cognitive effects to the interpersonal domain takes time, in part because of the natural stability of social labeling and social reinforcement patterns and in part because of the time needed to integrate newly acquired cognitive abilities. While improved social decision-making and problem-solving skills might reduce avoidant reactions and thus diminish absence and tardiness, a more direct estimate of interpersonal effects can be examined through sociometric indices. Prior to training in December, children in all classes were administered the Peer Attribution Inventory (PAI). The PAI is a peer nomination procedure with excellent test-retest stability and internal consistency, from which four summary scores can be derived: social appropriateness (sharing, liked by others), social inappropriateness (fighting, not waiting one's turn), social isolation (alone, being avoided), and peer leadership (helpful to others, positively self-reliant). Scores from the PAI have shown consistent significant relationships with teachers' ratings of students' behavior and self-concept scores (Elias, Beier, & Gara, 1989).

In our conceptualization, the social decision-making program sets into motion not only skill acquisition within individual children but also a process by which children begin to look at each other in new ways and reconceptualize their peer relationships. We believe that labels can become "unstuck" as children are taught to be more interpersonally aware and to consider alternatives and consequences in their everyday classroom interactions. To us, a comparison between children who received only the Instructional phase with those who received no training was the most meaningful analysis. Children were assigned scores that denoted whether they were in the bottom, middle, or top third of the nominations received for each sociometric item, based on the distribution of scores across *all* children (*E* and *C*). Using chi-square analyses, movement of children across major status groupings was compared for experimental (instructional phase only) and control (no treatment) conditions.

Significant results at or beyond the .01 level were obtained in two areas. First, experimental children made substantial gains in being seen as helpful to others and as self-reliant problem solvers—two behaviors that are a primary target of a social problem-solving program. Second, isolation was significantly reduced. Children who received Instructional phase training were much less likely to be viewed as sitting alone and having no friends. In control classrooms, patterns of social isolation that were seen at the beginning of the year tended to be stable or to intensify at the midyear assessment.

Absence and tardiness are well recognized as indicators of children who are likely to experience adjustment difficulty. Patterns of absence and tardiness are associated with school withdrawal and failure and, in our framework, imply a lack of proactive, constructive problem-solving strategies. Using multivariate analyses of covariance, the pattern of change of absence and tardiness scores was examined over the four marking periods for the children receiving the two-phase (instructional and application) curriculum or only the instructional phase. A significant multivariate effect was found only for change between the second and third marking periods, and again a group-by-grade interaction was found, with $p < .01$. Univariate analyses revealed major improvements in fourth graders who received the full curriculum, with reductions in absences and especially in tardiness. However, differences in the within-group variances across time periods suggest caution in interpreting the nature of the covariance adjustment of the initial group differences.

Thus, the ISA-SPS instructional and application phases have been associated with (1) increasing skills that are seen as important to social competence, (2) reducing deficiencies that have been clearly documented as placing children at risk for subsequent dysfunction, and (3) improving school attendance and punctuality, behaviors that are clearly predictive of future academic and interpersonal functioning (although greater caution should be noted with regard to the latter finding, when it is compared to the first two conclusions).

Behavioral changes resulting from readiness lessons were examined in one experimental and one control class of third-grade students. Training consisted of eleven formal lessons and follow-up activities. Teachers were asked to observe and rate the following behaviors in their students before and after the training period:

- *Sensitivity*—skills such as the recognition and expression of feelings, and giving help to others
- *Self-control*—skills such as listening carefully, following directions, and calming oneself down to concentrate on work or to resist provocation
- *Positive behavior*—social approach and group interaction skills such as using an appropriate tone of voice when conversing with adults or peers
- *Peer acceptance*—ability to be accepted by classmates and included in group activities
- *Teacher time*—the amount of time required by the teacher to help with individual social-emotional and academic problems

Experimental and control students were comparable at pretest in all areas.

The result of teachers' evaluations of students' social behavior strongly indicate statistically significant gains for the children participating in the program in each of the social behavior areas. They also improved significantly on the level of overall peer acceptance in the classroom and showed significant reductions in the amount of teacher time that was necessary for helping them solve academic as well as social and emotional problems. The control group made no statistically significant gains in any of the areas assessed. It is not possible, however, to be certain that trained teachers were not sensitized to look for certain behaviors and rate them more favorably than control group teachers would. Nevertheless, the validity of these changes is supported by observation by on-site project consultants and by school administrators, who subsequently approved the program for district-wide adoption.

Generalization to Academic Performance

The application phase of the curriculum contained specific lessons that integrated the use of a social decision-making and problem-solving approach into both social studies and language arts skills. Specific examples include activities designed to help children critically analyze current and historical events in a decision-making framework and worksheets designed to help children write more creatively and check their final product before submitting it to the teacher. It was reasoned that children who received the application phase from January to June would show significantly greater improvement in social studies and language arts report card grades compared with children who received only the instructional phase during that time.

Multivariate analyses of covariance were performed to examine changes between the first and second, second and third, and second and fourth marking periods. The grades for the second marking period were recorded at approximately the same time the application phase was begun, affording appropriate comparison points. No group differences were found between the first and second marking periods. From the second to the third marking periods, there were no significant main effects for experimental group or grade level, but there was a significant multivariate F for the group-by-grade interaction, with $p < .005$. Post hoc testing revealed that the differences were in language arts scores, with modest improvement noted in fifth graders who received the application phase. From the second marking period to the final marking period, a multivariate group-by-grade effect was again found, with $p < .0002$. In language arts, fifth graders who received the application phase showed the greatest overall improvement, while fifth graders who received the instructional phase were the only children to show virtually no change. In social studies, all groups improved; however, the greatest gains were made by fourth graders who received the application phase.

Although none of these analyses violated the assumption of homogeneity of slope of the covariate with the dependent variables, the pervasiveness of the group-by-grade interaction suggests a cautious interpretation of results. Nevertheless, it was found that instructional phase training used alone did not produce gains in social studies or language arts. However, generalization was accomplished by the incremental benefits when the application phase was added to the instructional phase. This suggests the critical importance of the application concept as a necessary component of preventive social problem-solving efforts.

Impact on the Transition to Middle School

An assessment of the generalizability of the program involved an examination of the impact of receiving full, partial (instructional phase only), or no exposure to the curriculum on reactions to the stressors that were encountered during the transition to middle school. Elias, Gara, Ubriaco, Rothbaum, Clabby, and Schuyler (1986) conducted a study involving 158 fifth-grade students in four elementary schools for whom parental permission was obtained (98 percent of the possible sample). There were 80 boys and 78 girls. Academically, they averaged approximately one year above grade level on standardized academic tests. All fifth-grade teachers were involved in carrying out the program under a delayed control design. Within the larger project, it was agreed that sufficient quality control could not be maintained if implementation was begun in all fifth-grade classrooms simultaneously; it was decided to begin instruction in two schools and use the two other schools as a delayed comparison group, while simultaneously meeting the concerns of parents that their children receive a high-quality program before entering middle school. To examine the nature of the adjustment among children who received no SPS training, a control group was used consisting of children entering middle school during the prior year. Thus, there were three quasi-experimental conditions: (1) no training, (2) full training, and (3) partial training (instructional phase only).

For the purpose of this study, two primary assessments were made. The first was assessment of children's transition to middle school. The instrument used, the Survey of Adaptational Tasks–Middle School, consisted of twenty-eight commonly occurring situations in middle school identified through behavioral analytic procedures as leading to difficulty, distress, or upset feelings (Goldfried & D'Zurilla, 1969). Examples of these stressor situations ranged from logistical concerns such as forgetting one's locker combination and learning one's way around a larger new building, to mastering new academic routines (having many different teachers, more homework, greater academic pressures) and new relationships with peers (being teased or asked to do things one does not want to do, being approached to smoke or drink, not being part of a desired group, undressing in a locker room). Children were asked to rate each stressor, stating that it was either not a problem, a small problem, a medium problem, or a large problem for them in middle school. In addition to patterns of response on the twenty-eight stressors, summary indices included problem frequency (number of stressors rated as being a small, medium, or large problem) and problem intensity (number of stressors rated as a large problem). The present measure has an internal consistency coefficient greater than .90 across different samples and has been predictive of Piers-Harris Children's Self-Concept Scale scores, school attendance, and teacher ratings of school adjustment using the Activity-Mood-Learning (AML) (Elias, Gara, & Ubriaco, 1985). In October of their first year in the sixth grade, all children who received social problem-solving training were administered the Survey. The preceding year, a comparison cohort entering the same middle school had also received the Survey. The second primary assessment involved children's social problem-solving skills, using the GSPSA.

For the three groups of children, it was found that those entering without receiving training were differentiated from those who received at least some training, in both the extent and severity of the situations they considered to be problematic, with regression analyses significant at $p < .05$. Stressors such as peer pressure, academic demands, coping with authority figures, and becoming involved in behaviors such as smoking and substance abuse posed significantly more difficulty to children in the untrained group. Further, a significant discrimination also could be made between children with different amounts of training, in the expected direction. Perhaps most importantly, an analysis of the relationship of all children's social problem-solving abilities to their responses to stressors indicated a significant inverse relationship of Problem

Analysis and Action and Specificity of Planning with severity of stressors.

Overall, the results indicate that there is a positive association between level of training and children's reports of coping with stressors and adjusting to middle school, and that social decision making and problem solving is an important aspect of this shared variance. These results cannot be accounted for by preexisting differences related to the children's elementary schools or to marked differences in the degree of stressors encountered by students from one year to the next. Empirical support was found to suggest that a consistent mediating factor in the way children responded to stressors was their social problem-solving skills—most specifically, Problem Analysis and Action. These findings were obtained approximately four months after the conclusion of any formal training, including an intervening summer. None of the cues traditionally associated with the maintenance of an intervention (for example, the same physical environment, prompts by a trained teacher, or continued contact with the group within which training occurred) were available to the children. Furthermore, they were subjected to a transitional life event—middle school entry—with well-documented destabilizing influences on a "normal" population (Elias et al., 1985; Lipsitz, 1977; Toepfer & Marani, 1980).

Other alternative explanations also merit consideration. The mixture of children from all four elementary schools within each middle school homeroom and then in further recombinations within subject area classes makes any hidden group effects unlikely. Perhaps the area most in need of replication and extension is the use of the self-report Survey of Adaptational Tasks–Middle School as the main criterion measure. Nevertheless, there is evidence that self-reports of stressors are reasonably accurate (Felner, Farber, & Primavera, 1983). Further, Lazarus and Folkman (1984) state that self-report measures allow for an assessment of an individual's appraisal of the impact of various life events, a construct found empirically at the core of stress and coping processes.

Claim 4: Children in high school who received the program in elementary school will show greater positive, responsible, prosocial behavior and decreased antisocial, self-destructive, and socially dis-

ordered behavior, compared to controls who did not receive the program.

The design of the study (Elias, Branden-Muller, & Sayette, 1990) involved a comparison of three cohorts of students (grades 9–11) who received social decision-making and problem-solving lessons in elementary school, with a corresponding no-treatment control group. Cohorts also received, with each group, different levels of instructional fidelity to the program.

Children did not know the purpose of the study, and the participation rate exceeded 95 percent. The measures used were the National Youth Survey (NYS) of Antisocial and Delinquent Behaviors (Elliot, Ageton, Huizinga, Knowles, & Canter, 1983) and the Youth Self Report (YSR) Rating Scale (Achenbach & Edelbrock, 1987). Both are self-reports, are standardized, and have been validated against external behavioral indices. The NYS consists of items covering vandalism; theft; use of various illegal substances; aggressive behavior toward parents, peers, and other adults; cheating at school; lying about one's age; facilitating others' lying about their ages; and school-based discipline problems. The YSR taps six factors: depression, unpopularity, aggression, delinquency, somatic complaints, and thought disorders (an additional factor, self-destructive/identity problems, is scored for boys only). There is also a competence assessment, including overall social competence and positive social activity.

Results of analyses of variance indicated that, relative to ninth-grade controls, ninth-grade students used significantly fewer alcoholic beverages and had fewer self-destructive/identity problems, higher scores in overall social competence, greater membership and participation in positive social organizations, a higher level of participation in nonsports activities, and a higher level of quality of work when they were employed. Tenth-grade control students were significantly higher than tenth-grade program students in vandalism against school property, attacking persons with intent to injure, hitting or threatening other students, self-destructive/identity problems, and unpopularity. They also showed lower scores in overall social competence. Eleventh-grade control students were significantly higher than eleventh-grade program students in vandalism against parental property, hitting or threatening parents, and use of chewing tobacco. Across grades, male controls significantly exceeded male program recipients in petty theft and in buying or providing alcohol for someone else. The overall pattern of findings also indicated that students who received the higher-fidelity program implementation generally showed better goal attainment than those who received lower-fidelity implementation, but this was not a statistically significant effect. It should be noted that these results reflect generally low base rates, no correction for attenuation, and no program of follow-up in the middle school.

Conclusion

Evidence has been presented in a number of areas that shows the diverse application and multiple effects of the social decision-making program. This reflects the nature of the skills being developed and their application to common situations such as classroom and peer relationship problems. The skills introduced in the elementary years provide a developmental foundation upon which subsequent preventive programs can be built; yet, as our data show, some benefits can be derived even without planned, systematic follow-up and reinforcement after training.

A caveat should be noted. The basic method of selecting treatment and control groups used a quasi-experimental design. Following the work of Peter Rossi, Richard Price, Raymond Lorion, and others concerning the evaluation of preventive and competence-promoting programs, our strategy has been to start with treatment groups that are relatively motivated, and not randomly assigned. The ISA-SPS team has remained in districts over long periods of time, and each stage of action and research has been affected by any previous work and teachers' differential familiarity with it. Thus, one is always working with nonequivalent control groups. Discerning researchers recognize the problems of this design and the potential limits on generalizability and selection-by-treatment interaction effects. Attempts to minimize these effects have used delayed control and incremental designs, close monitoring of program delivery and teacher and student receptivity and responsiveness, and examination of the mediating roles of these variables where possible.

A final issue of great practical significance is the maintenance and generalization of learnings from a program. Since the
inception of the ISA-SPS program, students, teachers, and administrators have been given feedback surveys to complete. The general
format of these surveys involved items asking about satisfaction
with lessons, ratings of detailed components of the lessons, and
open-ended questions on how the curriculum could be improved.
Results in Elias (1980, 1981) and Elias, Gara, Ubriaco, Rothbaum,
Clabby, and Schuyler (1986) indicate that children and teachers who
are involved in the program find it enjoyable and worthwhile, and
that they put the principles of the program to regular and frequent
use. Among teachers, over 90 percent surveyed have said that the
instructional phase alone was of great or some value in helping
them understand the feelings, thoughts, and problems of their students. Most felt that the curriculum truly provided students with a
much-needed strategy to turn to when they were faced with problems and that the application phase provided many benefits in
classroom management and significant carry-over into academic
and interpersonal school situations. Students consistently give
poignant examples of occasions on which they use SPS, particularly
in situations that are not directly included in the curriculum. Here
are some examples in the students' own words (Elias et al., 1986):

> "One day I forgot my homework at home. I told my teacher
> calmly after counting to ten and using the social problem-
> solving steps."
> "I used it on writing stories by thinking of the past or using
> my imagination."
> "At home when just my brother, sister, and I are there, my
> brother gets on my nerves. I go in my room and figure out
> what to do. I really only use the VENT system" (discussed
> on p. 122).
> "In school, a girl in my class always gets upset over nothing
> and I try to help her by going over the eight steps."
> "I used the problem-solving steps while I was riding my bike
> and this jeep came riding up and the men inside asked me
> if I would like a ride. They were kind of a help to me

because I thought of a solution and said no and rode away." (Elias & Clabby, 1989).

These "consumer satisfaction" findings have been replicated in the primary action-research site, Middlesex Borough, New Jersey, and in our initial dissemination/diffusion sites, including urban areas such as Perth Amboy, New Jersey. These findings, added to the history of long-term use of the program in various sites, suggest that the social decision-making and problem-solving approach encourages receptivity, responsiveness, and everyday use of the skills being taught.

It would be a conceptual error to think that the impact of the ISA-SPS Project derives solely, or even primarily, from a simple skills learning paradigm. The conceptual framework described earlier has guided the project in working with school environments as well as individuals. (Examples will be presented in Chapter Eleven.) Any effective preventive or remediative program ultimately must show social and ecological validity by affecting individuals, their environments, and their ongoing transactions. The ISA-SPS approach is associated with improvements in both social problem solving and social adjustment. It is essential to note that this approach consists not only of a set of curriculum materials but of extensive, field-tested procedures that include

1. Engaging in collaboration with school districts
2. Training teachers and key district personnel
3. Providing a supervisory and MEF/MOD structure
4. Assisting districts to develop the capacity building needed to make them efficient and effective in institutionalizing social problem solving while continuing innovative, careful, within-district expansion
5. Accessing districts to a resource exchange network that provides vehicles for sharing specific successful and unsuccessful implementation procedures, disseminating research findings, and obtaining needed consultation

Thus, our project is most properly conceptualized as a comprehensive effort to generate sustained change at organizational, group, and individual levels, which we maintain is possible for even small-scale, school-based interventions.

PART THREE

Key Elements
of Program
Implementation

Parts Three and Four show how the social, conceptual, and empirical foundations of the ISA-SPS Project are operationalized in specific and concrete terms. These parts, authored by John Clabby, are written "practitioner to practitioner." As noted in Chapter Four, the ISA-SPS approach is curriculum based but recognizes a variety of factors that must be addressed by the school-based practitioner or action researcher in bringing the approach to fruition. In Parts Three and Four, the emphasis is on simplification of these factors through the concept of *key elements:* the factors practitioners must attend to most carefully in their quest to fashion a social decision-making and problem-solving program that will be of maximum benefit for their particular populations and settings.

It is becoming clear that getting programs to work effectively—even those that have had successful field trials—is a major challenge facing school-based professionals and other practitioners (Price, et al., 1988). For over a quarter of a century, the National Diffusion Network—a branch of the U.S. Department of Education—has devoted itself to facilitating the dissemination of research-validated educational interventions in mathematics, science, geography, history, and other areas, including social decision making and social problem solving. It is an organization that has worked to help programs identify what they do to reach their goals.

Working from guidelines established by the NDN and other sources (Ralph & Dwyer, 1988; Westchester County Social Competence in the Schools Task Force, 1990; Zins & Forman, 1988), we can outline a series of key elements to make up the components of a plan that is likely to lead to the successful replication of a program in another site. The concept of key elements is designed to convey the idea that certain levels of comprehensiveness and intensiveness are necessary if an intervention is to be effective and if it is to be operated as intended by its developers and as suggested by field testing. Key elements help guide practitioners in adapting a program to local conditions so that they can avoid making changes in program practices that will compromise the program's effectiveness.

The key elements of disseminable school-based programs from a "practitioner-friendly" perspective are summarized in the acronym MATS/MEF.

"M," *matching and planning,* addresses the process of ensuring a match between a school district's goals and what a program can offer. It also relates to planning a "pilot project" with which to test program feasibility for a given site, prior to full-scale implementation.

"A," *appropriate classroom materials,* includes specified sets of curricula and related activities that are to be carried out by school personnel and that incorporate required instructional strategies, classroom arrangements, and instructional resources.

"T," *training,* covers orientation, staff training, and other professional development activities, both initially and over time.

"S," *special help for special circumstances,* articulates the components required to adapt the program to children with special behavioral or learning needs or to the special characteristics of a setting.

"MEF," *monitoring, evaluation, and feedback,* specifies management arrangements for supervising lesson planning, instruction, curricular inclusion, consultative support, building and district coordination, and continuity of resources, as well as ways to ensure that the program is being carried out as intended with receptivity and responsiveness by implementors and students, with recommended adjustments made to allow the program to achieve the desired goals more easily.

Chapter Five focuses on the key element of matching and planning; this is the area where the practitioner should start in the important first step of assessing and negotiating a "fit" between a school district's resources and an SPS program. Chapter Six focuses on the hub of any school-based program: the curricular and instructional component. The award-winning, NDN-approved social decision-making curriculum for the elementary grades (Elias & Clabby, 1989) will be presented, with some references to earlier, related programs. Chapter Seven extends the discussion to the challenge of developing curricular and instructional approaches to the middle and high school.

As noted in Chapters Three and Four, the social decision-making and problem-solving program has received strong empirical support; its approval by NDN's Program Effectiveness Panel and its designation as an educational program of excellence reflects the research that has been carried out to date. Nevertheless, for practitioners, it is essential to go beyond broad statements of effectiveness. As the ISA-SPS Project has worked to disseminate the program to various sites, practitioners have assisted program staff in classifying the key elements that allow the program to be successful when other seemingly related programs have not. All of the key elements indicated earlier correspond to specific action-research activities undertaken by the ISA-SPS team and school-based consultants and practitioners working with the SPS Unit of UMDNJ-CMHC. These elements are reviewed next as they apply to SPS program development.

Matching and Planning

An initial needs assessment and program planning conversation done in person or on the telephone is important to assure that an appropriate match takes place between the district's needs and the program's services. What someone reads about social problem solving may or may not be consistent with what is being offered by a particular social problem-solving program. Early discussions with school representatives sometimes reveal that school personnel have equated social problem solving with a behavior modification program. Regardless of their preconceptions, the SPS Unit and school leaders should engage in a thorough discussion of what social problem solving comprises, thus allowing the school system to make a determination about whether social problem solving, as they more properly understand it, would fit their needs.

An important step is for an already existing committee, such as a health curriculum committee, to take on management responsibility for the program. If this is not possible, a new committee can be formed specifically for social problem solving.

The committee should include individuals with direct relationships to the central administration of the school system, as well as teachers, a building principal, and other key staff such as a guidance counselor or child study team members. This committee will take responsibility for conducting needs assessment, selecting the grade levels for the program, designing the pilot and the full program, implementation, management, incorporating feedback into tailoring of local programs, and program evaluation. This committee should plan for a well-monitored pilot program and also for subsequent continuation and expansion of the program. Where the SPS Unit of the UMDNJ-CMHC is involved, it is expected that a contracted service agreement and a contracted evaluation plan will be completed on an annual basis. This model fosters quality control and allows updating, while also promoting local ownership of the program and substantial autonomy, particularly after two to three years.

Appropriate Classroom Materials

The district leadership should review many programs and select an appropriate one, based on such factors as local needs, expectations for training, costs, and implementation demands. Dissemination for the ISA-SPS Project is based on *Social Decision-Making Skills: A Curriculum Guide for the Elementary Grades* (Elias & Clabby, 1989). This is a set of coordinated, sequenced, and scripted lesson materials and follow-through activities for grades K-6 (or K-5, or K-4, if an elementary school is so configured). This document also contains a set of procedures that are used as the basis for staff development activities and ongoing program monitoring, feedback gathering, and evaluation.

The curriculum is obtained by the district for the program

instructors, school district consultants, and other selected members of the district's SPS committee. A major portion of Chapter Six will be devoted to a discussion of this particular key element.

Training

A two-day training program that focuses on teaching the program implementors to use the curriculum is a central program component. The focus of the chapters on training in this book is on teacher training. However, members of the district's SPS committee should seek out consultation from a program such as the SPS Unit to discuss ways of providing on-site supportive visits to the implementing teachers, as well as supplying the other aspects of program management such as planning for program maintenance, expansion, and program institutionalization. Such vehicles as a toll-free telephone "hot line" also may be used to provide follow-up consultation by the SPS Unit Staff.

Special Help for Special Circumstances

One of the SPS program's primary strengths is its use of classroom-wide instruction with all of the children in the class. Students with special problems need this level of intervention and often much more. Consequently, a solid SPS program is characterized by a school staff's familiarity with and use of such approaches as individualized counseling using the SPS paradigm. This principle is extended most comprehensively when SPS programs are implemented in special education schools. Part Four addresses this element in greater detail.

Monitoring, Evaluation, and Feedback

Through the action-research process, much has been learned about implementation standards for SPS programs. For example, the district administration should arrange a minimum of one instructional period a week in which teachers conduct lessons with students using curriculum-based procedures. For maintenance and generalization of gains, other follow-through activities are absolutely required, including the use of social problem solving in the basic academic areas; its use in counseling by appropriate staff members; use of the SPS framework in the routine exchanges that occur between children and such support staff as librarians, school nurses, and recess aides; the posting of SPS skills on bulletin boards throughout the school building; implementation of SPS workshops for parents; and the dissemination of flyers descriptive of SPS concepts and techniques to parents. The school district's social problem-solving and decision-making team is responsible for administering selected measures to monitor program implementation, as well as student gains and overall program effectiveness. The operation of this element was illustrated in the summary of program outcomes in Chapters Three and Four and in the specific measurement methods that were discussed. However, some additional program management concerns and procedures will be described at the end of Part Four, and ways in which feedback information is currently being used to address new implementation circumstances will be presented in Part Five.

Chapter Five

Getting Started:
Matching Program Concepts
to the School's
Goals and Resources

Early in the SPS program development process, the focus of school-based consultants is on the first key element in the MATS/MEF model: matching and planning. The goal in this regard is to ensure that there is an appropriate match between what the district needs, what its resources can sustain, and what a particular SPS program can provide. This particular key element moves the consultant into the exciting and challenging waters of assessing the varying interests, abilities, and resistances of the school system and its staff as part of pretraining and preimplementation planning. These political considerations are part of the courtship dance that goes on between a potential host environment and the consultant.

Getting Started

Because it is likely that the SPS Program will involve the expenditure of money for items such as the purchase of curriculum materials, the superintendent of schools and eventually the school board will need to be involved to provide the ultimate sanction for the program. Over the years, adults in many varied educational roles, including school superintendents and individual school board members, have introduced the concept of SPS into the district. With regard to the ISA-SPS Project in particular, because the project is a validated program of the NDN, summary information about the program is being actively distributed in each state by the state's NDN facilitator, whose duty it is to bring the research-validated programs of the NDN to as many classrooms in the state as possible. In recent years, the NDN has provided a key way to make the ISA-SPS Program known to educators. Others may come to know about SPS by hearing about it through the articles, chapters, and books on social problem solving that are available. The following are all examples of how an SPS project can be brought into a school system.

Introduction of SPS can begin when a front-line practitioner such as a teacher learns about it at a state teachers' association meeting. The teacher recognizes SPS as a way to help special education students learn self-control skills and brings the idea of SPS to the attention of a supervisor, for instance, the director of special education.

Similarly, a school psychologist may be consulting with a number of special education teachers whose children are having difficulty making friends. The psychologist, who has read about SPS in graduate school and sees its social awareness component as a way to satisfy the teachers' needs, will contact a supervisor such as the director of student services.

A building principal in a poor, urban neighborhood school may want to marshall a whole-school approach to arm the students with survival skills. Learning about SPS through the NDN, the principal sees the value of having the skills and language of social problem solving used by all the members of the school community, including but not limited to teachers, parents, cafeteria aides, the librarian, and the school nurse. When the principal is more fully informed about SPS, she or he will meet with a supervisor regarding this programming idea.

An increasingly frequent channel through which SPS can become known in a district has been a district's substance abuse prevention coordinator. This person may want a curriculum that focuses on developing children's psychosocial competence as a critical building block in a broader substance abuse awareness or chemical education program. In addition, because SPS teaches what might be considered "life skills," it is an approach that fits with other district goals in a variety of domains, such as mandates to provide help for disaffected youth, programs for family life education, or special projects to build children's self-esteem.

Most often, the school practitioner who first recognizes that SPS may be a programming match in the district will conduct further research in relevant aspects of social problem solving. This can be done by contacting the NDN facilitator in the state, the authors of relevant SPS-focused articles or curricula, or the leaders of regional or nationally recognized SPS programs. If the practitioner's early impressions of a positive match are reinforced by this additional research, his or her next step is to assemble a packet of program "awareness" materials. This is important because it will be the first concrete vehicle that will be shown to key program decision makers within the district. Program awareness packets have typically included a copy of the social problem-solving thinking steps, a list of the SPS self-control and social awareness skills, an overview of the curriculum or its table of contents, several sample lessons, information about the history and background of the particular SPS program, and a brief statement as to the known research outcomes of the program.

Prepared with this information, the practitioner meets with key district administrators. This is the beginning of a process of mutual assessment and negotiation to see if there truly is a fit between SPS services and district needs. Because it can be a confusing experience, a framework with which to approach this process can provide the SPS consultant with some clarity, direction, and structure. Maher and Bennett (1984) offer a number of ideas on this matter and suggest the usefulness of the "A-VICTORY" framework. This concept is attributed to Davis and Salasin (1975) and has been used as a model by others in the field (Godin, Carr-Kaffashan, and Moore-Hines, 1990).

The A-VICTORY framework can be regarded as a consultative readiness index. It can assist the practitioner in planning, preparing, and thinking through the program development process. It is a touchstone that obligates a practitioner to study the issues and dynamics that must be considered in order to match, recruit, and plan training. The A-VICTORY dimensions point to useful information early in the matching and planning process, and, because some of this information is only discovered as the pilot program unfolds, the consultant needs to be patient and flexible, and to deal with these matters as they become clear.

Ability

In the development of programs by the SPS Unit, the "A" in "A-VICTORY" refers to the *ability* of the host school to deploy an already existing committee, such as a crisis intervention team, a health curriculum committee, or a substance abuse prevention task force, to effectively guide the development of the SPS program. Ideally, the persons on this committee represent many constituencies and would include individuals such as teachers, a building principal, a person with central office influence, a parent leader, and other key resource people such as a guidance counselor, child study team member, or substance abuse counselor. If such a committee already exists, this group can take the responsibility, from the schools' point of view, of determining whether the SPS program matches the district's needs. For school districts that do not have a committee capable of adding SPS to its other responsibilities, the SPS practitioner may discuss the idea of the program with representatives from the school's administration. Once a district has formally agreed to sponsor a pilot program in SPS, a committee can be formed as the dates of the training approach.

A district, through its version of an SPS Committee, ideally has the ability to perform a number of important functions. One of the first tasks is to set and prioritize goals for the program. With regard to social-affective progamming, an early and important decision might be to decide if the goal of the first year's program will be to focus on regular education, special education, or both. Typically, the committee wants SPS to be known as a preventive and health-promoting program for *all* students. In some cases, however, the committee may want to focus on SPS as a remedial intervention for special education students who are already experiencing difficulty. Decisions will also include determining the target grades for the first year. Although some districts may adopt a whole-school approach, most districts will designate a subset of classes for the pilot year and then develop a multiyear plan. For example, the first year will focus on grades K-2, with the second year focusing on grades 3-5.

Success in these determinations rests in part upon the committee members' ability to use their experience, influence, and familiarity with the staff to choose teachers for the pilot program who would like to incorporate a program like SPS into their classroom and who have the competence and confidence to make it work.

Implicit within this structure is the committee's ability to make decisions regarding program design. With critical input coming from the SPS practitioner, the committee may determine, for example, that the focus of the pilot program will be on training teachers to implement SPS self-control lessons. Another possibility is that the SPS Committee will recommend a pilot program that focuses on teaching self-control skills while emphasizing instruction in the Eight-step SPS thinking strategy.

The SPS Committee should be composed of individuals who recognize the importance of orienting teachers to an SPS approach in the early stages and of responding to their input. For example, a brief overview of SPS could be presented to teachers as part of a faculty meeting by the SPS practitioner and/or members of the SPS Committee. The committee members will note carefully what questions or observations the teachers raise and use that information as a guide to help shape the design of the program and the training plan. For example, if the original pilot program plan was to focus on grades 1 and 2 but a surprising level of interest was generated by the kindergarten teachers, the SPS Committee may want to consider including these teachers in the training.

It is important for the SPS Committee to be able to negotiate the political waters of the district. For example, the committee must understand the nuances of securing the funding that may be required for substitute teachers if the SPS teachers are trained during the school day. The committee also should have the ability to arrange teacher training dates and to make appropriate logistical arrangements for training, such as securing a comfortable training room and supplying refreshments. The committee members should also have enough flexibility in their present job roles to visit the classrooms of the pilot SPS teachers in order to provide support, encouragement, and validation for their efforts. Finally, the SPS

Committee should have the ability to perform the monitoring, evaluation, and feedback functions that are described later in this book or to obtain technical assistance in this regard.

Values

The "V" in "A-VICTORY" refers to the extent to which the beliefs, attitudes, and philosophy of the SPS practitioner, the SPS Committee, teachers, and parents—their values—are congruent with one another regarding social problem solving. Experience has shown that what a program in social problem solving can provide for children may or may not be consistent with the school system's current values. Each interested person has his or her own value system that shapes an individualized perception of what social problem solving could be and how it could help. A parent or PTA president may want help for an overly shy or dependent eight-year-old child, a particular teacher may be overwhelmed with classroom management problems at a middle school, a principal may want to respond to the swelling demands from teachers for some help in the affective domain, or a vice-principal may see SPS as a behavior modification program designed to "shape up" or discipline children.

It is important for the practitioner to realize that regardless of how clear written materials may appear to be, each person has an idiosyncratic notion of what would constitute a successful first-year program. Because these values and expectations influence what the committee members feel that SPS can do best for them, it is important to be sensitive to these values. An exchange of ideas on this front allows practitioners to design a program that can be on target, within the domain of what they believe they can do best and what they think will help students the most. It is possible that a good match does not exist and this is important to know early, so that it can be dealt with.

There are other values that are germane to successful SPS programming. Do the teachers, parents, and administrators believe that a program to teach children to think critically will enhance or diminish the school's efforts to help students grasp the basic academic skills? Another important value is elicited through observing how the school community views the role of the teacher. Specifically, school systems that have had long-term success with programs such as SPS acknowledge that part of the modern teacher's role is to educate children in areas such as self-control, critical thinking, and substance abuse prevention as important complements to the important teachings that go on in the family.

Information

The "I" in "A-VICTORY" refers to the ideas and *information* and how they are shared within a system to solve problems and to maximize a program's success. What or who are the sources of program information? Will the district focus solely on feedback from the teachers or are the parents and students also included in this process? Are teachers' aides also solicited for important information about what is working and what is not? In addition, how does the flow of information about new programs traditionally circulate in the school? Are faculty meetings good vehicles for these exchanges? Do teachers have an opportunity to pair up and team teach? Are there grade-level and/or departmental meetings? Will the district encourage an end-of-the-year SPS meeting for all those who are involved? What is the status of prospective booster training sessions or refresher training? Does the school and/or district have a newsletter? How often can the SPS Committee meet to exchange information regarding program development?

Circumstances

The "C" in "A-VICTORY" refers to *circumstances*, including such environmental factors as the formal and informal school system politics that can influence the successful development of the SPS program. Individuals who guide an SPS program's development should be very interested in learning about the history of similar social-affective efforts. It is surprising to see how intact community members' memories are regarding the good or bad features of social-affective programs that may have been tried in the district years ago. Does the history indicate that such programming was only used with special education students? This could potentially mark all future social-affective programs as being pertinent only to those students.

Timing

The "T" in "A-VICTORY" relates to the *timing* of introducing the SPS pilot program. For example, initiators of new programs should be very respectful of the impact that site visits from state monitors have on school systems. A school system organizes and deploys all of its resources for these visits and it must do well in order to maintain accreditation. The psychological energy of a school system during this time is directed toward complying with the many quality assurance standards that are a part of these visits. Beginning a new program, unless it meets a monitoring need, is best put off for another time. Timing is also an issue when there is a change of classroom, school building, or district-wide leadership. A new fourth-grade teacher, a change in building principal, or a different director of curriculum can work either for or against an SPS program. Timing also refers to the seasoning and experience of the classroom teacher. Some teachers who have just completed their undergraduate training can add enthusiasm and energy that will make the program work. Other new teachers have enough on their hands just to acclimate themselves to their new role of teaching the basics. Similarly, some experienced teachers can be jaded or burned out, whereas others will look forward with enthusiasm to a program such as social problem solving. Timing also refers to deciding at what point in the academic year the SPS Committee should schedule its meetings and training events. For example, the opening of a school building in September and its closing in June are two enormous events, and those months may not be the best times to hold SPS meetings and training workshops.

Obligation

The "O" in "A-VICTORY" refers to the degree to which an *obligation* is felt by members of the school community to make the changes needed in order to accommodate health promotion or problem prevention programs such as social problem solving. Does the commitment put forth by the power structure of parents, school board, and administrators vary widely? Is there support for multiyear program development or does the feeling exist that one year's attention to a project will be sufficient and that the school system should focus on something new each year? Is SPS a potential "fad" in the district? How strong is the commitment to the goal that building educated *and* socially competent citizens is the long-term mission of the school community? Also, how committed is the district leadership to the continuing professional development of its staff? To what extent are in-service programs carefully planned, closely examined, and improved upon from year to year?

Resistance

The "R" in "A-VICTORY" refers to the level and sources of *resistance* that inevitably exist when a new program is brought into a school system. Are there staff members who feel that their status, influence, job satisfaction, and/or income will be negatively affected by a new program such as social problem solving? In one school system, teachers' unions discouraged teachers who volunteered to remain after school in order to learn more about social problem solving, because they wanted the teachers to be paid for the extra time. The teachers knew that there was no money in the school budget to pay them, but they were intrigued sufficiently by social problem solving to meet after school anyway. Rather than seeing that they are key to the success of such efforts as social problem solving, some guidance counselors, child study team members, and substance abuse counselors may feel that they are being threatened or overburdened. Attention should be given to identifying the altruistic and nonaltruistic interests of all potential team members in order to form a happy convergence of mutual self-interest (Elias, 1991; Elias and Clabby, 1984b).

Yield

Finally, the "Y" in "A-VICTORY" asks what *yield* can be envisioned if the program is implemented. It is important to have a clear-headed and objective view of what could benefit the children and the school as a whole as a result of SPS programming. Will a Herculean effort be required to overcome the system's resistance? If that is the case, it may not be seen as worth the effort. As a rule, a realistic and shared vision of the cost-benefit dynamics is quite useful. Many schools readily see the social and psychological benefits that will accrue to the children as a result of SPS. But unless it is pointed out, they may not see such radiating effects as improved classroom climate, better teacher morale, or improvement in teachers' own thinking skills.

Conclusion

The SPS practitioner is a person who has read and studied the research literature and policy considerations such as those presented in Parts One and Two of this book. Because of that, she or he believes in the worthiness of this particular approach to promoting children's social competence. The practitioner's knowledge base can give rise to a substantive and persuasive eloquence that can bring others to theoretical and philosophical agreement with this point of view. However, the knowledge can stay within the scholarly domain and never reach children in terms of a hands-on program unless it is integrated with an equally developed knowledge base of the political realities of practical program development. The SPS practitioner needs to look for and encourage the environmental features that will help the program enter into and match with a system whose staff can effectively plan for new program development.

Accordingly, Davis and Salasin's (1975) A-VICTORY framework is suggested as an important political and environmental screen that the practitioner can use to gauge whether there is an appropriate match between SPS and a school system's needs, as well as to determine if the district has adequate planning resources to make the program successful. Once it has been determined that there is a good match, attention should be turned more closely to the issue of allowing such gatekeepers as SPS Committee members, building principals, and school superintendents to become familiar with SPS curricula, a topic that is presented in the next several chapters.

Chapter Six

Comprehensive Instruction
at the Elementary
School Level

This chapter is devoted to the key element "A," appropriate classroom materials, in the overall framework of the MATS/MEF model.

There are a number of programs that focus on teaching SPS skills to elementary school–aged students; some of them are listed at the end of this chapter. Only one SPS curriculum, however, has the distinction of being recommended and supported for national dissemination by the U.S. Department of Education. It is this fact, as well as its comprehensive, lesson-by-lesson coverage of the full continuum of social problem-solving skills, that makes it an important model to study.

A Curriculum Guide for the Elementary Grades

Publishing a curriculum, like most other complex acts, encompasses opportunity and risk. As educators and parents become increasingly convinced that schools should be a place where children can learn social competence skills, there will be many professionals who want to use research-validated lessons such as those that form the base of the SPS Unit's services. Thousands of children can be helped if materials from high-quality social competence programs can be distributed to caring and serious educators. However, there is a risk concomitant with this opportunity. That risk centers on educators having access to the "lessons" without being aware of the theoretical background for the program, program development issues, and other information that could result in the most thoughtful and responsible use of the lessons.

This specific issue was joined when the leadership of the ISA-SPS team had to decide whether lessons on social problem-solving should only be distributed when an individual had participated in training. The decision was made to include both the lessons and extensive background material in one published volume. It was reasoned that the ISA-SPS project was started in the first place by a judicious use of the AWARE curriculum (Elardo & Cooper, 1977), which was available without a mandated training requirement. Accordingly, *Social Decision-Making Skills: A Curriculum Guide for the Elementary Grades* (Elias & Clabby, 1989) was written as a comprehensive social problem-solving document that could help individuals such as building principals in isolated school districts who did not have access to training or to the kind of written materials needed to initiate a sound program. The intention is that such persons, with careful reading, would now have enough written material to understand, implement, and monitor an SPS program at any point along the continuum of kindergarten through sixth grade. Perhaps an argument could be made that this curriculum is "too comprehensive" and has much more than is typically needed in beginning a pilot program. That may well be true. An individual practitioner may only be able to implement some of the ideal key elements because of job role constraints. There is no doubt, based on dissemination experts' experience, however, that to the extent possible, practitioners will benefit from having a comprehensive resource that they can go to when they are struggling with implementation issues.

The major portion of the document is the section containing scripted lessons. This includes curriculum materials corresponding to a readiness phase, which endeavors to teach the social skills of self-control and group awareness; an instructional phase, which teaches an eight-step cognitive decision-making strategy; and an application phase, which endeavors to encourage transfer and generalization of the skills. The document is a 255-page volume that includes historical background for the program, research validation for the social decision-making approach, practical questions and ideas on how to "begin" such a program, advice to guide the institutionalization of such a program in a school setting, specific scripts for parents' meetings, evaluation forms to test the students' acquisition of the skills that are taught, and guides to using social decision making in problem-focused dialogues with students.

In this chapter's presentation of the Elias and Clabby (1989) approach to the development of a comprehensive elementary school SPS program, sections of the curriculum are mentioned to illustrate key points. These sections have been selected and described in a manner that will allow all readers, including those who do not have a copy of the curriculum, to grasp the important concepts.

In Part One, "Introduction and Rationale," the argument is made for the critical importance of SPS skills. It was felt that individual practitioners may need this information in a convenient format in order to make a compelling argument to school board members, administrators, and other colleagues regarding how social decision-making skills can help students reach their academic and psychological potential, handle peer pressure and other day-to-day difficulties, and successfully make the critical transition to the middle school years. (Note that the present book begins in a similar manner, although with far more detail and depth.)

This section of the volume also describes how the book is organized and can be used. And, because one of the first questions on any teacher's mind is, "At my grade level, what lessons am I expected to teach and where do I begin?" a scope and sequence chart is included such as the one appearing in Exhibit 6.1. This skills-by-grade chart focuses specifically on a full K–6 program.

The second part introduces the teacher to social problem-solving skills by offering concrete examples of what it "looks like" when a student uses or does not use a particular skill. It is important for a teacher to be able to think about the children in his or her class and mentally draw a picture of how the absence of a particular SPS skill can lead to the difficulties a child manifests in the classroom. Understanding a student's deficits in mathematics allows the teacher to sensibly plan a remediation lesson. This is also true in social problem solving. Examples are provided to help teachers in

Exhibit 6.1. Skills-by-Grade Guide for the K–6 Program.

	K	1	2	3	4	5	6
Readiness: Teaching the skills of self-control and social awareness (pp. 53–86)							
Introduction to SPS meetings	•	•	•	•			
Learning to listen carefully and accurately	•	•	•	•			
Remembering and following directions	•	•	•	•			
Asking for help and giving help to others	•	•	•	•			
Keep Calm before problem solving		•	•	•			
Selecting praiseworthy and caring friends		•	•	•			
Starting a conversation and keeping it going			•	•			
Using affective exercises to pull your class together			•	•			
Resisting provocations and keeping control				•			
Sharing problems and decisions and sharing ways to keep in control				•			
Helping your class become a problem-solving team				•			
"If you can't say something nice, say what you see"				•			
Learning how to receive praise				•			
Teaching children how to role play				•			
Learning to care about one's classmates				•			
Readiness: reviewing the skills (p. 195)					•	•	•
Instructional: Teaching social-cognitive problem solving at the middle elementary level (pp. 87–143)							
Look for signs of different feelings					•		
Tell yourself what the problem is					•		

Exhibit 6.1. Skills-by-Grade Guide for the K–6 Program, Cont'd.

	K	1	2	3	4	5	6
Decide on your goal					•		
Stop and think of as many solutions to the problem as you can					•		
For each solution, think of all the things that might happen next					•		
Choose your best solution					•		
Plan it and make a final check					•		
Try it and rethink it				•			
Instructional: Teaching social-cognitive problem solving at the upper elementary level (pp. 87–143)							
Look for signs of different feelings						•	
Tell yourself what the problem is						•	
Decide on your goal						•	
Stop and think of as many solutions to the problem as you can						•	
For each solution, think of all the things that might happen next						•	
Choose your best solution						•	
Plan it and make a final check						•	
Try it and rethink it						•	
Instructional: Reviewing the skills (p. 196)							•
Application: Teaching transfer and generalization to academic content areas (pp. 145–165)						•	•
Application: Teaching transfer and generalization to real social problems (pp. 165–185)						•	•
Application: Teaching transfer and generalization to a combination of social and academic problems (pp. 185–197)							

Note: The presence of a dot indicates that the skill listed in a particular row is taught at the grade level listed in the column, in a K–6 setting (see Elias & Clabby, 1989, for guidelines for K–4 or K–5 settings). Page numbers refer to Elias and Clabby, 1989.

this diagnostic process. Following is an example of how a child who is not using the skill of generating alternative solutions to a problem may be affected (Elias & Clabby, 1989, p. 36):

> Step 4—*The Depressed Child*—The sad or unhappy youngster concerns us, especially with our heightened awareness of the serious problems of youth involved in self-destructive behaviors, suicidal gestures, driving at excessively high speeds, and the like. When children are depressed, their thinking processes lose some sharpness. Most important, their flexibility and their willingness to look at alternatives is diminished. . . . When children have a habit of thinking of alternative solutions, they are less likely to have, or remain in, a depression. Once depressed, however, students benefit from practice in seeing that there are other solutions, that problems can be solved, and that positive consequences are possible, too.

This part of the curriculum also includes a diagnostic checklist to help a teacher assess a student's problem-solving strengths and deficits. A presentation is made of the techniques, attitudes, and approaches that successful teachers use during their formal SPS lessons, and high-quality counseling and conversational exchanges with students are emphasized. An important goal here is to communicate to teachers and other implementers that an effective problem-solving program consists not only of lessons in decision making but in the creation of an entire classroom atmosphere or culture that is organized under the social decision-making model. This is a critical part of any high-quality social decision-making program. All teachers should talk to their children in a way that provides the children with practice in independent thinking, something that has come to be known as "dialoguing" (Spivack & Shure, 1974).

A natural question is how much the formal lessons and informal dialogues help the students to learn a framework that they can call their own. The curriculum makes it clear that this occurs to the extent to which implementers encourage independent thinking *outside* the confines of the formal social problem-solving lessons. Successful teachers will make use of powerful "teachable moments," such as the brief informal dialogues that may take place with students during recess or a social studies lesson. Such teachers also use compliments to reinforce the spontaneously expressed examples of social decision making that emerge from the students during the course of the day, use appropriate self-disclosure of their own use of social decision making, and "think out loud" to model the process for the students. To make these linkages clear, the SPS curriculum has a section on "The Major Techniques for Fostering Thoughtful Decision Making," which gives a variety of examples illustrating ways to make social problem solving come alive in the classroom. Following is an excerpt showing the kind of dialogue that is provided to a teacher to demonstrate how to ask questions that facilitate students' problem solving (Elias & Clabby, 1989, p. 43):

Mike: Tom left the game and wants to play with Ron and his friends . . . but they are not as good as we are.

Teacher: I wonder how that makes you feel?

Mike: Mad, burning mad. That's the last time I'm playing with Tom.

Teacher: I'm not following you too well. What's the problem?

Mike: It's not as much fun when Tom doesn't play.

Teacher: What is it that you want to have happen?

Mike: You know . . . I want to play kickball and have a good time.

Teacher: What ideas do you have?

Mike: What do you mean?

Teacher: You know, what are some ways you can think of that can help you play kickball and have a good time?

Mike: I can't think of any.

Teacher: C'mon, try.

Mike: Okay . . . Well, I could tell Tom I'll only play with him if he stops being Ron's friend.

Teacher: I wonder what else you could do?

Mike: Find some different people to play with.

Teacher: That's good . . . you already have two ideas . . . I'm thinking about another idea.

Mike: I could learn to be more patient with Ron.

Teacher: That makes sense also. Let's see. What would happen if you tried out some of these ideas?

Teachers of even the youngest children also thrive on learning explicit ways to allow the steps of clear thinking to become part of classroom lessons, even of telling stories such as "Pinocchio." Notice how identifying problems, acknowledging feelings, setting goals, and understanding consequences—key social problem-solving skills—all can be made part of a routine story discussion time, as is discussed in the curriculum and provided below. Each paragraph represents a section of the discussion and illustrates at least one technique that implementors can use to promote critical thinking in their students (Elias & Clabby, 1989, p. 45):

- Okay, we've just finished reading Walt Disney's version of the story of Pinocchio. Let's start by going over the main things that happened from start to finish. Who would like to tell how the story starts? Okay, go ahead, Clifton.
- Pinocchio, Geppetto, Jiminy, and their friends find lots of problems in the story. Let's take a look at some of them. Let's see, I think it would be most useful to pick a problem like something that could actually happen to some of you. We'll start with what happened when Pinocchio was on his way to school for the first time. How is he feeling? How could you tell?

- When Foulfellow the Fox came up to him, what was Pinocchio's problem? Who will try to put it into words?
- What do you think was Pinocchio's goal? What did he want to have happen?
- This is tricky because he left the house with a goal. What was that? Then what happened?

It is also obvious that providing children with the incentive to continue to use critical thinking is very important. High-quality SPS programs show teachers how to use systematic complimenting to help the children persevere. Too often, teachers and parents do very little complimenting or they offer well-intended but essentially punitive "back-handed compliments," for example, "Good job of being able to think of what would happen next, Robert. Now why don't you ever do that during our Reading?" Following is an illustration of how this issue is addressed in the curriculum (Elias & Clabby, 1989, p. 49):

How to Compliment Thoughtful Decision Making

1. Notice when your student demonstrates problem-solving thinking.
2. Get eye contact with the student.
3. Offer a "praise phrase" and vary it over time. Examples:
   "That's terrific!"
   "What a great job!"
   "You must be so proud of yourself!"
   "Wonderful!"
4. After the "praise phrase" describe the thinking or behavior that you want to encourage.
   "That's terrific that you *thought of another way to end the story.*"
   "What a great job you did in *trying out your good idea!*"
   "You must be so proud of yourself that *you thought ahead!*"

> "Wonderful! You *figured out* how to do that
> math problem!"
> 5.   Deliver your praise with an enthusiastic tone of
>   voice.

As suggested earlier, thinking out loud is also a very important technique, with which teachers can be shown how to harness the power of modeling. This is a point that cannot be overemphasized by leaders of SPS programs. The problem solving that goes on constantly in the mind of a teacher needs to be made more public so that it, too, can become a purposeful part of the hidden curriculum. Here are two examples:

1.   "Let's see. We finished the health lesson early. We could do our math now or we could do language arts. In math, we are up to a new topic and I'll need much more time than I have right now to explain it to you. In language arts, we could just pick up where we left off last time. Let's do language arts." (alternatives, consequences, planning, and choosing a best solution)
2.   "Whenever the videocassette player doesn't work, I get upset and start to worry about how I'm going to be able to do our lesson. When I notice myself getting nervous, I usually try to use Keep Calm." (feelings, problem identification, goal setting, and use of the readiness prompt for calming down when under stress)

The Phases That Organize the Lessons

The curriculum is organized around a series of topics or lessons. Each topic contains a variety of activities that can be taught in one class period or, more typically, broken down and dealt with over a series of class periods, depending on factors such as the attention span of the students and their ages. The lessons are organized into several developmental phases. It is important to give some background on the development of the curriculum. Through the action-research process described in Part Two of this book, it became quite clear that many younger students and special education students needed a "readiness" experience that would emphasize self-control and social awareness skills. From teacher feedback, it also became clear that if students were "only" to learn these kinds of skills, it would be a worthy accomplishment in and of itself. Additionally, students who have some familiarity with these readiness skills are better able to sit and concentrate on learning the eight steps of social decision making.

As a result of the action-research process, and as noted earlier, SPS skills began to be seen in terms of developmental phases of instruction. The lessons pertaining to social interaction skills were organized within a readiness phase, the original array of lessons that explicitly taught the cognitive problem-solving steps became known as the instructional phase, and an application phase assisted the teachers in helping the children transfer and generalize the skills to real-life and academic areas. In the early years of the program, teachers did not always remember to bring up social problem-solving ideas during the course of a social studies lesson or to use social problem solving as a framework to help guide students' thinking when they became involved in a classroom altercation. So the application phase formally included transfer and generalization lessons into the structure of the program.

The Readiness Phase

Realizing the seemingly infinite number of social skills that children need to master can be a disquieting experience. In the practical world of the classroom, this array must become finite, and decisions must be made about which specific social skills should be taught. Ultimately, theoretical and action-research considerations of the kind described in Parts One and Two for regular and special education populations led to a decision to focus on developing the self-control and social awareness domains listed under "Readiness" in the first part of Exhibit 6.1.

Based on the teacher input and instructional perspectives outlined in Part One of this book, it was felt that the format of a readiness lesson should emphasize a game-like approach. If that flavor could be captured, the teachers would be reinforced to keep teaching social problem solving. Correspondingly, the children themselves would not see it as drudgery and might actually look forward to their SPS class time. Consequently, each readiness lesson is composed of a variety of activities, allowing teachers to be flexible in their use of time. A teacher may take from fifteen to thirty minutes for a particular activity. To provide an example of format, the following is an excerpt from a self-control lesson entitled "Learning to Listen Carefully and Accurately" (Elias & Clabby, 1989, p. 64):

Instructional Activities

1. Begin by telling the children that good friends are not easy to make or keep. Ask them whether they think it is more important to be able to be a good talker or a good listener when trying to make friends with someone. Help them recall how they feel when they are not listened to.

2. The following activity is designed to show the children how hard it is to be a good listener. Read the words from the list below at a rate of about one word per second. Ask the children to clap only when they hear the word "cow." Note both performance errors (clap on another word) and nonperformance errors (no clap on "cow").

3. Have the children share their difficulties. Then ask them to share the things they do to help them listen carefully and accurately. Be sure to mention the following:

    "Listening position"—Sit or stand straight, with at least one foot on the ground; if sitting, your rump should be on the chair; face the speaker (or source of sound).

    "Concentrate"—Do not interrupt or let anything distract you.

    "When the speaker is finished, ask questions"—Ask if you do not understand what is said or if you want more information about who, what, where, or when.

One of the word lists in this lesson consists of the following, used in this order: cart, seat, cow, cup, pig, crow, cow, seat, cart, cup, crow, cup, pig, cow, crow, cart, sea, pig, cart, crow, pig, crow, cup, cow, pig, seat.

Notice that an effort is made in the first activity to connect this game-like activity to an important social competence skill. In this case, making a good friend rests to a certain extent on a person's capacity to be a good listener. Children and teachers must be able to see tangibly and clearly the practical, everyday benefit of the lesson. It is particularly important for teachers to realize the connection between such a game-like activity and the goal of improving social competence, because they may be called on to explain the rationale to an interested parent, administrator, or school board member.

Note that in this sample of a readiness lesson, the concept of "listening position" is introduced. "Listening position" is what you did as a child when you were misbehaving and your teacher, mother, or father gave you a serious "stare" from across the room. Many of us recall that we responded to such looks by becoming quiet, sitting up straight, and looking attentive. "Listening position" in this curriculum is taught in its component parts as a self-control skill. Once it is learned in a lesson and practiced, a teacher can use the words "listening position" as a prompt by saying, "Okay, children, everyone please show me 'listening position.'" A key instructional principle of many of the SPS lessons is an array of *prompts* that a teacher, parent, building principal, school bus driver, or aide can use to cue students to access a skill that they have been taught in an SPS class lesson.

The social awareness lessons of the readiness phase follow the same game-like format as the self-control lessons. The following is an excerpt from the social awareness lesson "Learning How to Receive Praise" (Elias & Clabby, 1989, p. 79):

Instructional Activities

1. Ask the children to recall a time when they were praised and to write an example of this on a piece of paper. Have them also write what they did or

said or how they felt when they received this
praise.

2. Have several children share their answers. Focus
   particularly on how they responded to the praise.
   Tell the children that when someone praises
   them, they must let that person know that they
   heard and that they liked it.

3. Have the children suggest things that they can say
   after they have been praised. Keep a list on the
   board or on a poster paper.

4. Pick a child who is relatively comfortable with
   receiving praise. Give him or her a compliment
   and have him or her respond. Gently offer constructive feedback, using VENT as part of the
   guidelines you give children for properly receiving praise. Then select two children and have one
   praise and the other respond. Ask the children to
   comment on what each child does.

Note that in activity 4 the teacher is asked to use a prompt
known as VENT. In an earlier self-control lesson, VENT was introduced as an acronym to help students monitor themselves so that
they will remember to speak in a calm Voice, look the person in the
Eye, use Nice language, and stand Tall with a good posture. It
is amazing to observe in classrooms how this particular prompt
becomes an internalized frame through which children filter their
social approach skills. The students can self-check their interpersonal presentation to others, avoiding overly passive or aggressive
styles.

The Instructional Phase

In special education classes, the readiness phase may be emphasized
for quite a long time, well into the elementary years. Children in
regular education classes at the third- and fourth-grade level, and
special education children when they are ready, can begin to learn the
eight social cognitive problem-solving steps in a formal lesson format. Keep in mind that even while readiness skills are being taught,

it is important for teachers to use facilitative questioning to help their students practice the skill of critical thinking. The use of formal lessons on "clear thinking" was where the ISA-SPS Project began in 1979 and it is where most SPS programs begin their work. An important issue for teachers to keep in mind is that feedback is relatively clear when readiness skills such as "listening position" are taught, because readiness lessons teach a behavioral skill that can easily be seen. Teachers who are focusing primarily on the cognitive problem-solving steps cannot see the fruits of their labors as easily. These teachers need to be reassured that the acquisition of clear thinking is indeed less visible than the acquisition of readiness skills. Clear thinking has major payoffs that in time will manifest themselves in a variety of ways. But it is a complex, integrative skill, like reading and mathematics, and therefore time and opportunity must be allowed for teaching component abilities and providing for their continuous and ever more challenging coalescence and application.

During the instructional phase, the eight social decision-making skills noted in Part One are taught. Because great value is placed on the children learning the eight steps "by heart," recitation of the steps is built into the program. The program emphasizes successful practice opportunities. The children are helped to apply the steps to hypothetical, age-appropriate, and open-ended social conflict stories. This format emphasizes the importance of learning a discrete skill and then linking that skill to others in order to maximize its retention and use. There is a clear emphasis on review and enjoyable practice that reflects an intent to help the children go beyond the acquisition of knowledge to the acquisition of skills.

Once the children have demonstrated improvements in the self-control and social awareness skills, they begin a journey through twenty-two topics in which the eight social decision-making skills are taught. As a result of many conversations with teachers and curriculum specialists, and by creating many versions of the lessons, trying them out in the classroom, and obtaining feedback about them, we determined the following format to be one of the most effective ways of organizing lessons to teach children social problem solving:

1. Define a purpose for the lesson. This should provide a focusing and organizing goal statement for the teachers' benefit.
2. A listing of the social problem-solving steps that have been taught thus far should be included, along with the new step that will be taught in the present lesson.
3. A detailed "Leader's Guide" also should be included that provides a detailed script for the teacher to follow.
    a. Open with a sharing circle—This is an opportunity for the children to say hello to one another and briefly state what is on their mind. It is introduced in the readiness phase as a skill-building lesson in and of itself.
    b. Review the previous lesson—This reminds the students of what has been covered thus far, similar to what a teacher does when introducing a new math or science lesson.
    c. Introduce and explain the new lesson or the new concept— This alerts the teacher as to what will be highlighted in this lesson.
    d. Offer a practical rationale—Emphasis is placed here on trying to make the lesson meaningful to the students in some way. It is a response to the student-centered question, "Why should I pay attention to this lesson?"
    e. Participate in practice activities for the middle elementary grades—This usually consists of reading a hypothetical social conflict story involving school issues that are appropriate for third, fourth, and fifth graders.
    f. Participate in practice activities for the upper elementary grades—These practice activities provide slightly more developmentally sophisticated practice stories that are read by the teacher. On occasion, videotaped segments from educational television programs are shown.
    g. Participate in follow-through activities
        i.   Social applications—Students are encouraged to use the skill that has been taught that day and apply it in the real world of neighborhoods, friends, recess time, and the classroom.
        ii. Academic applications—Teachers are given some suggestions about how the skills that have been

taught in the lesson can be applied to the basic academic skill areas.

h. Use teaching tips—This is an important category that compiles hints and suggestions made by teachers over the years who have learned how to overcome problems in teaching a particular skill to children and how to maximize the children's learning experience.

The following are examples of how this format comes to life in a classroom. As mentioned, the teacher first sees a "purpose statement" that distinctly describes the goals and context for the lesson. For example, one topic introduces problem-solving step 8, "Plan it and make a final check." This lesson will be used as an example of how an instructional lesson can be formatted.

The following is the purpose statement from the lesson entitled "Plan How You Will Try Out Your Solution" (Elias & Clabby, 1989, p. 123):

Children will learn that, even after they carefully select a way to solve a problem, they must attend to the time, place, and circumstances of carrying out that action. This is what we call planning or the "politics" of social decision making and problem solving. Children will also learn the habit of making a final check—anticipating the obstacles to their plans that might arise—before carrying out a solution. Making a final check helps keep us from trying to carry out our "best solution" at the incorrect time, using the wrong words, or with inappropriate people.

The teacher would then see a list of the problem-solving steps that have been taught to the children thus far (p. 123):

This topic's problem-solving steps are:
1. Look for signs of different feelings.
2. Tell yourself what the problem is.
3. Decide on your goal.

4. Stop and think of as many solutions to the prob-
    lem as you can.
5. For each solution, think of all the things that
    might happen next.
6. Choose your best solution.
7. Plan it and make a final check.

The topic is then continued with a scriptlike lesson plan for
what can be a series of lessons. The lessons open with a "sharing
circle" (which would have been introduced as an introductory lesson to the idea of even having class problem-solving meetings),
where the children express their ideas or feelings in an open, informal, and friendly way. It is important to note that as the material
to be covered increases in complexity during the latter stages of the
instructional phase, teachers sometimes have questions about how
much time should be devoted to the sharing circle. This is an individual judgment call for each teacher. The material that is
brought up in a sharing circle may be considered important enough
for a genuine, class-wide problem-solving discussion. For example,
if several of the girls are claiming that they do not have equal access
to the kickball field and that the boys seem to dominate, the teacher
may see this as a topic that should be discussed in an SPS way. In
this case, the formal, scripted SPS lesson may be put off until
another time. In other circumstances, if a teacher realizes that the
children are not planning a good solution to a problem, the teacher
may limit the sharing circle to a seven-minute experience, so that
she or he can change the lesson to skill instruction in planning.
There are, of course, all kinds of creative ways of controlling the
time spent in a sharing circle, such as asking the students to limit
their contributions to one phrase or asking every other person in the
circle to share.

The sharing circle in the instructional phase is followed by
a teacher- or student-led review of the skills that were taught in the
prior lesson.

In the lesson emphasizing the skill of planning, the teachers
are instructed to ask the students to take a moment and think of an
interesting way to review the first six problem-solving steps (for

example, by using a certain tone of voice or image or by dividing the class into subgroups for recitation).

The new thinking skill is then introduced. In this particular lesson, a hypothetical challenge is presented in which each student plans how, when, where, and with whom he or she will talk to the music teacher about a problem. The teacher is given the following instructions (pp. 123–124):

B. Ask each student to imagine that he or she was constantly getting into trouble in music class along with the students around him or her. Say, "Imagine that you've gone through six problem-solving steps and the best solution seems to be asking the music teacher, Mr. Petro, to allow you to sit with some other children. What are some ways this could be carried out?"

C. List some of their ideas on the board. If they have any difficulty grasping the idea of planning, ask them how each of the following might work out:
    Interrupt the fifth graders' rehearsal and ask Mr. Petro to change your seat.
    Yell your idea to Mr. Petro from the back of the class.
    Ask a friend to speak to Mr. Petro for you.
    Come with fifteen friends to ask Mr. Petro.
    Demand that your seat be changed.
    Beg that your seat be changed.
    Find Mr. Petro during his lunch break and talk to him then.
    At the end of your next class, ask for a few minutes of Mr. Petro's time. Share your concerns with him.

D. Ask the students if they ever made plans that got snagged, messed up, stopped, or ruined. Label such events or circumstances as "obstacles."

To maximize the students' attention and interest in the lesson, the teacher is provided with a practical rationale section that endeavors to show the students why or how the particular skill can make a real difference in their day-to-day lives. In the lessons on "planning," the teachers are asked to "let them know that no one can really know for sure what is going to happen when you put a solution to work in the real world. Life is full of surprises. We can best prepare ourselves for the unexpected if we plan our ideas, and then are ready to calm ourselves and to come up with a new plan if our first one does not work out well. Tell them that this is an important part of problem solving and that you are confident that they can learn how to plan and anticipate obstacles" (p. 124).

This section is now followed by two practice activities: one for the middle elementary grades (grades 3-4) and one for the upper elementary grades (grades 4-5). A teacher can choose one of these two activities based on his or her sense of which one would best meet the developmental needs of the students.

At the upper elementary level, for example, the teacher reads a story, "The Trouble with Susie's Solutions." Here is an example from that stimulus material: "Some children were jumping rope, and Susie wanted a turn. She thought that they would let her play if she said 'please,' so she said, 'Please let me play' (said in a commanding or nasty way). The other children said, 'No.' *Why didn't Susie's solution work?*" (p. 125).

The discussion that follows should emphasize that *how* things are said can make a difference in how people will react and that it is not enough to ask or say "please." The teacher is then asked to practice the new skill with the class (p. 125):

1. Discuss how Susie was good at considering alternatives but that she didn't use problem-solving step 7. Have someone say aloud step 7, and ask the children to review the things to think about when planning a solution. Suggestions include:
    —"When" should I do it? (timing)
    —"How" should I do it? (tone of voice)
    —"Whom" should I include in my plan? (pick the right people)
    —"What" can I learn from other times when this has happened?

            —Should I act right now or wait for a better
            time?
    2.   Apply these ideas to Susie.

    This practice activity is followed by a summary, which in-
cludes a recital of the steps in a further effort to help the students
"overlearn" the problem-solving steps. The teacher is again encouraged to use the important technique of appropriate self-disclosure
of her or his own use of the SPS skill being taught.
    Next, follow-through to the social and academic worlds is
emphasized, and the students are asked "to take a few moments to
plan a nice surprise for someone or several people in their family.
This could mean preparing a thoughtful snack, cleaning part of the
house, and the like. Help them focus on the goal, alternatives, and
consequences and then on choosing their best idea. The key to this
assignment is that the students then carefully write their plan
'where,' 'when,' and 'how' they will carry out their idea. Finally,
have them write down any of the obstacles that they can think of
and to plan around them" (p. 125).
    Additionally, suggestions are made for ways in which the
teacher can apply the planning step to the academic domain. In the
area of language arts, the teacher is asked to help the students understand how the idea of planning is a part of many of the stories
that they read. Teachers are asked to choose a suitable story and to
have students identify a plan and any obstacles that were encountered and perhaps overcome through anticipatory planning (that is,
"final checks"). The students can also be encouraged to write or
share with the class a story involving a plan, a final check, and some
obstacles that occurred in spite of the final check.
    Next, a "Teaching Tips" section is provided, including ideas
such as the following: "As the children learn the skills and as you
become increasingly more comfortable with the framework, you can
be more flexible in leading the lessons and modeling your own
social decision making and problem solving. Most of all, enjoy the
process of teaching the children these skills" (p. 126).
    Finally, the last section in the instructional phase lessons
may include some additional social decision-making stories if the
teacher feels the need for more skill practice opportunities. Brief

vignettes such as the following are included: "You have been invited to Jim's party and the only person you know there is Jim. He's
very busy talking to a lot of other people. You are beginning to feel
uncomfortable because you are standing alone and not talking to
anyone" (p. 126).

The Application Phase

The curriculum's approach to teaching social decision-making
skills devotes a final major section of lessons to systematically teaching the children to transfer and generalize the skills that they are
learning to real day-to-day and academic problem situations. From
the beginning of the ISA-SPS Project, efforts have been undertaken
to minimize the chance that children would only use the SPS skills
during the social problem-solving class. Hence, there is an emphasis on teachers using SPS dialoguing and related techniques
throughout the course of the day, including self-disclosure of their
own use of SPS skills. In the early days of the ISA-SPS Project,
teachers were encouraged to adapt the SPS framework to the academic areas and to the way that they were handling discipline and
classroom behavior problems. However, it was soon learned that far
too many teachers, although they were well-intentioned, did not
have the time to develop such adaptations, especially in the academic areas. Rather than letting this important feature go by the
wayside, application phase lessons were developed.

There are twelve application topics, with titles such as "Alternatives to Stereotyping and Prejudice," "Solving the Problem of
Moving to a New Grade or School," " A Problem-Solving Strategy
for Starting and Completing Projects," and "A Decision-Making
Approach to Social Studies." The lessons make frequent use of
frameworks that can be adapted and used repeatedly with changing
content. Overall, the format of the lessons is similar to the format
used in the readiness phase, with the main sections being "Purpose," "Instructional Activities," and "Teaching Tips."

To illustrate, a common problem students experience as they
approach the middle school years is that of organizing themselves
to write a "report." These kinds of assignments will increasingly
become a major part of their academic responsibility through high

school and beyond. Following are some of the questions that appear in a worksheet format entitled "Taming Tough Topics" (Elias & Clabby, 1989, p. 157):

> *First, define your problem and goal.*
> - What is the topic? . . .
> - What are some questions you would like to answer or learn about the topic? . . .
>
> *Second, list alternative places to look for information.*
> - Write at least five possible places where you can look for information . . .
> - Plan which one you will try first . . .
> - Who else can you ask for ideas if these do not work? . . .

This approach has proved to be a fine way to encourage children to bring the skills of clear thinking to a variety of academic areas including AIDS, science, and the Native Americans of New Jersey. Other worksheets act as a bridge to real-life social problem areas.

Additional Sections

Elias and Clabby (1989) include a separate section that summarizes the research findings that provide the empirical underpinnings for the program. There is also a major section that presents specific strategies to help make an SPS program "work" as it is brought into a classroom, school building, or school district. This section describes how social problem solving fits with the other objectives held by those in general academic education and by those who are concerned specifically with the primary prevention of mental health, behavioral, and emotional difficulties. Recommendations are also made concerning use of the lessons in both the regular education and special education classrooms.

Because the program is used in both special education classes and classes in which special education students have been mainstreamed, a separate section is included that provides some guidelines and principles for the practitioner, including the following:

1. SPS represents a hierarchy of skills, with new skills being added once mastery is achieved with more basic skills.
2. The language of SPS should be shared by as many of the people in the student's life as possible.
3. The practitioner should keep in mind all of the instructional identities that he or she can bring to the situation, such as being a support system for students, being a facilitator of their critical thinking, and being a prompter of their use of the readiness skills.
4. The practitioner must continue to cultivate the qualities of patience, persistence, and a sense of humor, qualities that have helped many people prevail in challenging circumstances.

Suggestions are made for district-wide program development, including strategies for parent involvement and techniques for monitoring and personalizing the lessons. The parent involvement suggestions are drawn largely from the substantive parent handbook entitled *Teach Your Child Decision Making* (Clabby & Elias, 1986), which contains techniques, guidelines, and worksheets on social problem solving for parents as well as leaders of parent groups. Finally, evaluation forms are included that can be used to assess the students' acquisition and use of the SPS skills.

Other Elementary School SPS Programs

What a program defines as "appropriate classroom materials" provides the clearest view into its value and mission, and the way it implements them. This chapter can be considered such a window into the curriculum-based social decision-making and problem-solving program. This program is ambitious in its comprehensive inclusion of the ingredients that are seen as important to interventions designed to equip children with clear social thinking skills. However, it is important to also mention other social decision-making/problem-solving approaches, obtainable without a mandatory training requirement, that have been influential in shaping our thinking. This complements the streams of influence described in Chapter Two. Each program contributes something unique in its goals, approaches, and level of appropriateness for a school system. Indeed, the reader may already have recognized familiar aspects and activities in the description of SPS. Certainly, the ISA-SPS Project believes that much of its worth is in compiling the best of what is reflected in the programs listed next, and in synergistically improving the resulting approach by attending to a broad spectrum of key elements.

It is therefore fitting for this chapter to conclude with a listing of some of the most salient programs that have forged our approach. They are presented in grade-level order.

ICPS: A Mental Health Program for Kindergarten and First Grade Children (Shure & Spivack, 1974) is a fifty-five-lesson curriculum with material allowing twenty minutes of instructional time for each lesson. There is a section of lessons within this curriculum that emphasizes problem-solving word concepts; the two problem-solving steps that are taught are (1) alternative solution thinking and (2) consequential thinking.

Think Aloud: Increasing Social and Cognitive Skills—A Problem-Solving Program for Children. Classroom Program Grades 1-2 (Camp & Bash, 1985a) is a thirty-lesson curriculum that focuses on these four SPS skills: (1) What am I supposed to do? (2) What are some plans? (3) How is my plan working? and (4) How did I do? The authors state that thirty minutes of instructional time should be allowed for each lesson.

The Rochester Social Problem-Solving Program (SPS): A Training Manual for Teachers of 2nd-4th Grade Children (Weissberg et al., 1980) contains forty lessons with the suggested time for each lesson being twenty minutes. The six SPS steps emphasized in this work are (1) say exactly what the problem is, (2) decide on your goal, (3) stop to think before you act, (4) think of as many solutions as you can, (5) think ahead to what might happen next, and (6) when you have a really good solution, try it.

Camp and Bash followed up their program for grades 1 and 2 with *Think Aloud: Increasing Social and Cognitive Skills—A Problem-Solving Program for Children. Classroom Program Grades 3-4* (Camp & Bash, 1985b). There are thirty-one lessons in this curriculum that rest on the following four-step framework: (1) What is my problem? (2) How can I solve it? (3) Am I using the best plan? and (4) How did I do? The authors suggest that teachers set aside thirty minutes for each of these lessons.

As mentioned in Chapter Three, Elardo and Cooper's (1977) *AWARE: Activities for Social Development* was the first curriculum used in the ISA-SPS project. Designed for eight- to ten-year-olds, this volume has seventy-two "discussion activities," each designed for a minimum time of thirty minutes. The three steps of decision making included in this work are (1) understanding and recognizing the thoughts and feelings of others, (2) being able to define a problem, and (3) being able to understand the consequences of each alternative for all people involved.

The Friendship Group Manual for Social Skills Development (Elementary Grades)—Interpersonal Problem-Solving Training for Friendship-Making (Urbain, 1985) is a twenty-four-lesson program designed for children in grades 2 to 6. The leader of each lesson should allow at least ninety minutes of instructional time. This curriculum also includes some supplementary team-building activities in the form of cooperative games. The manual teaches the following four-step approach to SPS: (1) stop and think (What is going on here? What are the consequences of what I am doing?), (2) put yourself in the other guy's shoes (listen for feelings—How do I feel? How would I feel if that happened to me?), (3) brainstorm: think of different ways to solve the problem (What different ideas can I try in this situation?), and (4) make a plan (What is the best idea to try first? What will I do if my best idea doesn't work?).

Shure and Spivack (1982) also developed *ICPS: A Mental Health Program for Intermediate Elementary Grades,* which contains fifty-one lessons with a thirty- to forty-minute amount of time required for each lesson. Twenty-nine lessons make up a "Pre-Problem Solving Skills" section focusing on such skills as remembering things about people and sensitivity to feelings. Twenty-two lessons teach the following three-step problem-solving strategy: (1) alternative solutions thinking, (2) consequential thinking, and (3) means-end thinking (the ability to plan, step by step, the means to reach a stated goal).

The third curriculum in the Camp & Bash series is *Think*

Aloud: Increasing Social and Cognitive Skills—A Problem-Solving Program for Children. Classroom Program Grades 5-6 (Camp & Bash, 1985c). There are twenty-three lessons in this particular volume and a teacher should allow thirty minutes of class time for each lesson. The same four-step strategy that was used in their curriculum for grades 3 and 4 is used here.

In the following chapter, the discussion of curricular and instructional procedures as essential vehicles for conveying social decision-making skills to students is extended to the middle and high school years. Practitioners no doubt share the experience of our project that serious developmental issues come to the fore during this period, and that demands for interventions intensify. The SPS Unit found itself turning to the social, conceptual, and empirical foundations and key elements of the SPS approach as a starting point for addressing these demands. The status of this work, while still in progress, is presented in Chapter Seven.

Chapter Seven

Addressing the Needs of Middle and High School Students

The implementation of an elementary school–based intervention sets up the next challenge: the cohorts of elementary school–aged children with whom educators are working will mature and enter middle school and, eventually, high school. As the SPS Unit faced this situation, the staff began considering more and more the idea of developing strategies to keep the concept of social problem solving alive within students as they entered the world of secondary education. The focus of this chapter will primarily remain within the "A" domain of the MATS/MEF framework, centering on "appropriate classroom materials." Incorporated also are extensive considerations of matching and planning as practitioners address the changing developmental realities for students as well as attempting to find a comfortable niche for the program within a departmentalized organizational structure.

The Case for Programming
at the Secondary Level

A school-based practitioner who can succeed in convincing a school system and its teachers at even one grade level to adopt and implement an SPS program has achieved a great deal. It is a special accomplishment when a school system is persuaded to adopt a change, such as a new program, especially when that new program is in the nontraditional social-affective area.

Many practitioners can relate to the experience of striving to get a foot in the door of a school system for a first-year pilot program. The goal is to survive and prevail that first year and, if the program proves successful, to use that credibility in order to persuade the school decision makers to expand the program upward or downward in order to ensure multiyear programming. In that way, the children do not receive one year of the program only to forget the knowledge and skills they have learned by the following year. Consequently, school-based practitioners who truly respect what it takes for a student to acquire and begin to use a skill such as social problem solving will be looking for program continuity throughout as much of the educational life cycle of the student as the host school system will permit.

If a school district's leaders are intrigued by a practitioner's explanation of social problem solving, they will probably have a specific grade level in mind that is causing particular difficulty for the staff. Most often, educational leaders will ask for programmatic help for the district's adolescent students. SPS practitioners who identify themselves as preventionists will do their best to convince these school leaders to allow some programming to take place with the district's younger children, presenting the concept of building up the students' skills before they get to the adolescent years. Although they sometimes are successful at moving the district's efforts to the lower elementary grades, there are many occasions when the school district's leadership remains unpersuaded. Rather than rejecting the district's point of view, the practitioner should look for ways to bring SPS interventions to adolescent students in the challenging host environment of departmentalized secondary education. A push from the schools for assistance with their adolescent students served as an important impetus for the SPS Unit to begin looking at an SPS program at the secondary level. As was stated earlier, an additional impetus has been the project's concern with follow-up. The primary question that has guided the work reported in this chapter is "What can be done to provide experiences that can help adolescent students further develop their skills in social decision making?"

Developmental Characteristics Influencing Program Structure
for Middle and High School Students

The developmental changes that occur in children up to the age of nine may be more generally known than those that are experienced by early adolescents. Because of this, a summary of some of the developmental challenges that confront the early adolescent is included in this section for the use of the SPS practitioner.

In recent years, fortunately, increasing attention has been given to understanding the challenges confronting school-based practitioners who have as their goal creating programs for middle and high school students. The Center for Early Adolescence at the University of North Carolina at Chapel Hill has taken on a leadership role in helping others better understand the dramatic jolt that students and their families experience when the particular developmental changes of adolescence encounter the tremendous school organizational changes that occur within a departmentalized curriculum. Indeed, these factors are a major cause of stress and a major reason why the SPS Unit was established with a prevention focus in the first place.

Early adolescence is defined as encompassing the ten- to fifteen-year-old range and therefore includes students who are found in elementary, middle, and high school settings. The significant developmental changes affecting this group will be discussed in terms of physiological/sexual, cognitive/intellectual, and social/emotional areas (Dorman, Geldof, & Scarborough, 1984).

Physiological/Sexual Changes

At some point in early adolescence, a youngster experiences rapid physical growth, becoming both stronger and taller. Energy and interest are invested in testing out this new body strength and size, which in turn can lead to restlessness, impulsivity, and risk taking. The capacity to reproduce also emerges during this period, marked by ejaculation in boys and menstruation in girls, and secondary sex characteristics appear, such as body hair, breast development in girls, and broadening of the shoulders and deepening of the voice in boys. Sexual maturity can strike like a thunderbolt, with its accompanying sexual feelings and interests, as well as hormonal changes that manifest themselves in a variety of ways including moodiness and the emergence of facial blemishes. Although not entirely over by age sixteen, these changes have stabilized to a great extent by that time.

Cognitive/Intellectual Changes

On the cognitive/intellectual side, there is a tentative ability by the young adolescent to reason abstractly. These young people are not as accepting of adult ideas and values as they were in middle childhood. They test adults' statements and evaluate their views and positions on every imaginable topic. Their new ability in abstract reasoning can also give rise to an increased concern about others and about what other people might be thinking, leading to a belief that others, in turn, are thinking about and/or watching them. This contributes to feelings of self-consciousness, a reluctance to self-disclose (especially in mixed-gender groups), and a consequential push to "hide out" in peer conformity. Adolescents prefer school activities and instruction that have a game-like component. By the time students reach sixteen years of age, they are much more solidly and consistently able to use formal operational skills, characterized in part by an increased reflectiveness, a longer attention span, and an improved capacity to retain abstract concepts. In addition, because they have accumulated more and varied experiences with the skill of abstract reasoning and have reality-tested the fact that their actions and attitudes are not so conspicuous after all, older adolescents begin to feel more comfortable with their now-stabilizing physical presentation and to have relatively greater self-confidence. They also become somewhat more receptive to the world of learning and ideas.

Social/Emotional Changes

The social/emotional world of the early adolescent might be considered, in part, as a reaction to the fledgling skill of abstract reasoning. Many early adolescents have an inner world marked by feelings of inferiority and of not measuring up to their peers. Thus, they may be relatively thin-skinned, appearing to be quite uncomfortable with criticism. On one hand, they are shown respect for beginning to move into the highly regarded age group of young adulthood by being awarded such responsible jobs as that of paid babysitter in charge of an entire household. On the other hand, they are not given the kind of independence, privacy, and status that would normally accompany such responsibility. These privileges do not come until later adolescence. Younger adolescents can become very self-absorbed and cliquish but may still be disarmingly childlike and refreshing in their views about relationships. Strong bonds to particular teachers can highlight their impressionability and search for positive role models and identities.

At about sixteen years of age, as a high school student, the young person has greater options for time alone and privacy. Curfews are more extended and, in some cases, these adolescents are ready to acquire and use automobile drivers' licenses. Older adolescents do not need to rely on the security of the clique as much as they once did and may begin to experiment with dating on a one-to-one basis. Because they are given greater autonomy now, many older adolescents can engage in regular, sustained paid employment, and the resulting income that allows them to buy holiday gifts for friends and family and clothes and snacks for themselves are all, of course, ego-enhancing experiences. Moreoever, greater numbers of formalized socialization opportunities are now available to older adolescents who, if they are not working, can become involved in high school athletics and clubs, using such domains to test out their emerging identities. Unfortunately, they too often follow confusing media and cultural messages promoting "autonomy" from parents, whereas a more appropriate social-emotional goal would be for them to establish respectful interdependence with adults (Elias, 1990b; Gilligan, 1987).

Finding a Fit for Social Problem Solving
in the Middle School

Although it can be a major challenge to find a niche for SPS programming in the crowded, academic schedule of the elementary level, this quest can move to a higher level of complexity in secondary education. It is a challenge that requires creative programming efforts to match the different needs of middle and high school students. The approaches undertaken by the SPS Unit staff in middle schools are presented next.

Middle School: An Infusion Approach

For early adolescents, superimposed on their developmental changes is a major sociological change—the move away from the elementary school experience of having a single "primary" teacher all day long. The elementary school teacher traditionally gets to know a child quite well, shepherding that child to lunch and assemblies, following up on missed homework assignments, and perhaps even becoming acquainted with the parents. With the onset of middle school or junior high school, all of this changes. The youngster may be riding a school bus for the first time and the social interactions occurring on those bus rides are legendary. In addition, the child may be going to a larger building, because the middle school and the junior high school typically are regionalized schools, fed by several "sending" elementary schools and with many of the students coming from neighborhoods that will be new to the child. There are demands on the young adolescent to master locker combinations, do well in physical education class, and handle six, seven, or eight teachers, each of whom may have a different set of organizational demands and tolerances.

Joan Lipsitz (1980) of the Center for Early Adolescence asserts that there is no more widely heterogenous group than young adolescents. In one middle school homeroom, a teacher can observe a full six-year span in biological development between a rapidly developing girl and a slowly developing boy, and this refers only to the dimension of physical growth. When one considers the challenges that each young adolescent juggles—physiological/sexual, cognitive/intellectual, and social/emotional—programming for an intact class of middle school students who are the same chronological age becomes incredibly difficult.

For these reasons, programming for the early adolescent has truly challenged SPS consultants' efforts to stay faithful to the key element of providing an adequate matching and planning process. It is a complex dynamic to design an SPS intervention for middle school students that gives this widely variable group what they need, and that does it in a way that can be supported by the complex institution of the middle school. For this reason the SPS program has utilized an *infusion approach*, in which the building of SPS skills is incorporated into already existing formal and informal structures in the middle school. To do this, a wide variety of SPS vehicles have been designed and implemented.

Examples of informal infusion reflect an attempt to capture the high energy level and limited attention span of some of the students, often through the vehicle of contests. For example, a contest was organized to encourage students to create artistically engaging posters concerning the benefits of being a good social decision maker and problem solver. The school's student calligraphy club judged this particular contest and gift certificates donated by local fast food restaurants were given as prizes. One middle school guidance counselor organized a social problem-solving contest in which groups of middle school students held discussions of ways to solve interpersonal problems. A faculty panel judged their use of social decision-making skills and then awarded gift certificates donated by a local music store to the winning group of students.

To incorporate more fun and variability and to deemphasize competitiveness, some teachers have written songs with SPS lyrics. One teacher and class collaborated to write and perform an SPS rap song, which they filmed on videotape, complete with a dance routine that they choreographed themselves. One school produced SPS T-shirts and buttons with slogans such as "Be Your Best" and "Ridgemont Kids Make Good Decisions" printed on the front.

Other teachers have focused on taking a problem-solving approach to instruction in traditional content areas. Locked tightly into schedules designed to impart instruction in basic academic skills, these teachers have been receptive to having SPS concepts infused into the teaching of middle school science, mathematics, language arts, and geography. Examples of those activities are discussed in the next sections.

SPS and Language Arts: Into the Video Age

One of the most engaging middle school classes the SPS staff saw was a language arts/journalism class in which students learned how to conceive, plan, and produce their own newspaper or music video program. It was an obviously exciting class for the students, in which they learned the basics of journalism, the elements of media persuasion, and how to view commercials, advertisements, and motion pictures in a thoughtful, discerning way. In so doing, they learned that a producer had to be a good social problem solver and have a goal in mind, as well as a plan regarding how she or he was going to meet that goal. Considering the power that the media wields in such areas as persuading young people to smoke tobacco or use alcohol, it is important to help youngsters develop a critical, problem-solving view of the persuasion techniques used by the media. (This method is derived from elementary-level SPS application phase lessons.) The lesson, which appears in Appendix C, is an example of how an SPS-trained or oriented school-based consultant can create a vehicle that is matched with students developmentally and that also fits well within a departmentalized curriculum.

It is also important that the structure of this lesson allows it to stand alone, and that is not dependent on students having received prior or concurrent SPS instruction, because the schedule of a busy middle school teacher may only allow enough time for a limited number of such lessons. However, the same lesson *structure* can be used in many different situations by the teacher. This kind of lesson can be used in a variety of academic classes and can be broken down and taught over time. It also represents an effort to match SPS to an already demonstrated adolescent interest, in this case, the media.

Alchemy Lives: Turning SPS Questions into Academic Worksheet Gems

In one middle school, the SPS staff encountered a very common situation: the acquisition of basic academic skills as evidenced by the students' scores on standardized academic achievement tests was the overt, explicit, and main mission of the school. This goal found its way into each teacher's annual formal professional improvement plan, which had been developed with the building principal. Signs posted throughout the building encouraged improved scores on national tests of academic achievement and the mission was mentioned quite often by the building principal in faculty meetings and in conversations with the SPS staff. Part of this schoolwide goal was a push for improvement in the student's prose writing skills. In fact, all of the school's teachers, regardless of their subject, were required to have four creative writing assignments completed by the children during the course of the year.

Having assessed these aspects of the school climate, the SPS Unit staff strongly felt that in this type of middle school, teaching social problem solving using a traditional instructional phase cumulative curriculum approach would vary from what most teachers saw as their mission. The teachers' end-of-the-year performance evaluations were not going to be based on their students' improved social competence but on whether their scores on nationally standardized tests of academic achievement had improved. Consequently, the SPS Unit staff suggested that SPS academic worksheets be developed that would correspond to the mathematics, science, social studies (geography), reading, and language arts missions of the school.

Once again, the upper elementary school–level application phase served as a jumping-off point for SPS staff and middle school teachers, whose creative collaboration resulted in SPS academic worksheets. These worksheets were a good match because first, their successful completion demanded narrative writing skills that meshed well with a schoolwide academic goal; second, the format of the worksheets allowed them to be used again and again by the teachers; and third, they were timely, because the prospect of once again teaching seventh graders about the wonders of world geography was filling some teachers with dread.

The following is an example of SPS questions that have been used successfully (developed with the assistance of Howard Rubinstein during his participation in a graduate-level practicum with the ISA-SPS Project). A worksheet was developed in which geography was brought alive for a seventh grader when it was linked to a newspaper article describing tensions between the farmers of the Brazilian rain forest and international environmentalists regarding the pros and cons of clearing land for cultivation.

1. What is the topic of this article? ("How environmentalists and farmers are fighting over the burning of the rain forests.")

2. When and where is it happening? ("It's happening now, in Brazil.")

3. Put the topic into words as a *problem*. ("The farmers are burning the rain forest because they need the land, but the Brazilian government and environmentalists say it's bad for the earth.")

4. What people or groups are involved in the problem? ("Brazilian farmers, the government of Brazil, and environmentalists.")

5. What are the different feelings and points of view about the problem? ("The farmers need the land to farm so they can live, the Brazilian government is pressured by other countries, and the environmentalists really just want to save the forests.")

6. If you were involved in this problem, what would be one of your goals? ("I would try to stop the burning of the forests and find other land for the farmers.")

7. What do you know about features such as the size of the country, climate, weather conditions, and so on that might help you solve the problem? ("I know how the rain forests affect the oxygen level and how they would affect global warming. Also, understanding the political situation is important.")

8. Name some different solutions and consequences. ("To tell the farmers to stop. The forests would begin to grow back. Another possibility is that the farmers could become homeless." "To let the farmers only burn a limited number of forests, then some of the forests would remain untouched. Also, the farmers might use up all the land and need more." "To tell the farmers to stop and find them other jobs. The forests would begin to grow back but the farmers might not be as good at other jobs as they were at farming.")

9. Which of your solutions do you think would best solve the problem? ("To tell the farmers to stop and find them other jobs.")

Learning world geography, no matter how it is taught, certainly involves the memorization of information about continents, the countries within those continents, the topography and various climates of the region, and major cities. Unfortunately, if the instructional plan always relies on the approach of having students read a textbook, memorize the facts, and be tested on their knowledge of those facts, the process can be quite dull for the early adolescent, who attaches little meaning or personal experience to these facts.

Infusing SPS into world geography can be seen by teachers as consistent with academic goals and also can breathe some life into what might otherwise be a fairly static class. As shown in the sample responses to the worksheet questions, knowledge of geographical location, climate, and their interplay could now be seen by middle school students as facts that were critical for solving a dangerous social problem that they frequently heard discussed in the news media and popular culture. The student responses to the issue of the Brazilian rain forest illustrates how engaged students can become with this kind of approach—including students who have traditionally been labeled as "disaffected" or "at risk."

The middle school practitioner who wishes to actively infuse SPS into the academic area needs not only creativity but also great familiarity with SPS and students' developmental levels. When a good match is created, the tailored result can be and has been, in our experience, an exciting, charged, powerful learning and growth experience.

Other Curriculum Approaches for the Early Adolescent

Additional resources are available to the practitioner that adopt an infusion approach to bringing SPS skills into the academic mainstream for early adolescents and their teachers. For example, *Decision Making Skills for Middle School Students* (Bergmann & Rudman, 1985) is an eighteen-lesson curriculum that is designed for social studies and language arts classes. Each lesson is planned as a twenty- to twenty-five-minute experience and is based on the following eight-step decision-making strategy:

1. Problem finding: What is the decision to be made?
2. Problem defining: What are the important elements of the decision—the who, the what, and the where?
3. Information gathering: What information do I need?
4. Information prioritizing: Rank ordering the data in order of importance

5. Values assessment: What do I believe in and what part will my beliefs play in my decision?
6. *Alternatives and consequences:* What are the probable solutions and outcomes?
7. *Action:* What will I actually do about this decision?
8. *Evaluation:* Was my decision consistent with my beliefs and the data gathered?

   Decision-Making Infusion: A Supplement to a Social-Cognitive Approach to the Prevention of Adolescent Substance Abuse, Intervention I: Sixth Grade (Consultation Center of the Connecticut Mental Health Center et al., 1989) is a compilation of 134 lessons from a wide array of sources with varied formats; this collection includes some lessons that are appropriate for the academic areas.

   There are other middle school SPS curricula that do not focus on the academic areas but teach SPS as it applies to social problems. Following are three examples that may interest the SPS practitioner who wishes the more direct instructional approach. The Consultation Center's (1989) infusion curriculum just mentioned is, as its title states, supplemental to *A Social-Cognitive Approach to the Prevention of Adolescent Substance Abuse, Intervention I: Sixth Grade Student Curriculum: Project New Directions* (Cohen, Brennan, & Sexton, 1984). This curriculum contains twelve topics or lessons, each of which is designed to be taught in a forty- to fifty-minute period. A six-step social decision-making strategy is the organizing framework for this curriculum. These steps are (1) define the problem, (2) generate all possible alternatives, (3) narrow down the list of alternatives, (4) identify positive and negative consequences for self and others, (5) identify risks, and (6) choose the best alternative for yourself. Six of the lessons focus on how decision making is influenced by one's role in the group and how to get help from others in decision making.

   A Social-Cognitive Approach to the Prevention of Adolescent Substance Abuse Intervention II: Eighth/Ninth Grade Student Curriculum: Decision-Making (McLaughlin et al., 1984) is a twelve-lesson/topic curriculum. The suggested time for each lesson is forty-five minutes, and there is an emphasis on the importance of personal values. Seven problem-solving steps provide the framework for these lessons: (1) define the problem, (2) identify alternatives, (3) identify consequences and risks associated with the remaining alternatives, (4) identify your personal values influencing the decision, (5) identify any group or peer pressure that may influence the decision, (6) decide if more information is needed before making this decision, and (7) decide which alternatives would be your best choice.

Finally, *The Positive Youth Development Program: A Substance Abuse Prevention Program for Young Adolescents* (Caplan, Jacoby, Weissberg, & Grady, 1988) is a twenty-lesson/topic curriculum designed for use with sixth and seventh graders. An estimated time length for each lesson is not provided. This curriculum is organized around a four-step problem-solving strategy: (1) stop, calm down, and say the problem, (2) think of different alternatives, (3) think ahead to the consequences, and (4) go ahead and try the best plan. Some of the lessons focus on stress management, self-esteem, substance abuse, assertiveness, and social networks.

The next section moves to a discussion of SPS at the high school level. Developmental issues are followed by SPS curriculum approaches.

High School: A Curriculum-Based Approach

Many high school students, especially those sixteen years old and older, have already sustained their major growth spurts and have had some practice and experience with their emerging physical, cognitive, and emotional capabilities. This gives them a greater sense of poise than they had as twelve-year-old seventh graders. Also, older adolescents have started to venture out from the structure and predictability of the peer group. Opportunities to work, to learn how to drive a car, and to be more responsible for their own schedule have allowed them to begin to see how they might fit into the adult world.

Because they have been using their abstract thinking skills to an increasing degree and because they are seeing a much more expanded world, these older adolescents are able to recognize the connection between SPS and their potential for success in that world. Their motivation to participate in SPS programming, if it can be shown to be a way to help them manage in the adult world, may be higher than it was in middle school. During those years, their defensiveness, uncertainty, and a fragile ego often stopped them from admitting when they did not know something that they needed to know. Older adolescents realize more and more than they are not the subject of everyone's gossip, and they are less self-conscious. They may still talk to friends about very personal matters on the telephone, but they no longer have to rely on its relative anonymity and can also have such talks in person. Older adolescents are able to absorb more abstract academic content areas, such as chemistry and political science, and in their reflectiveness they can begin to "think about thinking." They not only can benefit from an infusion approach but can be given a cumulative curriculum approach to SPS similar to the one used in the elementary school. They can participate in a sharing circle and contribute something personally meaningful (without becoming very embarrassed) more easily than when they were in middle school. Talking in front of members of the opposite sex about hypothetical dating problems they saw in a video can be done with less of the anxious giggling and joking that characterized the uncertainty of such discussions held in early adolescence.

In school systems where the SPS approach had become well established with programming at the elementary and middle school grades, encouragement grew for the program to "move up" into the high school with an SPS program that could provide some conceptual continuity. This is an extremely important point. In fact, one district in which the SPS program was being used had several different kinds of "decision-making" or "critical thinking" problem-solving programs going on at different grade levels. Each of these programs used a different array of SPS steps; students were expected to synthesize a five-step decision-making model in the elementary years, a six-step model using different terminology when they entered middle school, and a four-step model using still different terms and language when they entered high school. The school system's central administration and the SPS Unit staff both felt that the students could easily become confused.

The school leadership in another district was interested in incorporating a high school SPS program for students who were educationally classified as emotionally disturbed. In collaboration with the staff of the SPS Unit, the district wished to use the same eight-step social decision-making strategy and language that were used at the elementary level with special education students who had been in the SPS program. There were some features of the elementary curriculum that were especially valued and desired as part of the high school program. For example, the procedure of teaching these eight steps in a gradual, cumulative fashion was seen as important, as was the skill of self-calming as a response to the stress of interpersonal problems. Also valued was the inclusion of lessons that taught the students the importance of transferring and generalizing the SPS skills to real-life problems in an application phase. Finally, because several topics in the elementary curriculum had very successfully used videos of stories to capture and sustain the students' attention, it was felt that this feature should be greatly expanded at the high school level. All of these features were included in the development of a high school SPS curriculum that was termed *ASPIRE: Adolescent Problem-Solving Interventions with Relaxation Exercises* (Clabby, 1992).

An Overview of ASPIRE

ASPIRE can serve as an illustration of how an SPS curriculum can be developed to fit a specific school system's needs. In the case of ASPIRE, there was a need to provide motivation for older adolescents to participate in SPS classes. If the right focus and instructional vehicle could be identified, there would be a match that would work. The motivational focus here was money, which students would obtain by securing and keeping jobs. Therefore, a job-related slant was woven into many of the vignettes, stories, and exercises that were chosen for the instructional phase topics. It also was obvious that it would be best to focus the entire application phase on how SPS could help students secure and keep jobs. With regard to the *vehicle* for learning the skills, it was determined that the tradition of having active SPS discussions of hypothetical problems would still be the main activity but, as mentioned earlier, this activity would be greatly enhanced in the instructional phase by the inclusion of many engaging video stimulus stories.

The same instructional philosophy that guided the development of the elementary curriculum (see Part One and Elias & Clabby, 1989) guided and continues to guide the development of ASPIRE (Clabby, 1992; see Chapter Eleven of this book for a discussion of the action-research background of the ASPIRE approach). ASPIRE reflects a belief that one of the best models for teaching the skills of social cognitive problem solving is drawn from observing how other complex skills, such as driving a car, are taught. Generally, these skills are taught slowly and gradually, with the next step being taught after the prior ones have been fairly well learned. There is an instructional phase in which a student learns driving skills through an engaging format and instructor, followed by an opportunity to practice in a safe environment, such as an empty parking lot. This is followed by supervised driving in real traffic. The skills of driving a car are first remembered by a novice driver in a relatively rigid, mechanical way, but with enough time spent in guided practice, these skills begin to blend more comfortably and become more or less automatic. This approach corresponds to the way that ASPIRE endeavors to teach social decision making: slowly and cumulatively.

ASPIRE contains thirty-two lessons, which are organized into a nine-lesson readiness phase, a fourteen-lesson instructional phase, and a nine-lesson application phase. The lessons might also be considered "topics" in that a particular "lesson" might pertain to a skill or theme that a teacher may cover over a number of class periods. Each lesson has enough material for at least one forty-five-minute class.

All of the lessons contain a list of the objectives, a list of the required materials (important when the video programs are used), a Lesson Outline, and a detailed, scriptlike Leader's Guide. In curriculum work in the area of social decision making, outlines are very useful, because they allow a busy teacher to scan the material to visualize the goals and the instructional flow. A teacher who is well trained in SPS and who understands the research and practice literature as presented in Chapters One through Three is well able to understand the goals of such lessons. With repeated experience in teaching SPS lessons such as the ones in ASPIRE, a teacher may gradually rely less on the detailed Leader's Guide as a script and more on the outline as a guide. As with the elementary SPS program, ASPIRE begins with readiness phase lessons, which are discussed next.

The ASPIRE Readiness Phase

The nine social awareness and group-building lessons within this phase focus on such topics as developing a sense of empathy, growing comfortable with self-disclosure, and helping others. The self-control lessons review and reinforce the skills of keeping calm under stress and self-monitoring one's interpersonal presentation. In harmony with how the elementary readiness lessons were designed, these high school readiness lessons have active learning formats to engage all types of learners. For example, in the readiness lesson, "Developing a Classroom Team," there are three objectives: (1) to help the students grow in comfort about sharing their ideas and feelings, (2) to facilitate the feeling that they are members of a cooperative team or group, and (3) to call attention to the importance of observational skills.

Accordingly, the topic begins with a class discussion of the practical rationale for "attending," such as being alert enough to notice that there was a mistake on your paycheck and that you were underpaid. One of the suggested activities integrates the three objectives of the topic and is called "Keeping Alert." This exercise consists of a series of questions that tap into the students' observational skills. The teacher and/or class members can add to this activity by developing questions that are particularly tailored for their school and class. Here are some examples of the questions that appear in this lesson:

1. What is the color of the carpet in the library?
2. Who is the superintendent of schools?
3. What movie theater is closest to school? Where exactly is it located?
4. Who is usually the first student to arrive in class?
5. What is the first name of our principal?
6. What are the names of all of the fast food restaurants in our town? Where are they located?

7. Name the pizza restaurant that is closest to our school.
8. Name all of the elementary schools in our district.
9. How many total credits do you need to graduate from high school?
10. Which two students are the best listeners in our class?
11. Name the room number of our classroom.
12. Who appears to be the happiest person in our group?
13. What service station has the least expensive gasoline in town?
14. Who in our group seems to be the most patient?
15. Earlier we discussed several situations where keeping alert and paying attention can really help us. Name two of these situations.

Following the students' participation in this and a number of other such activities on this topic, the teacher ends the day's SPS lesson by complimenting the students for their efforts (when appropriate) and especially their specific efforts at paying attention during class.

The teacher then summarizes the main themes of the lesson: (1) the importance of being a good observer and (2) the fact that we all belong to groups, such as our family, our class, and our place of employment, and that to be happy and successful we all need to find a way to cooperatively use our individual talents.

The ASPIRE Instructional Phase

The fourteen lessons of this phase all correspond to the eight SPS steps, with "solutions" and "consequences" being introduced simultaneously. In the instructional phase lessons, the readiness skill of being able to calm oneself by using relaxation techniques is seen as essential in engaging adolescents' ability to be reflective under interpersonal pressure and stress. It is also seen as a valuable instructional tool to "punctuate" the beginning and end of each lesson. Consequently, each lesson begins and ends with a brief self-calming exercise. The lesson then reviews whatever skills were taught in the preceding lesson. Again, the emphasis is on "over-learning," so that the skills can move toward the automatic level. Next, a new social decision-making skill is introduced, defined, and explained. The leader then works with the students to help them uncover a *practical rationale* to describe why learning this skill might be useful to them. (Leaders often find it helpful to use some appropriate self-disclosure at this point to explain how this skill is valuable for them.)

ASPIRE's instructional phase makes consistent use of video-taped stimulus stories, an engaging modality that is too rarely used in social problem solving and related curricula. ASPIRE uses fifteen-minute video programs from the "On the Level" videotape series produced by the Agency for Instructional Technology (1990). "On the Level" is broadcast on a number of educational public television stations and is stocked by many audiovisual libraries and educational resource centers, thus making it widely available.

It is worthwhile noting that by the time some educational video materials are produced and find their way to schools, certain features of the production, such as clothing styles, can appear dated. However, it has been our experience that the power and attractiveness of this medium as an instructional tool greatly override this issue. The practitioner who believes that "datedness" will be an issue is encouraged to acknowledge this with the students *before* the video is shown. This can help a great deal. For the "On the Level" series, this issue has rarely created a problem. The teachers and students seem to genuinely enjoy the video programs. "On the Level" was specifically selected for ASPIRE because many of the open-ended social conflict stories that the students in the videos experience have some connection to the world of work. They are portrayed through developmentally relevant, open-ended plots that lend themselves very nicely to discussions that use the social decision-making framework.

It is important for anyone leading video-based lessons or consulting to a video-based SPS program to remember that good video programs have a wonderful capacity to involve the audience in the plot, character development, and so on. Thus, there is often an "instinctive drift" pulling the leader into an extended discussion of the *content* of the video. In so doing, the leader can lose sight of the fact that the content is only important to the extent that it helps the student learn social decision-making skills. SPS program consultants have often run into this kind of difficulty with first-time teachers and other group leaders. To combat the tendency to "drift," ASPIRE makes use of SPS video worksheets that help focus the students and their instruction on the main goal of the lesson.

Within the ASPIRE lesson, typically the teacher introduces the class to the characters they will observe in the video. The students are then oriented to the SPS video worksheets, which require that they view the program with an active eye and ear to see how well or poorly the characters are using the particular social decision-making step that is the focus of the lesson. Once the students have viewed the program, they have a brief, focused discussion regarding what they have seen. A full social problem-solving discussion takes place at the follow-up lesson. (Ideally, the follow-up lesson would take place during the same week to maximize content retention. Because that often is impossible, it may take place during the next week, with the completed video worksheet being used as a helpful reminder of both the program and the skills taught.) At times, the ASPIRE lessons also have additional practice activities. Each lesson closes with a summary and a brief relaxation activity. The two consecutive lessons that focus specifically on the skill "Decide on Your Goal" are presented in their entirety in Appendix D.

The ASPIRE Application Phase

As has been discussed with regard to the elementary curriculum (Elias & Clabby, 1989), it is wise not to assume that the students will automatically take the skills that were taught during the social problem-solving class and apply them to situations outside of the class. For that reason, a phase of real-life "application" lessons also was developed for ASPIRE. One of the main guiding principles in the development of ASPIRE was to be responsive to the interests of these high school students, who, as their teachers reported, would be able to connect with an affective education type of class if the experience corresponded to the practical incentive of securing money through working. The goal was to encourage the students to become "thinkers" when they were faced with the task of looking for and keeping a job, including a part-time job after school. There are eight ASPIRE application phase lessons covering such topics as generating multiple ideas regarding job and career opportunities, developing a résumé, dealing with interpersonal conflicts at work that involve coworkers and supervisors, handling constructive criticism, being planful, and controlling anger at work. This last topic appears in the curriculum as "Lesson 31: Using Problem Solving to Control Your Temper at Work" and is included in its entirety in Appendix E.

Other Curriculum-Based Approaches for High School Students

Additional resources are available to the practitioner who is working with high school students. *A Social-Cognitive Approach to the Prevention of Adolescent Substance Abuse, Intervention III: Tenth/ Eleventh Grade Student Curriculum: Decision-Making and Stress* (McLaughlin, Jacoby, Grady, & Snow, 1986) is a twelve-lesson/ topic curriculum with each lesson projected for use in a forty-five minute class. In addition to a main focus on cognitive decision making, there are also lessons on how values affect that process. This program's problem-solving framework uses a four-step model: (1) learning to identify the problem, (2) generating alternatives, (3) identifying positive and negative consequences, and (4) selecting the alternative that is the best choice.

A Resource Manual for the Development and Evaluation of Special Programs for Exceptional Students—Volume V-C: Affective Curriculum for Secondary Emotionally Handicapped Students (Francescani, 1983) was written for junior and senior high school students who were classified within the special education system. In all, the manual has seventy-two lessons. Most lessons begin with a thirty- to forty-five-minute skill introduction component followed by a thirty-minute skill practice section. Included are lessons that focus on self-control, communication, and behavioral interactions such as assertiveness, as well as lessons teaching the following seven-step decision-making strategy: (1) identifying the problem, (2) choosing a desired outcome, (3) generating several possible solutions, (4) anticipating the consequences of each solution, (5) choosing the best solution, (6) making a plan to implement the solution and then implementing it, and (7) evaluating the plan.

A program designed for both junior and senior high school

students is the *Adolescent Issues Project* (Brion-Meisels & Selman, 1982), which contains twenty-five lessons that focus on the content of work, twenty-five that focus on drug use, and twenty-six that focus on sexuality, with each lesson/topic designed to be taught within a sixty-minute class period. This program teaches a five-step decision-making strategy: (1) *ask* what decision has to be made, (2) *list* two or more alternative solutions, (3) *think* about the consequences of each solution for yourself and for others, (4) *decide* on one solution and try it out, and (5) *evaluate* your decision and try again. There are also some major sections that apply SPS to such "academic" areas as juvenile law, government, and drug use.

Conclusion

For the practitioner, the prospect of bringing an SPS program into the schools to help students is looking more and more feasible. Within the MATS/MEF model, the practitioner has been a sensitive negotiator in efforts to shape a proper match between what a school district wants and what its resources can support in terms of a pilot project. Once the practitioner has become acquainted with a variety of potentially appropriate classroom materials, he or she can focus on the key element of training. Well acquainted with the concept of social problem solving and its research underpinnings, and convinced of the importance of its place as a school program, the practitioner can skillfully bring that knowledge and belief to the minds and hearts of teachers in a well-planned and well-executed two-day training experience, which is the subject of the next two chapters.

PART FOUR

Guidelines
for the
Practitioner

The key elements defined by MATS/MEF assist informed practitioners as they sensitively guide the initial development of the pilot program. The needs and resources of the school district have been carefully matched with an SPS curriculum. The next step in the progressive review of the key elements, training, is the focus of Chapters Eight and Nine, in which a detailed look is offered at the ways in which practitioners can effectively implement the goals of a well-planned training agenda. Note that for those in the role of program developer and trainer MATS/MEF functions to define a *minimum unit of effective programmatic intervention.* A curriculum-based approach often is a school-based practitioner's best "calling card," because it includes the aspects of a program about which school staff, administrators, and parents are most likely to be concerned. However, applications of social problem solving can be equally relevant to a program targeted for one grade level in one school, for a single multigrade special education class, or for an entire school building. In each case, attending to the MATS/MEF elements enhances the likelihood of obtaining positive results that are sustained over time (Commins & Elias, in press; Hord et al., 1987).

Part Four also addresses the "S" in MATS/MEF, special help for special circumstances, which joins the role of trainer to an ad-

159

ditional role, that of counselor. At the most common level, it is clear
that a number of school-based professionals are unique in the
school system because of the fact that they have been trained in the
principles and practice of mental health counseling. This is a role
that will remain with the individuals who are available to assist
students who are troubled because of learning or emotional handicaps, chronic or stressor-triggered family discord, or developmentally related problems. No one curriculum has the flexibility, focus,
and specificity to meet the needs of all children in these types of
special circumstances (Elias, 1990b). Thus, Chapter Ten describes
ways in which the school-based counselor can implement the principles and methods of social decision making and problem solving
into disciplinary situations, problems related to academic disorganization, counseling, and psychotherapy.

It is necessary for there to be no perception of "competition"
between the role of developer and consultant to a curriculum-based
program and the role of clinician. Optimally, the counseling role
provides a much-needed complement to the presence of an SPS
program. Part Four shows how an expectation must be created for
levels of service delivery, so that when a curriculum-based program
uncovers students' serious, personal problems or concerns or fails
to remediate preexisting problems for particular students despite its
effectiveness for the class as a whole, there is a link to follow-up
counseling. Part Four provides specific information to help practitioners create a culture of caregivers who will support the growth
of students' social problem-solving skills.

Chapter Eight

Procedures for Successful Teacher Training: Initial Activities

Attention will now be centered on the activities that take place with the key element of training in the MATS/MEF model of program development. Setting the stage with important considerations regarding training styles, this chapter focuses on the practical implementation of day 1 of training teachers to use the Elias and Clabby (1989) elementary curriculum.

Training Styles

Although there are certain core attributes that are usually found in all successful trainers, such as a respect for audience expertise, there is no one best "style." For example, if the presenter is a person who can use humor well and can comfortably fit it into the context of the presentation, then humor should be used. However, someone who is not particularly comfortable with humor should not feel that she or he has to learn to be humorous in order to be an effective trainer. Trainers should get to know their own skills and attributes. Some individuals have a calm, confident, composed, and deliberate style that quickly puts a group at ease. Others work with a wonderfully engaging, high-energy style that is contagious. Their enthusiastic spirit encourages the participants, in turn, to become excited about the work they are embarking on in social problem solving.

Still other presenters are steeped in the research and/or clinical underpinnings of social problem solving and can use that knowledge to persuade others of its value, and some, in their self-examination, recognize that they work most effectively if they co-lead a workshop with another practitioner. As has been noted, some trainers effectively use humor, and certain presenters may be comfortable in demonstrating, in a self-disclosing way, the use of the SPS skills that are being taught. For example, if the overhead projector is not working satisfactorily, a trainer may comment out loud that he or she is using the readiness skill of Keep Calm or the problem-solving step of Decide on Your Goal as a way to handle the situation.

Clearly, trainers do not have to become clones of one another in order to be effective. All of the attributes or attitudes just mentioned belong to effective trainers. There is one feature, however, that successful trainers share and that is to make certain that they are adequately prepared. For practitioners in the role of trainer, this may involve, for example, having a "rehearsal" prior to the training event. Practicing out loud either alone or with family members and friends helps the presenter to build up a sense of confidence and mastery of the material, and it can also provide an opportunity for positive corrective feedback. Thinking out loud shapes the conceptual and practical material and allows the presenter to change and modulate ideas for an even more effective presentation. In this way, as the trainer goes into the actual workshop with the inevitable accompanying performance anxiety, a greater sense of confidence prevails. If the trainer is rested and healthy and knows the material well, she or he will be in the best position to relax and use humor and self-disclosure in an engaging manner.

In training teachers to implement an SPS curriculum, the practitioner should prepare and organize for at least a two-day training experience. If possible, these two days should be spaced several weeks apart to allow between-session practice of the skills that have been taught. Training is a complex task that involves such logistical planning as securing an adequate training room, acquiring curriculum materials, duplicating handouts, and making arrangements for refreshments during the breaks. It also involves preparing minilectures, demonstrations, and experiential exercises, a task for which an agenda is an indispensable organizer.

Developing an Agenda: A Key Planning Tool

An agenda is a key planning instrument that forces presenters to confront the practical realities of seeing how their training goals will sensitively fit within the time and resources that have been provided. Social problem-solving, in many cases, is regarded as "just another new program." In preparing for a workshop, therefore, it is healthy for the trainer to imagine what a skeptical devil's advocate might be thinking: "How is a training experience in SPS going to be any different from all those other useless workshops I've attended?" It is helpful to keep remembering how precious everyone's time is.

Well-prepared workshop leaders first identify the key concepts that they want to get across. Next, they find the best ordinal position for each concept in the menu of topics that they want to present. They then determine how much time will be needed to make each module effective. In this effort to operationalize the ideas, workshop leaders can quickly gauge whether they are under- or overambitious with their plans. Moreover, when leaders are co-presenting with colleagues, the agenda-planning experience permits them all to be on the same wavelength as to when a colleague can be expected to be finished with his or her section, so that the execution of the plan can be well coordinated.

Additionally, distributing an agenda to all the participants permits them to see what major points will be covered. It also communicates to them the respect the practitioner has for their time and shows them that the practitioner is planful and earnest.

Trainers, as they are planning their agenda, are strongly encouraged to use multimodal vehicles such as lectures, overhead transparencies, active recording of participants' observations on the chalkboard, handouts, modeling of skills, and experiential exercises. Distributing these and other approaches across the training experience respects the fact that the participants possess varied learning styles. Also, by avoiding straight lecture approaches in the early afternoon, the trainer can minimize the natural sleepiness and passivity that takes place after the luncheon break.

An agenda for the first day of a two-day curriculum-based training session based upon the Elias and Clabby (1989) curriculum is presented in Exhibit 8.1. The time divisions are presented for the trainer's benefit.

Introduction of the Trainer (8:45–8:50 A.M.)

The lead-in activity for this module provides an informal opportunity for participants to chat among themselves as they drink juice, coffee, or tea accompanied by a light snack. It may be useful to have a respected building or district-level administrator energetically open the workshop with welcoming remarks, as well as inform the group about some basic details such as where the restrooms are located. The remarks might include a brief history of the work that has taken place on the local level to provide a context for events leading up to the training event:

> Welcome, everyone. I am very excited about this day. As many of you know, our district has been interested for a long time in giving our students some additional help in the social-affective area. We are very happy to be bringing the social problem-solving program into our district. A committee that includes (name the participants) has been meeting for three months making certain that the social problem-solving program matches what we think our students need, and I am very happy to say that we think it does. I thank all of you for your gracious participation and I would like to introduce our trainer: Ms. Irene Galliard, who many of you know has been the school psychologist on our Child Study Team for the past two years.

At this point, the trainer introduces herself; if she is already known to the participants, she may want to share some additional professional or appropriate personal information about herself that may not be well known, such as where she went to graduate school,

**Exhibit 8.1. Agenda for First Day of Two-Day
Curriculum-Based Training Session.**

Teaching Social Problem Solving: The Curriculum Approach
A Workshop Presented for the Middletown School System
October 20
Presenter: Irene Galliard, M.S., School Psychologist
Day 1

8:30–8:45 a.m. (15 minutes)	Morning Refreshment
8:45–8:50 a.m. (5 minutes)	Introduction of the Trainer by Martha Dolan, Ed.D., Assistant Superintendent of Schools for Curriculum
8:50–8:55 a.m. (5 minutes)	Presentation of Workshop Goals and Agenda
8:55–9:30 a.m. (35 minutes)	Introduction of the Participants
9:30–9:45 a.m. (15 minutes)	The Importance of Social Problem Solving in Our Children's Lives Today
9:45–10:00 a.m. (15 minutes)	What Is Social Problem Solving?
10:00–10:10 a.m. (10 minutes)	Break for Refreshments
10:10–10:30 a.m. (20 minutes)	Effectively Facilitating SPS Thinking
10:30–11:30 a.m. (60 minutes)	Practicing and Processing Facilitative Questioning and Dialoguing
11:30 a.m.–12:00 noon (30 minutes)	Keep Calm as an Example of an SPS Readiness Skill
12:00 noon–1:00 p.m. (60 minutes)	Luncheon Break
1:00–1:05 p.m. (5 minutes)	The Value of the Curriculum-Based Approach
1:05–1:20 p.m. (15 minutes)	Overview of the SPS Curriculum
1:20–1:55 p.m. (35 minutes)	Readiness Phase: format, demonstration, and discussion
1:55–2:20 p.m. (25 minutes)	Instructional Phase: format, demonstration, and discussion
2:20–2:25 p.m. (5 minutes)	Stretch Break

**Exhibit 8.1. Agenda for First Day of Two-Day
Curriculum-Based Training Session, Cont'd.**

2:25–2:40 p.m. (15 minutes)	Application Phase: format, demonstration, and discussion
2:40–2:45 p.m. (5 minutes)	Summary and Homework
2:45–3:25 p.m. (40 minutes)	Preparing for the Curriculum Labs of the Next Workshop

a description of her practicum placements, how she became interested in SPS, or whether she is a parent. Although this introduction may take only a minute, five minutes is scheduled to allow a cushion in case the workshop starts later than scheduled.

Presentation of Workshop Goals and Agenda (8:50–8:55 A.M.)

The trainer presents the overall thematic goal for the day: "The main goal for this morning will be for all of you to have an understanding of what social problem solving is. This is an important step that will prepare us for reaching the goal for this afternoon, which is to help you get acquainted with how SPS lessons are taught in the classroom." The trainer can then move from the general to the specific by distributing the day's agenda to each person and discussing each item. It is important for the trainer to mention that the workshop approach will blend didactic presentations, opportunities to watch others using SPS, and experiential activities. The trainer can also mention any outstanding housekeeping details, such as providing information about the breaks and lunch arrangements.

Introduction of the Participants (8:55–9:30 A.M.)

Securing the cooperation and, eventually, the commitment of the participants is an important goal for the trainer; whatever is learned about the participants' values and interest will help form the way the trainer will approach the training tasks to effect that outcome. Toward that end, the introduction of the participants helps a trainer to gain additional knowledge about the group by inviting them to briefly present information about themselves, such as the kind of work they do and what they would like to learn at the workshop. This can be considered to be an example of the sharing circle, which is the warm-up activity that begins many SPS class lessons.

The trainer can begin introductions by asking the attendees to respond to an invitation such as "Please tell us your name and then describe the kind of students you are teaching this year" and then can follow up with a mildly personal question; the answers to these questions can be drawn upon later during the workshop. For example, participants might be asked, "If you were not in education, what would your ideal job be?" or "Tell us about the event, person, or experience that may have especially inspired you to work with children" or even "What would your ideal vacation be?" The workshop leader should give the participants a few minutes to pull their thoughts together. The leader should then go first and model the kind of self-disclosure that is appropriate in this type of exercise. This experience may seem time consuming, but it provides an invaluable assessment of potential commitment to the SPS program. It also creates an atmosphere that encourages a sense of play and collaboration and sets the stage for everyone to realize that the workshop will be an interactive learning experience in which everyone's ideas are valid and important.

The Importance of Social Problem Solving in Our Children's Lives Today (9:30–9:45 A.M.)

As has been mentioned, a program like social problem solving may be regarded by participants as "just another new project." Consequently, it may appear to be competitive with other goals that teachers have been assigned or have given themselves, such as improving the students' skills in phonics. Because of this skepticism, it has been the SPS Unit's tradition to present an intriguing and persuasive theoretical, policy, or research rationale (or some combination thereof) regarding the importance of providing children and the adults who deal with them with the skills that are important in preventing psychological problems and promoting health. Even if the participants are known to be cooperative and supportive, it is still very helpful to spend some time early in the workshop validating for the participants that now, more than ever, they are critically important in the fight for children's psychological and physical health.

The material in Chapter One provides a rich resource for such arguments. In addition, the SPS Unit staff has presented the following six topics alone or in combination as a further way to engender the commitment of participants:

1. The connection between social-affective education and basic academic skills education (see also Cartledge & Milburn, 1980). Study after study has demonstrated that such social skills as independence, attention, persistence to task, self-control, compliance to teacher demands, and the ability to follow directions all correlate highly with grades and academic test scores.

2. Research underpinnings for social problem solving. The possession of SPS skills significantly discriminates between poorly adjusted and normal preschool children, psychiatric populations and matched controls, and relatively better adjusted children in residential treatment (Higgins & Thies, 1981; Spivack et al., 1976). One year of preventive SPS in elementary school was significantly related to reductions in the severity of middle school stressors (Elias et al., 1986).

3. Social factors straining the family (see also Stephens, 1980). The mobility of the American family has increased (an average family moves every five years). This can lead to isolation and lack of support; the effects of stress before, during, and after separation and divorce; and the confusion of values generated by the entertainment and information industries.

4. Pressure on today's children (see also Elkind, 1981). There is enormous pressure on children today. Parents are anxious for their children to acquire the knowledge, skill, boldness, and aggression needed to succeed in the twenty-first century. Because they are anxious, they look for ways to measure their own and their children's progress in this area. This, in turn, leads to the stressors on children of achieving "excellence" in grades, athletics, and the social arena.

5.   Social competence research (see also Putallaz & Gottman, 1982). Research indicates that peer acceptance and the ability to establish at least one intimate relationship are two major, research-derived factors that influence psychological social competence.
6.   Chronic inability to negotiate everyday problems (see also Stone, Hinds, & Schmidt, 1975). This sets up a negative cycle: the child feels *incompetent,* which leads to a feeling of *underconfidence* and being undervalued by others; this in turn can lead to a child being excluded from mainstream socialization opportunities and becoming open to deviant ways of thinking, relating, and behaving.

This compilation of arguments for SPS can also be adapted into a handout or overhead transparency for use during the workshop.

What Is Social Problem Solving? (9:45–10:00 A.M.)

If participants can be helped on a personally meaningful level to understand what social problem solving is, they can then generalize and see many kinds of applications that such a framework can make possible. It is desirable to help the participants see the benefits accruing to children in the variety of roles that they occupy, such as student, member of a soccer team, daughter, and friend. Social problem solving can also be seen by participants as helping adults in their various roles, such as teacher, coach of the soccer team, parent, and friend.

While the concept of social problem solving has already been well introduced in Chapters One and Two, the following brief summary definitions have been used by John Clabby during training sessions as the basis for verbal remarks, handouts, and overhead transparencies:

1.   Social problem solving concerns itself with what goes on inside a person's head and heart just before he or she acts in a problem situation.
2.   The goal of an SPS program is to give children a feeling of "I can." SPS is a strategy that can become an effective and familiar friend youngsters can go to when they have difficulty.

3. Social problem solving is the purposeful use of a strategy to calm down, reorganize oneself, and think clearly, even under stress.

4. Spivack et al. (1976) posit that SPS is characterized by these features: conflict defined as a social problem, brainstorming solutions, articulating a step-by-step process of solving a problem within the context of sensitivity to the reactions of others, considering the consequences of those actions, and understanding how what you feel and how you act may influence or be influenced by others.

5. In addition to the above definitions, Elias and Clabby (1989) add that SPS also involves the skills of self-control and social awareness, being able to recognize one's own personal signs of stress and feelings, positive self-efficacy, an ability to plan, and the skill of self-monitoring.

6. Social problem solving comprises the skills that are needed to handle the full range of decision-making situations ranging from the everyday ("What should I do first: eat breakfast or get dressed?") to the more serious ("What should I do if Bob tries to get me to do drugs again?").

The following presentation is a portion of a script, based on definition 1, that John Clabby has used as a workshop leader:

> Social problem solving concerns itself with what goes on inside a person's head and heart just before he or she acts in a problem situation. One way of looking at this is that all of us are pursuing various goals. At a given point in time, some of us may want a certain kind of fruit at the supermarket, others may want to get a particular parking place or a certain seat on the bus, and others among us may want to watch a certain television program. Inevitably, we will be on the edge of bumping into one another psychologically or perhaps even physically when several people want the same fruit, the same parking space, the same bus seat, or control over the television set. What happens? Usually, there is not a major fight over these issues.

One person usually winds up with the parking space, and it is usually determined in a fairly peaceful manner with no head-on collision. In a matter of a few quick moments, some fast and clear thinking was done that resulted in a safe and good decision. This is what social problem solving is all about and it is what we want to give to children: the ability to make safe and sensible decisions when they are confronted with life's stressors.

Asking the participants to recall the many decisions they made that very morning is also very useful. Getting directions to the workshop site, deciding where to sit, and choosing whether to take notes are examples elicited at workshops that communicate the high frequency of decision-making situations that confront all of us.

At this point, it is important to explain, in practical terms, the SPS steps. These steps can be considered the backbone of the one-to-one problem-focused dialoguing experiences that a teacher, parent, or counselor would have with a youngster. As with any concept, it is important to present this in a way that fits with the practitioner's own teaching style. Keep in mind that most teachers have been exposed to steps such as these before. They may have used them as an approach to solving math problems or to describe the scientific method of inquiry, to name two examples. The following list provides some succinct definitions for each of the steps and can also be used as a guide for oral remarks, a handout, or overhead transparencies.

1. *Look for signs of different feelings.* Recognizing the early idiosyncratic signs of one's own feelings and stress as well as those in others.
2. *Tell yourself what the problem is.* Being able to describe one's upset in specific, behavioral terms.
3. *Decide on your goal.* Determining specifically what one wants to have happen.
4. *Stop and think of as many solutions to the problem as you can.* Brainstorming solutions that relate to the goal.

5. *For each solution, think of all the things that might happen next.* Anticipating consequences.
6. *Choose your best solution.* Making a selection from among some well-considered options.
7. *Plan it and make a final check.* Mentally rehearsing when, where, and how a best solution will be implemented as well as anticipating and dealing with potential obstacles.
8. *Try it and rethink it.* Implementing the planned solution and reviewing the outcome.

The realistic workshop leader remembers that participants will be constantly assessing what is being presented in terms of its practical implications. Regardless of how well the eight steps of decision making are presented, the translation by some adults regarding how children use these steps in the real world can be disquieting, because to these adults the steps may sound impractical. Participants may express questions privately or publicly, such as "This sounds fine, but isn't it a bit drawn out?" They may also be asking themselves questions such as "Is a child who is on the brink of a fight in the schoolyard supposed to ask everyone to freeze so he can dig into his pocket for his eight-step social problem-solving handout?" These are realistic concerns that must be addressed. Therefore, after presenting the eight SPS steps, the trainer should take time to elicit questions or comments, to which she or he can respond in a number of ways. In a curriculum workshop for teachers such as the one discussed here, the leader can explain that the steps are taught deliberately, slowly, and cumulatively. Multiple, successful practice opportunities combined with rote learning allow the children to get to "know" the steps. They then start collapsing the steps into what for them will become a personally meaningful and useful strategy.

Break for Refreshments (10:00–10:10 A.M.)

Fueled and excited by a strong belief in the importance of SPS for children, some trainers tend to overteach, which can result in bombarding the participants with too much material, too quickly, and in one sitting.

The skilled and experienced trainer realizes that many people go to a presentation or a workshop to enjoy the experience as much as to learn something. SPS program staff have learned the hard way not to resist this truth and to join with it. It is therefore important for trainers to suspend their human vanities during the workshop. A trainer may have critical content that he or she feels absolutely must be presented; however, if it is presented there may not be enough time for the break that was planned. Consider this decision carefully. Participants, especially for a full-day workshop, and even for an evening parents' workshop, look forward to some refreshment, a chance to chat informally, and even time to use the restroom. Take this opportunity for a ten-minute break.

Effectively Facilitating SPS Thinking (10:10–10:30 A.M.)

One way to open this segment is by encouraging the attendees to recall a conversation they had with a person who helped them with a personal problem. The workshop leader can then ask the group to discuss what it was about that person's style that helped. This exercise can also be introduced by the use of imagery such as asking the participants to close their eyes and remember where this problem-focused conversation took place. The trainer can ask the participants to recall what the "helping" person's face looked like at the time, what clothes the person was wearing, what color the room was, and whether there were any other sounds in the area. Next, the participants can share in a group discussion the qualities that their "helper" projected. Often, what is heard is, "He really listened," or "She didn't try to take over and tell me what to do," or "I could tell he was interested in what I had to say because he took the time and just seemed attentive."

Elias and Tobias (1990) have categorized many of the behavioral domains that are relevant to effectively facilitating another person's problem-solving thinking. These include *nonverbal style* (eye contact, head nods, appropriate gestures, and appropriate body posture), *verbal style* (using a voice tone that fits the content and using an appropriate rate of speech), *general verbal skills* (paraphrasing content and feelings, reviewing content, praising signs of decision-making thinking, clarifying, linking ideas together, and using self-disclosure appropriately), and *SPS verbal skills* (encouraging the use of readiness skills, using follow-up questioning, and encouraging a sense of positive self-efficacy). Domains such as these can be made into checklists to provide feedback for teachers' dialoguing or SPS lesson-leading skills.

As some of these qualities are presented, it may be important to acknowledge that different people will demonstrate different subsets of these traits and that it is unlikely or even unrealistic to have all of them demonstrated in a single dialogue or lesson presentation. As well as serving as a good summary of verbal and nonverbal facilitating skills, awareness of these domains is a great help to the practitioner and others who may visit classrooms and support teachers of SPS lessons.

Earlier, the participants were exposed to the eight social problem-solving steps in their declarative form; now it is time to show them these skills in their questioning format. The trainer can list the following questions for use in a handout and/or overhead transparency (Clabby & Elias, 1986):

1. How are you feeling? Am I right in thinking your voice sounds a bit nervous?
2. What would you say is the problem?
3. What do you want to have happen? What's your goal in doing that?
4. What are all the different ways you can think of to reach your goal?
5. If you _____, what might happen? What do you think might happen if you do that? What else?
6. Which of your ideas do you think is best for you? Which idea has the best chance of meeting your goal?
7. What will have to happen so that you can carry out your idea? What do you think could possibly go wrong or block your plan?
8. What happened when you tried out your plan? What did you learn that might help you next time?

Facilitative questioning garners this much attention during in-service training because it is such an integral part of the Elias and

Clabby (1989) curriculum. One of the best ways of bringing this point to life is for the trainer to show a videotape example of a teacher actually doing facilitative questioning with a student or a class of students. Because the trainer is familiar with the content of the videotape, she or he can point out the moments when good facilitative questioning took place or, perhaps equally important, did *not* take place. Before the videotape is shown, the participants can be asked to note at what point certain SPS steps were used, which step seemed to provide the greatest challenge for the "counselee," and how successful the facilitator was in establishing an encouraging atmosphere, as described in the prior discussion.

Practicing and Processing Facilitative Questioning and Dialoguing (10:30–11:30 A.M.)

The eight problem-solving steps, as used in facilitative questioning, may be taught most effectively by having the trainees pair up and actually practice facilitating the progress of someone who is dealing with real or hypothetical difficulty.

To the extent that it is possible, the persons in each dyad should turn their chairs so that they are completely facing each other, with full eye contact. One person can role play the facilitative adult and the other can become the student with the problem. The workshop participants can have fun determining who should be the student and who should be the adult: the person whose birthday is next or who lives closest to the training site could be the person with the problem. It may be helpful to assign a problem for the whole group, such as "I am upset because I got an 'F' on the math test" or "Ricky is pushing me around." This saves precious time, if that is an issue. Distribute to the facilitating adults a copy of the SPS steps in a questioning format to use as a guide. Inform everyone that the goal of this exercise is simply to help them develop a "feel" for using social problem solving as a dialoguing tool. The "students" should realize this and not make it too difficult for the helpers to progress in their assignment.

The leader can also ask the "students" to mentally note some of the qualities their helper uses to establish an encouraging atmosphere. Let the group know that you will be circulating around the room providing constructive support and guidance, and answering their questions.

Within the one hour of workshop time that has been provided for this vital skill practice, the leader can allow five minutes to orient the participants to the activity, fifteen minutes for the actual dialogue, and another fifteen minutes for group processing of the experience. The leader can then ask the participants to reverse roles, introduce a new problem, and begin the sequence again.

As part of the processing, the participants who assumed the helper role can initiate comments on what the experience was like for them and/or respond to such leader-initiated questions as

"What step seemed to be most useful in encouraging your 'student' to really think?"
"How was the 'problem' described?"
"What step seemed to be the most challenging for you and/ or your students?"
"What was your student's goal?"

For their part, the "students" who role-played the individuals with a problem can comment on the interpersonal qualities emitted by the adult that led to a feeling of comfort, support, and, it is hoped, progress in dealing with the problem.

These elicited qualities can be written down on a chalkboard for everyone's observation and comment. Some workshop leaders also record the comments and categorize the observations in some way (for example, as "verbal qualities" and "nonverbal qualities").

People who are first learning about social problem solving sometimes mistakenly think that *all* of the SPS steps must be used in order to have an effective dialogue. This is an excellent opportunity to reassure those individuals. Emphasize to the group that the main goal is to help students remember to think before they act. This may mean that in a brief contact (one to two minutes) or even in five or six counseling sessions, efforts may best be placed on only one or two of the eight steps, such as telling yourself what the problem is and deciding on your goal. This is good SPS dialoguing at work! Well-intentioned, dedicated, and overly responsible workshop participants sometimes must be taken off the hook and explicitly hear from the workshop leader that a pressured or "rushed" conversation in which all eight SPS steps are forced into the conversation is a counterproductive experience. More often than not, the role of the facilitator is to focus on the student's struggle with one or more of the problem-solving steps and be ready to sensitively ask the appropriate questions or make helpful comments that could allow that youngster to become unstuck.

Keep Calm as an Example of an SPS Readiness Skill (11:30 A.M.–12:00 noon)

A more complete understanding of social problem solving involves a grasp not only of the importance of a step-by-step cognitive decision-making strategy but also of the importance of self-control and social awareness skills to the process of solving stressful social dilemmas. Some of the material in Chapter Six from the Elias and Clabby (1989) curriculum will be helpful in this regard. The need to calm down is generally seen as an important prerequisite to thinking clearly. The skill of Keep Calm, which is taught in that curriculum, is a good example of the kind of self-control skill that can be adapted to provide the participants with a feeling for this concept.

Over the years, some SPS workshop leaders have found it quite helpful to use an adaptation of Ladd and Mize's (1983) method to organize the teaching of such concepts as the self-control and social awareness skills. What follows next is an abbreviated version of the way in which one trainer, after explaining the importance of "readiness" to social problem solving, demonstrated Keep Calm as an example of such a skill.

Step 1 is "state what the skill is," which in this case, of course, is Keep Calm. Step 2 is "provide a practical rationale for the skill." The leader could mention here that it is very hard to be a good problem solver and concentrate on a task when one is tense, upset, or anxious. Each of us can use a skill that we can rely on during those times. Step 3 is "define the skill." Keep Calm involves saying to yourself "Stop. Calm down," inhaling through your nose to the count of 5, holding it to the count of 2, exhaling through your

mouth to the count of 5, and then saying to yourself "Keep calm."
It is recommended that this exercise be done twice.

Step 4 asks the trainer to "model what the skill is," which
can be done directly or by showing a videotape of a teacher training
her class to use Keep Calm. Step 5 asks the trainer to "model what
the skill is not." In this case, the trainer can show how the procedure is not done with one's eyes closed or how holding air much
longer than two seconds leads to greater tension! The sixth step is
to "encourage practice for the skill." Here the trainer can ask the
participants as a group to practice the skill and can follow up by
answering questions that they might have. The seventh step is to
"assign practice," such as asking the participants to personally use
Keep Calm four times per day.

Luncheon Break (12:00 noon–1:00 P.M.)

When possible, an hour's lunch break is recommended. This allows
time for the trainer to eat and, if necessary, to review and adjust the
plans for the afternoon. If volunteers are needed to demonstrate any
lessons on day 2, and these volunteers have not yet been identified,
the trainer will use this time to decide who to approach and then
will follow up by asking these key people for their assistance.

After lunch, it is advisable to briskly and energetically welcome the group back for the afternoon session, take the time to go
over the balance of the agenda, and announce any adjustments that
have been made. The luncheon break marks a transition from an
emphasis on understanding SPS to a focus on how SPS is taught
in actual classroom lessons. It is reasonable to expect that, after the
lunch break, teachers would have the idea, "Okay. Now I think I
have some idea of what is meant by social problem solving, and I'm
ready to see how this can work in my classroom."

The Value of the Curriculum-Based Approach (1:00–1:05 P.M.)

It is helpful to ask teachers what features they believe allow children
to learn the basic academic skills such as reading and math. They
will often make the following suggestions:

- Academic skills should be taught to children from a very young age, in a slow, careful, and cumulative manner.
- A new skill should be taught after the child has mastered the previous skill, as multiplication skills are taught after addition skills.
- Ideally, an emphasis should be placed on explaining a concept, modeling it, and learning its key "rules" or "steps," followed by multiple, guided practice of the skill by the children in the classroom.
- Good lessons are characterized by a shared feeling of satisfaction, with everyone experiencing some measure of success because the practice opportunities are geared that way.
- Progress is greatly enhanced when the children, with their teacher's encouragement, practice this skill outside of the class, for example, by completing useful homework assignments.

Teachers can be told that this approach for basic academic skill instruction is equally valuable in the area of SPS skill development.

Overview of the SPS Curriculum (1:05–1:20 P.M.)

At this point, curriculum materials, which presumably have been preordered, should be distributed to the teachers, who are ready to have some hands-on contact with the lessons they will use. It is important to go through the table of contents; explain that the lessons are grouped into readiness, instructional, and application phases; and briefly mention the purpose of those phases as discussed in Chapter Six. Good trainers continue to remain tuned in to their trainees' unspoken apprehensions or feelings of being overwhelmed. Thoughtful trainers will reassure the teachers that their first-year effort in social problem solving is a learning and training year. It is important to affirm that the major goal of any new program is to help the teachers gradually learn and grow comfortable with the new material. Teaching social problem solving is not a competitive experience in which they are expected to hurriedly cover all the assigned topics in a certain amount of time. Rather, the teachers are being asked to carefully teach formal SPS lessons on a weekly basis. At this point in the workshop, it is also beneficial to review with the participants the fact that sanction has been obtained from the district curriculum leaders to teach social problem solving in lieu of or as a part of certain lessons, for instance, in health or social studies classes.

Readiness Phases: Format, Demonstration, and Discussion (1:20–1:55 P.M.)

In a sense, the entire workshop can be considered a "demonstration"; toward that end, this segment marks the beginning of a series of demonstrations of what the SPS lessons look like. Since the skill of Keep Calm was introduced before lunch, and because most teachers will usually begin by teaching readiness lessons to their students, the trainer's demonstration of formal lessons should begin with one of the first readiness lessons, the one in which Keep Calm is taught. In addition to the Keep Calm prompt, two other readiness vocabulary terms are introduced here for the first time: the concept of "feelings fingerprints," which are the signals that each person's body uniquely feels as a sign of upset feelings, and "trigger situations," which are the times and/or situations in which a person is likely to lose control. In addition, two SPS teaching techniques are demonstrated for the first time: the appropriate use of teacher self-disclosure of his or her own use of SPS and the encouragement of having children provide "testimonials" regarding how the readiness skills that they are learning have helped.

Chapter Six is a good source for the trainer to draw from in providing a ten-minute explanation of the format of this and the other readiness lessons; it shows teachers that they are going to be able to teach these skills and that they and the children will even enjoy participating. Accordingly, the trainer should now go beyond the didactic explanations and distribution of written materials and find a way to bring the lessons to life.

The trainer can take fifteen minutes to demonstrate key activities from the "Keep Calm Before Problem-Solving" lesson or play a videotape of the trainer or a teacher leading some of this lesson's activities with children. Again, the participants can be prepared to make observations on the leader's style based on the characteristics that are important in establishing an encouraging atmosphere they can be asked to focus primarily on the students' reactions, or they can be asked to decide which of the activities (or adaptations thereof) would be particularly useful interventions for their students. The subsequent ten-minute "processing" can be an outgrowth of these other observations.

Instructional Phase: Format, Demonstration, and Discussion (1:55–2:20 P.M.)

Chapter Six is also a good source for the trainer to draw from in planning a ten-minute overview of the format of the instructional phase lessons in which the eight steps of cognitive decision making are taught.

 Since the participants are looking into these lessons for the first time, it may be advantageous to pick a lesson from the first group of instructional phase lessons, such as the topic that teaches the skill "Learn How to Decide on a Goal." Because only three steps are featured (feelings, problems, and goal setting), it may be easier to explain the format. The ten-minute demonstration can involve an introduction of the skill of goal setting, a reading of the social conflict story from the curriculum materials, and the application of these three steps to focal characters in the story, with an emphasis on goal setting. Again, the participants can be oriented to be active observers (or participating observers if it is a "live" demonstration) in the same way as in the previous segment. Five minutes should be set aside for group processing.

Stretch Break (2:20–2:25 P.M.)

Even workshop leaders benefit from one of these!

Application Phase: Format, Demonstration, and Discussion, (2:25–2:40 P.M.)

As noted in Chapter Six's discussion of format, the lessons in this phase focus primarily on worksheets and discussion guides in which the children are shown ways to transfer and generalize SPS skills to academic subjects, such as history and creative writing, and to the world outside of the classroom, such as advertising and the media and racial prejudice. Five minutes are set aside for the discussion of format, an additional five minutes can be used to demonstrate the use of the eight SPS steps in teaching current events, and five more minutes can be devoted to finding out how this approach to the academics blends into what these teachers may already be doing with their students.

Summary and Homework (2:40–2:45 P.M.)

Good educational practice dictates that the key points and themes of the day be summarized. The agenda will be a useful guide for this segment, which again should be delivered with energy and enthusiasm. The participants should be expected to practice SPS facilitative questioning as a regular part of their conversational discourse about the problem situations that their students or colleagues are having. They should also be encouraged to use the readiness skill of Keep Calm themselves and teach it to the children. For the purposes of this chapter, it is assumed that the host school system has agreed to release its teachers to come to two days of training because it has determined that these teachers will implement and integrate SPS into their classroom routine. In a curriculum-focused training, the participants will need copies of the lessons to benefit from the workshops; if the workshop days are scheduled at least one week apart, the trainer should encourage the teachers to have at least one SPS class with their students. The trainer should make a specific assignment of deciding what that lesson should be for each grade level. In some cases, the trainer may ask the teachers to sample specific activities from several lessons.

After the trainer has encouraged the participants to do the SPS homework, she or he can mention that the second day of training will focus on the presentation by some of their colleagues of activities from a total of four SPS lessons in a curriculum "lab" approach. The trainer will then assign two participants to each of the four labs; one person is to provide positive feedback regarding the verbal style of the lab teacher and the other person will comment on the teacher's nonverbal style. Giving these assignments marks the end of the first day of training.

Preparing for the Curriculum Labs of the Next Workshop
(2:45–3:25 P.M.)

One of the most singularly valuable components of a teacher training experience may well be the use of a curriculum lab, which takes
place during the second day of a curriculum-based workshop. This
is an opportunity for teachers to take instructional activities from
selected SPS lessons and demonstrate them in front of their colleagues, who role-play students.

If the trainer knows the teachers in the district, then some
weeks before the first workshop, he or she can approach four
teachers who are good-natured, confident, and skilled and ask if
each of them would, with the help of the trainer, be willing to
model some lesson activities during the second day of training.
They are also told that their colleagues will be giving them positive
feedback at the end of the lab.

The goal of the labs is to help the workshop participants
become even more familiar with lesson formats, as well as to show
them that these lesson activities can be learned by teachers. Two
readiness phase lessons, one instructional phase lesson (social-
cognitive problem solving), and one academic application phase
lesson are chosen for this second workshop day. The trainer can
select several interesting, engaging, and easily learnable activities
from each of these lessons for the teachers' presentations. The application phase lesson selected for the second day of training involves integrating SPS into social studies and current events. The
teacher responsible for this lesson might be advised to pick a content
area with which the "students" are familiar, such as Columbus's
discovery of the New World.

This is an opportunity for the teachers who will be leading
curriculum labs to review the purpose of the labs as well as to go
over their assignments. The trainer carefully takes the teachers
through the lesson scripts and gives them the agenda showing when
each particular lab activity will be demonstrated.

The trainer's role at this time is not only to provide technical
guidance but also to provide encouragement and support. The
trainer assures the teacher that she or he will be available if help is
needed and the trainer also tells the teacher that the "audience" of

other workshop participants will be asked to be a helpful, cooperative "class" because the purpose of the lab is to help everyone become more familiar with the lesson material, not to demonstrate classroom management skills.

It is important to note that curriculum labs have also been done in regionalized trainings that take place over two consecutive days, with the demonstrating teachers being selected at the end of day 1. In these cases the trainer approaches teachers who seem particularly interested in SPS, as evidenced, for example, by their attentiveness and the kinds of questions they ask. They are oriented at 2:45 P.M. on the first day and are offered additional consultation on the telephone that evening or early in the morning of the second day of training. This approach has worked out very well in these workshops.

Conclusion

An SPS program brings many new dimensions to the role of school practitioners. Our perspective on SPS requires a commitment to program planning and training that may seem at odds with typical psychoeducational in-service models. It is fundamental for a trainer of social problem solving to personally master social problem-solving in both theory and practice. Knowing and experiencing a personal definition and application of SPS builds trainer confidence. The trainer can then find creative ways of explaining this concept to professional colleagues and of designing meaningful, skill-building practice opportunities for workshop participants. Additionally, the well-informed trainer should make use of the principles of adult learning techniques to design skill-training modules that will be accepted by the host school. What follows next is a continuation of our discussion of the key element of training in the MATS/MEF approach to program development, beginning with the return of workshop attendees after their initial training day and their intervening practice experiences.

Chapter Nine

Procedures for Successful Teacher Training: Providing Practice and Orienting Parents

This chapter takes our discussion of the key element of training to the next phase by illustrating the proceedings of the second day of teacher training. Orienting teachers to the SPS lessons is an important but limited first step in preparing them to actually teach SPS lessons to children. During the second day, participants will have their opportunity to demonstrate lessons from the readiness, instructional, and application phases and make observations regarding their SPS teaching style. In addition to bringing closure to the discussion of teacher training, this chapter also addresses the issue of outreach to parents, suggesting the specifics of organizing and presenting a seventy-five-minute parents' presentation on the SPS elementary school program.

Providing Practice

A sample agenda for the second day of teacher training is presented in Exhibit 9.1. Ideally, the first item on the agenda is preceded by an opportunity for refreshment and casual conversation among the trainer and participants. This provides an excellent informal opportunity for the trainer to determine how comfortable the trainees are with what they have been learning and practicing.

**Exhibit 9.1. Agenda for Second Day of Two-Day
Curriculum-Based Training Session.**

Teaching Social Problem Solving: The Curriculum Approach
A Workshop Presented for the Middletown School System
October 21
Presenter: Irene Galliard, M.S., School Psychologist
Day 2

8:45–8:50 a.m. (5 minutes)	Welcoming Remarks by Martha Dolan, Ed.D., Assistant Superintendent of Schools for Curriculum
8:50–9:00 a.m. (10 minutes)	Presentation of Workshop Goals and Agenda
9:00–9:25 a.m. (25 minutes)	Sharing Circle
9:25–9:35 a.m. (10 minutes)	Review
9:35–9:40 a.m. (5 minutes)	Overview of Curriculum Labs
9:40–10:20 a.m. (40 minutes)	Lab 1: Learning to Listen Carefully and Accurately (p. 64)
10:20–10:35 a.m. (15 minutes)	Break
10:35–11:15 a.m. (40 minutes)	Lab 2: Selecting Praiseworthy and Caring Friends (p. 85)
11:15 a.m.–12:00 noon (45 minutes)	Lab 3: Practice Creative Thinking (p. 108)
12:00 noon–1:00 p.m. (60 minutes)	Luncheon Break
1:00–1:45 p.m. (45 minutes)	Lab 4: A Decision-Making Approach to Social Studies (p. 162)
1:45–2:00 p.m. (15 minutes)	Break
2:00–2:50 p.m. (50 minutes)	Planning for the Pilot Year
2:50–2:55 p.m. (5 minutes)	Summary and Feedback
2:55–3:00 p.m. (5 minutes)	Closing Ceremonies

Welcoming Remarks (8:45–8:50 A.M.)

To provide continuity, if a building or district-level administrator opened the first day of training, that person should also open the second day. If possible, this should be done with an acknowledgment of the cooperation and effort that the teachers have been putting into becoming familiar with the SPS program and trying out portions of it.

Presentation of Workshop Goals and Agenda (8:50–9:00 A.M.)

The trainer also welcomes the group and then crisply takes the participants through the goals of the day with an item-by-item presentation of the agenda. As the participants will readily see, the day is primarily organized around a hands-on tour of the SPS curriculum and provides opportunities to practice and participate in some of the SPS activities they eventually will be teaching their students.

Sharing Circle (9:00–9:25 A.M.)

By this time, the participants all know that the sharing circle in which they participated as part of the opening of the first day is a traditional way to begin an SPS lesson. By repeating this experience as an opening activity for the second day of training, the trainer models the importance of providing a consistent structure for SPS lessons. Additionally, this activity can illustrate the innumerable contributions that a sharing circle makes: a comfortable environment in which the quieter participants make a brief comment, a team-building experience, and, at times, an opportunity for skill development (such as practicing memory skills by recalling what others have said). A useful day 2 sharing circle activity consists of discussing the homework by asking when and how the participants used the skills of SPS facilitative questioning and Keep Calm.

Review (9:25–9:35 A.M.)

Even if this workshop meets on the day following the first workshop, there is a need to recenter the participants within the context of social problem solving. A review of SPS concepts helps the participants to make the transition from thoughts of what the traffic was like on the way to the workshop or concerns they may have about their families to concentration on the task at hand. With the agenda from day 1 as a guide, the important concepts to review are (1) what SPS is and why it is important, (2) the eight SPS steps and how they can be used as a guide in dialoguing with children, and (3) how the SPS curriculum is organized and formatted.

Overview of Curriculum Labs (9:35–9:40 A.M.)

It is helpful for the trainer to consider that she or he has two constituents at this point: the participants who will be watching the lesson demonstrations and those who will actually be doing them. The job of the trainer is to adequately explain the purpose of the curriculum lab so that the participants can get the most out of the experience and to do so in such a way that the demonstrating teachers feel reassured and protected by the trainer.

The most helpful way to introduce the concept of the lab is to go back to what was said during the overview of the SPS curriculum presented during day 1. Here is a sample script used by John Clabby:

> Remember that the major goal of any new program during the first year is to help you to gradually get to know and grow comfortable with new material. The purpose of the curriculum lab is to make you more familiar with SPS lessons that you have never seen before.
>
> Therefore, we have designed this series of four labs as a journey through the readiness, instructional, and application phases of the curriculum. Since most of you will be concentrating on the self-control and social awareness areas, two of the labs will be taken from the readiness phase and one each will be taken from the other two phases. To help us out, four teachers have graciously agreed to take a risk and present some lesson activities. We know you will be a

kind and supportive "class" for your colleagues, who have only had a small amount of time to read this material.

The format of the labs is rather simple. I will introduce each teacher, who will then lead us through some activities. I think that we realize that each of us brings something unique to the students in the form of our teaching style. As part of our discussion following the lesson demonstration, several teachers have been assigned to look specifically for verbal or nonverbal behaviors that seem particularly positive, similar to the procedure we used during our first workshop. Nonverbal characteristics may include voice tone or the way a teacher makes eye contact, uses the chalkboard, or moves around the room. Time permitting, the rest of us can also be ready to share our observations regarding particularly positive ways in which the teacher got us to participate.

Keep in mind that although many of you teach special education children or even regular education children who may be having behavioral problems, I will be asking you to role-play a *well-behaved* group of students for these labs. That's because our main goal is to have all of us see the content of SPS lessons come to life rather than to teach behavior management skills, although they could be the subject of another workshop that the district might sponsor.

Lab 1: Learning to Listen Carefully and Accurately
(9:40–10:20 A.M.)

The following script shows one way that John Clabby has, as a trainer, introduced the first curriculum lab:

Remember that the first group of readiness lessons concentrates on self-control skills such as getting better at following directions and learning ways to calm down when we are under stress.

Imagine that it is the last week in September. You are all third graders and, of course, are a well-behaved and interested group of third graders who have had an introductory class in social problem solving. You have already done a sharing circle, enjoyed it, and know that one of the rules is to raise your hand in order to be called on by your teacher. The lesson today is called "Learning to Listen Carefully and Accurately," which is a self-control lesson from the readiness phase [Elias & Clabby, 1989, p. 64]. Our teacher for this second lesson in SPS is Mrs. Barbara Salney, who is a special education teacher from Swampnut Elementary School.

This lesson from the Elias and Clabby (1989) curriculum is a good example of the kind of lesson a trainer should use in a series of curriculum labs because it introduces a readiness prompt such as "speaker power." This technique, which may have been mentioned in day 1, encourages the lab teacher to select an object such as a stuffed animal that gives the person holding it the right to speak. The technique also offers an easily led and often enjoyable activity in which a series of words are read to the students and they are asked to clap their hands on certain words, as a lead-in to a discussion of the techniques of good listening.

Following Mrs. Salney's demonstration, the trainer can acknowledge and support her work by saying something like: "Let's all give a big round of applause to Mrs. Salney for taking that risk and to all of you for being such a cooperative group of third graders!"

The trainer can initiate the processing discussion by asking the curriculum lab teacher to share what the experience was like or to describe how he or she prepared for the lesson. The trainer can then ask the "official" observers to provide their *positive* feedback of the verbal or nonverbal features of the teacher's style. Others can join if time permits.

The trainer can also move the discussion to the content of the lesson by having everyone turn to the page of the curriculum that corresponds to the lesson activities that have been taught and then generating a group conversation regarding ways in which the participants might teach this lesson. For example, teachers of communication-handicapped children may explain that they would greatly slow down the speed with which they would read the word list to their students because of their special needs.

Break (10:20–10:35 A.M.)

Some refreshments should be available at this time.

Lab 2: Selecting Praiseworthy and Caring Friends (10:35–11:15 A.M.)

It cannot be overemphasized that a key issue for the trainer is to select lessons that make it easy for the demonstrating teacher to gain full group cooperation. This lesson from the Elias and Clabby (1989) curriculum is a readiness phase lesson that teaches social awareness. In it, the class must complete a simple worksheet entitled "What Makes a Friend a Friend?" By using this lesson, the teachers get hands-on experience using an SPS worksheet for the first time. This particular activity asks the participants to write down the names of up to five friends and then write down next to each name the person's positive qualities. The activity can also be adapted to ask children to list characteristics that they would *not* want to see in friends.

The other curriculum labs, which also use lessons from the Elias and Clabby (1989) curriculum, follow the same procedural flow: the trainer introduces the lab teacher and the lesson title, the lab teacher demonstrates the lesson activities and comments on the experience, the "official" observers give feedback, and, time permitting, others join in the discussion.

Lab 3: Practice Creative Thinking (11:15 A.M.–12:00 noon)

As this teacher workshop is designed, the instructional phase skill "Practice Creative Thinking" was selected for the third lab. One of its activities asks students to generate as many ideas as they can for sample drawings. This lesson is designed for fourth and fifth graders, who have acquired the self-control and social awareness skills that were taught in readiness lessons. Accordingly, the teacher who teaches this lab can assume for demonstration purposes that the workshop participants will now be role-playing fourth graders with skills in the areas of self-control and social awareness. Trainers can set up this expectation in their introduction:

> We would like all of you to now imagine that you are fourth graders. Last year, as third graders, you worked all year on learning self-control and group awareness skills. It is now January and we have recently returned from our winter holiday vacation. As a class, we have spent some of September and most of October reviewing and brushing up on the readiness skills. Since then, we have been learning the first three steps of social cognitive problem-solving: look for signs of different feelings, tell yourself what the problem is, and decide on your goal. Our teacher for this next lesson, which is an instructional phase lesson, is Mr. Douglas Hildman, who is a fourth-grade, regular education teacher from James Elementary School.

The teacher then demonstrates the lesson activities followed by discussion.

Luncheon Break (12:00 noon–1:00 P.M.)

As in day 1, a full hour's lunch break is recommended, followed by the trainer briskly welcoming the group back and briefly mentioning the goals of the afternoon session.

Lab 4: A Decision-Making Approach to Social Studies
(1:00–1:45 P.M.)

In this workshop, the fourth and final lab is an application phase lesson entitled "A Decision-Making Approach to Social Studies." Here, the trainer may assume that the class is now in sixth grade and has been exposed to all of the readiness skills taught in the third grade as well as all eight SPS steps, which were taught during the fourth and fifth grades. Once again, this lesson was chosen because it maximizes the success of the lab teacher. The lesson encourages the use of a student worksheet entitled "Thinking About Important Events." One part focuses on an SPS view of events in history and another focuses on an SPS way of examining current events.

As mentioned before, the lab teacher is advised to use a content topic with which she or he feels all of the "class" is familiar. This demonstration is followed by the processing discussion.

Break (1:45–2:00 P.M.)

Even if the workshop is off schedule, it is essential to break at this time.

Planning for the Pilot Year (2:00–2:50 P.M.)

It is now time for the trainees and members of the SPS Committee to turn their attention to the logistics of establishing a regular rhythm of teaching SPS lessons and to discuss how they can continue to get supportive help. This provides an opportunity for a discussion of such issues that may continue long after the workshop is over.

A fine way for the trainer to begin this segment is by encouraging the participants to have reasonable expectations of themselves and of one another. They should be reminded that the goal during the pilot year is for the teachers to become comfortable with the material and, in doing so, to find a "fit" for SPS. The trainer can say that for this to happen the teachers should teach a minimum of one formal SPS lesson per week. The SPS Committee members (who should be part of the training, and perhaps even coleaders) along with building principals and/or district-level administrators with curriculum responsibilities can play an important role in validating this expectation and offering some options as to how SPS can fit in such areas as social studies, language arts, and health. The SPS Committee or school administrators should be able to respect and deal with teachers' concerns that SPS may be perceived as an "add-on" to an already packed schedule. This can be done by showing how SPS can be infused into or used as a part of preexisting curricular domains. In addition, the SPS Committee should be prepared with suggestions regarding how the district can provide ongoing support during the pilot. For example, each SPS teacher might have an opportunity once each week to meet with fellow SPS teachers or a member of the committee in order to review a lesson that has already been covered or to plan an upcoming lesson.

It is advisable at this point for the trainer to ask the teachers to consider two general areas. First, they need to plan logistics: when they will start regular SPS classes, what days of the week SPS will be formally taught, and what time of day the lessons will be taught. Second, the teachers need to talk about ways of getting continued support from one another and from other members of the SPS team such as guidance staff and child study team members.

It may be helpful for the trainer to divide the participants into small groups according to the issues they have in common, such as fourth-grade teachers, special education teachers, and third-grade teachers. A member of the SPS Committee can chair each group and help participants decide when the lessons will begin and how each teacher can receive support with initial implementation, for example, by making SPS a regular discussion item at grade-level meetings. This section is completed by bringing the entire group back together for general sharing of the plans that have been made thus far.

Summary and Feedback (2:50–2:55 P.M.).

Consistent with the practice begun at the close of the first day, this is the trainer's opportunity to review the key points of both days, as well as to thank the trainees for their attention, interest, and good-spirited participation. It is also an opportunity to extend appreciation to the hosting school and the SPS Committee for handling the arrangements. At this point, the trainer can obtain feedback from the group regarding the workshop by asking them for their reactions to the experience, by conducting a final sharing circle, or by putting such questions into a written consumer satisfaction measure or a workshop evaluation questionnaire.

Closing Ceremonies (2:55–3:00 P.M.)

It is helpful to close a workshop with some kind of ceremony, for example, having the trainer read a brief inspirational poem or taking a photograph of all of the participants in a group. The staff of the SPS Unit has successfully used both of these techniques, as well as the ceremony of bringing in a large print of a sea voyage and comparing the beginning of a pilot program in SPS to the launching of a boat on its maiden voyage. This is a rich metaphor that allows the trainer to say that a voyage is successful when all of the right supplies are on board and are in sufficient quantity, when the captain watches out for hidden mines or dangers, and when the first voyage for the boat is of reasonable duration and does not over-stretch the limits of the craft. In addition, a successful voyage is marked by excitement, enthusiasm, promise, and adventure.

Orienting Parents

It is a significant accomplishment to have trained teachers in the delivery of an SPS curriculum. The attention of the SPS practitioner now turns to bringing in parents as partners in the process of teaching SPS.

Parents want and need to be informed about the SPS program so that they can bolster their children's skill development. Knowing the busy lives of most parents, planful leaders of social problem solving are first concerned with the need to make parents aware of the SPS skills their children are learning in the classroom. Therefore, the first efforts at school-based parent outreach are often best situated within the "curriculum awareness" and education domains.

Trainers who are parents themselves realize that after a long day of working, parents need to feel welcome, comfortable, and enlightened enough by a school program so that they will be willing to come again for other such visits on behalf of their children. Incidentally, this may be an especially challenging prospect when the SPS leaders invite parents of special education students. For years, these parents have been called by the school for negative reasons, usually to talk about problems their children are having. Careful preparation and sensitivity on the leader's part can result in an appealing invitation and program. A formal presentation made to parents, for example, at a PTA meeting, is a high-visibility venture, so careful planning is very important. Parents merit the same kind of respect that is given to teachers; therefore, the SPS leader should develop and distribute agendas, secure arrangements for refreshments, and arrange for a formal introduction of the presenter by the PTA president and/or district or building administrator.

Exhibit 9.2 shows a sample agenda for a seventy-five-minute presentation for parents that could be given at a PTA meeting, one of the most widely used vehicles for in-person parent outreach.

Welcome (8:00–8:05 P.M.)

If real concern is felt about possible parent resistance, there is no substitute for the support that SPS practitioners get from an explicit formal endorsement of the pilot SPS program by key school system administrators. Again, this can be crisply and enthusiastically handled through an official welcome to the parents given by a school administrator with high credibility and by the PTA president.

Introduction of the SPS Teaching Staff and Presenters (8:05–8:10 P.M.)

It is very important to give recognition to the administrators and teachers who are collaborating on the pilot program for what it is hoped will be a fine SPS classroom program. After all, it is they who work directly with the children. Depending on the number of parents present, it may also be desirable for the parents to introduce themselves. In a large group, for example, twenty-five and above, it may be useful to at least ask the parents for a show of hands in response to questions such as who among them has heard about SPS from their child, or who has more than one child in the school. A sharing circle format with a "light" question ("If you could go on your ideal vacation without any of your children, where would you go?") serves as a helpful icebreaker.

Exhibit 9.2. Sample Agenda for Parents' Meeting.

Social Problem-Solving in Your Youngster's Classroom
A Presentation for the South Middletown
Parent-Teachers' Association

Date:	Wednesday, November 21, 8:00 p.m.–9:15 p.m.
Presenters:	Patrick Jackson, Third-Grade Teacher
	Sheila Laurence, Fourth-Grade Teacher
	Wendy Marshall, School Psychologist and
	Consultant
8:00–8:05 p.m.	Welcome by PTA President Frances Hannigan
(5 minutes)	and Assistant Superintendent Patricia Arnt
8:05–8:10 p.m.	Introduction of the SPS Teaching Staff and
(5 minutes)	Presenters
8:10–8:20 p.m.	What Is Social Problem Solving?
(10 minutes)	
8:20–8:30 p.m.	Why Is Social Problem Solving So Important
(10 minutes)	for Today's Child?
8:30–8:50 p.m.	A Demonstration of How SPS Is Taught in the
(20 minutes)	Elementary Classroom in South Middletown
	School
8:50–9:00 p.m.	Discussion
(10 minutes)	
9:00–9:15 p.m.	Refreshments and Informal Conversation
(15 minutes)	

What Is Social Problem Solving? (8:10–8:20 P.M.)

As parents sit down for a seventy-five-minute presentation, there
may be as many different notions about what social problem solving is as there are parents in attendance. Accordingly, a major early
challenge with such a limited time frame is to succinctly define
what SPS is. Chapter Eight contains a number of useful ideas; one
particularly good approach is to elicit from the parents a list of the
many decisions that they and their children make from the time they
get up in the morning until lunchtime. Typically, the list is quite
long and parents can appreciate the fact that we live in a decision-
oriented world that requires a great deal of clear thinking. This can
be followed by defining social problem solving as the skills that are

needed to handle the full range of problem situations and social decisions, from the everyday ("How can I relax enough to do well on this test?") to the more serious ("How can I handle that group of kids who want to beat me up?"). This definition can be embellished, as needed, by the other definitions: SPS is what goes on just before someone acts, SPS is what gives children a sense of "I can," SPS is the capacity to think clearly when under stress, SPS is a step-by-step process of solving problems, and SPS is being able to use self-control and to be effective in school and peer groups.

Why Is Social Problem-Solving So Important for Today's Child? (8:20–8:30 P.M.)

It is advisable to take some time to explain the importance of SPS. Clabby finds the six rallying calls that were described in Chapter Eight to be an excellent practical source of this information. Of particular relevance to parents may be the concern all of us have for the child who has a chronic inability to solve everyday social problems (Stone et al., 1975). This establishes a negative sequence of self-perception that can be repeated. First, a child begins to believe that he or she does not have the skills it takes to succeed socially. This, in turn, leads to a lack of self-confidence and the child can begin to turn away from the usual school and social activities, which are so fraught with failure, and be more vulnerable to deviant ways of acting.

Other arguments that have successfully and positively affected parents can be used to augment this section, such as the positive connection between social-affective education and education in basic academic skills (Cartledge & Milburn, 1980), the research foundation for SPS (Elias & Clabby, 1989), and acknowledgment of how social strains on the American family give children a greater need for instruction in skills such as SPS (Stephens, 1980).

A Demonstration of How SPS Is Taught in the Elementary Classroom in South Middletown School (8:30–8:50 P.M.)

Parents benefit by learning about the curriculum-based approach to SPS that their children are experiencing and by seeing how it fits in as a regular part of the classroom routine. This includes hearing about some of the skills that are emphasized as well as about such logistics as the time of day SPS lessons are taught. As in teacher training, the focal point of a curriculum-focused presentation for parents is a demonstration of a sample lesson or sample lesson activity.

The readiness lesson from lab 1 of the teacher training, "Learning to Listen Carefully and Accurately" (Elias & Clabby, 1989, p. 64), is also a good source of activities that allow parents to experience what an SPS lesson is like. In addition to the prompt "speaker power," the prompt "listening position" (sitting straight, with at least one foot on the floor, and facing the speaker) is introduced here. It is a prompt that the leader can demonstrate and recommend the parents use with their children at home. Ten minutes can be devoted to this segment. A second source for a presentation to parents can be the readiness lesson topic 4, "Keep Calm Before Problem Solving" (Elias & Clabby, 1989, p. 66), which was showcased during the first day of teacher training. Encouraging the parents' participation by teaching them the skill of Keep Calm provides them with a prompt that can be of practical use at home. Ten minutes can also be set aside for this activity.

Discussion (8:50–9:00 P.M.)

At the close of the meeting, the leader can summarize what has been discussed and take advantage of the opportunity to see if the parents would be interested in other such meetings. The PTA president can be an important person in this discussion. While this workshop was primarily geared toward showing parents the SPS readiness skills as taught in the curriculum, future workshops can focus on how the children are taught the eight steps of clear thinking through the instructional phase lessons, and how all of these skills, as taught in the application phase, can be transferred and generalized. Another major workshop focus could be that of teaching the parents SPS facilitative dialoguing skills and of showing how this approach can be woven into everyday discussions with their children.

It is also possible that the parents may ask questions regarding the future of SPS in the district. Here again, the presence of a central office administrator such as an assistant superintendent or building principal can be quite helpful. Parents may want to know if their child will receive SPS programming in the next year. Also, it is not unlikely that parents from other parts of the district where the SPS program does not exist may be present and may ask if and when the pilot program will come to their school. Gathering the feelings of the parents will be an important activity that will help the administrators and members of the SPS Committee keep informed as they make their program development decisions.

Refreshments and Informal Conversation (9:00–9:15 P.M.)

Because a major benefit of such a meeting is that parents can network and enjoy the company and support of other parents, it is important to allow time for this activity. Serving refreshments provided by the PTA can be very helpful in creating a relaxed atmosphere. Because these SPS orientation presentations have been designed to allow parents to experience the kinds of activities that their children are learning at school, they are usually very well received.

It is wise to note, however, that this refreshment time also provides another occasion during which parents can raise questions or observations to the presenter that they were reluctant to communicate in the more public arena of the large meeting.

It is possible that some parents may question whether their roles are being usurped, especially in relation to "values" that are being taught. In this case, teachers can explain that the goal of SPS is not to tell the students "what" to think, but "how" to think. Teachers can tell the parents that they want to encourage the children to do more thinking on their own, a skill that is of critical importance for academic as well as social success. The actual decisions the children will make are based primarily on the values they have learned at home from their family and friends.

Although parents want their children to grow up physically and psychologically healthy, they vary in their beliefs regarding how to help a child reach that goal. Some parents believe that heredity is the primary influence. They leave little or no room for other explanations or factors: "She's that way because it's in her blood. Her father is the same way." Other parents maintain that setting limits and giving direct advice is the only road to take in helping children reach their potential. Still others may concentrate on "acknowledging feelings," believing that this is the major contributor. The list of preferred explanations can go on and on. The SPS practitioner can deal with this by acknowledging that there are many opinions regarding how a parent can best "be." It is the practitioner's role to make the case, in as nonthreatening a way as possible, that SPS should also be considered important in helping children reach their optimal human development (Clabby & Elias, 1986; Elias, Clabby, & Hett, in preparation). Leaders of SPS parents' meetings must avoid provoking parental resistance in their zealousness by leaving the impression that SPS is the only way to raise children. The thoughtful trainer will plan a way to honestly acknowledge that social problem solving is best considered as an approach to parenting that has some excellent qualities, and that parents should consider adding it to their repertoire.

As a final note, the trainer who wishes to go beyond the awareness stage with parents and move into actual parent training in SPS will find many available sources for worksheets, handouts, and practical suggestions (Clabby & Elias, 1986; Clabby & Elias, 1987–88; Elias, 1988; Elias et al., in preparation; Shure & Spivack, 1978).

Conclusion

Even with the thoughtful matching and planning of an SPS program, proper selection of materials, and sound training, there will be a need for further tailoring of SPS interventions. For the many students who fail to successfully negotiate the problems of everyday living, curriculum-based approaches must be supplemented. Specific aspects of the overall school environment can be modified to reflect a problem-solving approach. Ways in which practitioners can provide special help for special circumstances form the focus of Chapter Ten.

Chapter Ten

Supplementing Formal Instruction to Meet Special Needs and Circumstances

Clearly, the bedrock of a social problem-solving program is the actual instruction provided by a teacher who is using a curriculum-based approach. The concerned and creative practitioner, however, is always alert for other opportunities to provide special help for special circumstances, which is symbolized by "S," the next key element in the MATS/MEF model.

A role that many practitioners routinely fill is one in which they provide counseling services to a child who has been identified as needing special help, for example, one who has been so afraid of school that he avoids coming. This is a significant and necessary reactive role for the practitioner. It is important to mention, however, that although counseling troubled children is indeed an important special circumstance demanding the practitioner's expertise, it is not the only "special" domain. The idea of special help for special circumstances does not limit itself to a person-centered deficit and trait-oriented approach. It embraces a continuation of the proactive, prevention-oriented stance of anticipatory guidance that is provided, for example, to the children of alcoholics, children of divorce, or adolescents who are at risk of contracting AIDS or becoming pregnant. These students may not yet be in need of, or appropriately treated by, services such as counseling. However, children who are in communities that may be anticipating a significant change such as a major factory layoff might have a special discussion of this issue in a sharing circle. Or a group might be formed to help children cope with the problems and decisions facing their families when a breadwinner is laid off. For the purposes of this chapter, direct counseling work with children who are already troubled is the primary special circumstance discussed. Other resources exist for practitioners who are interested in preventively oriented group applications (Elias & Tobias, 1990).

The next section begins with a discussion of how SPS can be used in the brief, time-limited counselor-counselee encounters that are so typically found in schools. Attention will then be focused on the ways in which SPS can be applied to academic organizational difficulties and school-based behavior problems. A later section is devoted to a discussion in which a practitioner is shown using SPS as a professional guide to develop a treatment plan for a self-destructive adolescent. In this case, a presentation is also made regarding how this adolescent was taught SPS to reduce his risk. The chapter closes with some suggestions regarding techniques for school-based practitioners using SPS in formal or informal counseling contexts.

SPS Counseling in Brief Conversational Exchanges

Students, faculty, and staff work hard to try to keep pace with the packed schedules of classes, lunch periods, physical education periods, and after-school activities. Because school systems most actively support activities that appear to directly affect the acquisition of basic academic skills, there may be little institutional support for ongoing counseling that takes place during the school day, even though the counseling would directly enhance the academic as well as the personal well-being of the student. School-based practitioners must assume a leadership role in persuading policy makers of the importance of psychological counseling in the schools. In the meantime, however, one of the most likely counseling contacts remains the valuable one- to two-minute supportive conversations that counselors have with students when they stop by the office on their way to class or when a counselor checks in with a student who has had recent family difficulties. The SPS framework provides a goal-directed way to encourage independent and clear thinking on the part of students and thereby help them deal with psychological discomfort.

Perhaps the counselor has had some prior contact with a particular student. If so, the counselor can assess the student's social problem-solving strengths and weaknesses and use that information to help the student in a focused way. For example, if the student is known to have difficulty setting personal goals, the counselor can help him or her determine a target to aim at. Following is an example of a brief counseling exchange with a student who has the problem of not being goal directed.

Michelle is a seventh grader who is easily frustrated with the confusing social scene of middle school and early adolescence. Her counselor knows that she can lose her focus regarding what she want to accomplish and sees his job as trying to steer her thinking toward setting a goal for herself. Notice how the counselor, with just a few questions and observations, makes good use of the SPS framework in a short amount of time.

Mr. McGowan: What's going on, Michelle?

Michelle: Everything's fine, Mr. McGowan.

Mr. McGowan: Yeah, but I know you. You don't look so fine.

Michelle: I'm mad.

Mr. McGowan: What about?

Michelle: I hate lunchtime.

Mr. McGowan: How come?

Michelle: There's no one to sit with.

Mr. McGowan: *What is it that you want to have happen?*

Michelle: Oh, I don't know. To find someone to sit with, I guess.

Mr. McGowan: It sounds like that's your goal.

Michelle: It sure is.

Mr. McGowan: Good thinking, Michelle. Tell you what, why don't you think of a couple of solutions and we can talk more about it in my office at lunchtime?

Michelle: Okay.

Michelle may or may not take advantage of Mr. McGowan's offer to continue the conversation. Nonetheless, Mr. McGowan has helped a student who often is directionless to focus on a goal. He did this primarily through the italicized question in the dialogue. It may very well be that as she goes through the rest of her day, Michelle will come up with solutions of her own as a result of the focusing question that Mr. McGowan asked.

The following example describes a counselor talking to a high school student after school play practice. Although this student is actually quite capable of generating alternative solutions, he usually forgets to use this skill and is dependent on others for ideas. Notice how the counselor stays true to her own goal of helping him develop confidence in his ability to solve his own problems:

Frank: Mrs. Gertrude, I really need to have a job this summer.

Mrs. Gertrude: Well, that's a fine goal to have, Frank. What solutions have you been thinking about?

Frank: That's just it. I can't think of any solutions. Can you help me?

Mrs. Gertrude: Sure. The best way I can help is by helping you think through this. Where could you look for a job?

Frank: I could ask friends.

Mrs. Gertrude: Good! Where else?

Frank: The newspaper . . . or maybe I could ask people in my neighborhood.

Mrs. Gertrude: You know, Frank, you're doing a fine job of coming up with solutions on your own. What's your next step?

Frank: I'm not sure. Maybe I need a day or two to think this over. Could I talk to you later this week?

Mrs. Gertrude: Absolutely . . . and, Frank, good job of thinking this through.

Frank: Thanks, Mrs. Gertrude.

Mrs. Gertrude, as an experienced counselor, has many ideas of where Frank could go for additional information about summer jobs, but her goal is to help him believe in his own ability to generate solutions. Mrs. Gertrude held back on her own ideas and "bit her tongue" as she patiently encouraged this young student's own independent thinking.

Counselors like Mrs. Gertrude and Mr. McGowan are often the persons to whom a student is sent for a "talk" about a particular academic or behavioral problem. This may involve a one-time discussion or it may develop into a short-term counseling contract. Either way, the SPS approach can be used as an organizing framework to allow students to examine a situation from a problem-solving perspective. The next section illustrates how SPS can be applied in challenging special circumstances, as when students have academic organizational difficulties.

Academic Organizational Problems

The inability of students to organize themselves for their academic responsibilities can become a major source of conflicts between parents, students, and teachers and can also be a major reason why many students are given detention. It is a problem that becomes more apparent when students make the transition from having the same teacher all day to having many teachers in a single day. As was discussed before, many students are most comfortable with the support of an elementary teacher who shepherds them and monitors their work. It is also reassuring when elementary teachers keep in close contact with parents.

Students may be quite startled by their first year in a departmentalized curriculum. They may now have a minimum of four teachers in four different rooms and these teachers each have different demands and expectations. Sometimes teachers wrongly assume that youngsters know how to organize their academic work and keep track of all their assignments and projects. While it is a phenomenon that is often seen in the early adolescent, this organizational problem may be witnessed at all ages. One approach that has been helpful for school-based professionals is based on the idea of constructing and using an SPS worksheet that is specifically designed to promote academic self-monitoring and organization.

The following list of SPS questions can be put in the form of an "academic self-responsibility worksheet" (Elias and Tobias, 1990, pp. 90–92). The responses of a hypothetical sixth grader are also included here.

1. Read over this list and underline the problems that give you difficulty:

   <u>Not doing my homework</u>
   <u>Forgetting to do my homework</u>
   Coming to school late
   Coming to class late
   Losing my books
   Losing my pen or pencil
   Not writing down my homework assignments
   Leaving my completed homework in my locker or at home
   Not finding what I need once I'm in class
   <u>My teachers telling me my homework is half-done</u>
   Forgetting or losing things I need for gym

   List any others that relate to you.
2. Look at the problems that you have checked. Which two or three of them give you the most trouble? ("Not doing my homework, forgetting to do my homework, my teachers telling me my homework is half-done.")
3. Which one would you *most* like to change? ("I want to change 'not doing my homework.'")
4. What is your goal? How do you want things to be different? ("My goal is to get my homework done.")
5. Describe one time when this problem bothered you or got you in trouble. ("I didn't do my math homework so I was sent out to do it while the rest of the class corrected their homework. I was sent to detention, too.")
6. What are some things you could have said or done *differently*

so that the problem would have been made smaller or would not have been there at all? Write down the consequences, too.

"I could have done my homework each night after dinner—I'd get a C or a B."

"I could have done my homework right away after school—I'd miss being with my friends, but at least it'd be done soon."

"I could have my parents check on me to make sure I did it—they'd be on my back all the time about homework."

"I could try to get it done during study hall—I'd miss fooling around with my friends during study hall."

7. Look at your solutions. Now, put together your best ideas and develop a step-by-step plan that will help you reach your goal.

"I'll hang up my coat and have a snack."

"I'll organize my books so that I know what I'm going to do first."

"I'll make sure I have everything else I need, like a dictionary or ruler or markers."

"Once I start something, I'll finish it before I go on to something else."

8. Look over your plan. What could happen to keep your plan from working and how would you handle it? ("I might just put off homework until later but probably never really get to it.")

9. If these things happen, how would you handle it? ("Maybe I could also try to get some homework done during study hall so I wouldn't have a lot to do at home.")

Although this set of questions has been used primarily in the middle school, it is an approach that is quite adaptable to other age groups. The number and wording of the questions can be changed and, if the questions appear in a worksheet format, the "white space" on the document can be adjusted in size and spacing or accompanied by pictures or sketches to fit the developmental and learning levels of the students.

There are several factors to consider when using this kind of approach with students. For example, a common academic organizational problem for early adolescents is coming to class late following a change of class. Usually, this is the result of students enjoyably talking to friends in the hallway between classes. It is well known by veterans of the school scene that, for many middle school students, socializing is the main reason they go to school. If a student is chronically late for class because she or he is talking to friends in the hallway, the practitioner and student need to work together to examine the advantages of arriving on time. Incentive systems must be analyzed from a child's-eye view. For example, the few minutes of extra "talk time" in the hallway may result in after-school detention that effectively takes away thirty to forty-five minutes of prime after-school socialization time. These connections can be framed as choices and decisions that students can make.

The same principle is true for other major academic organizational problems, such as not completing homework because of a poorly kept homework assignment pad or procrastination. Success for the practitioner in such academic problem areas involves helping students see how a change in their organizational and time management behavior will be followed by positive consequences in areas that are personally important to them.

A second problem is that, for many of their academic years, students who have had academic organizational problems have been told didactically by well-meaning parents and educators what they should do about the difficulty. Use of SPS dialoguing and SPS worksheets gives ownership of the problem back to the student. It is hoped that by being provided with a chance to develop a personal remedial strategy and to be the key participant in the development of the solution, the student will feel respected and will be more likely to change.

A third problem occurs when students are noticed by practitioners because of their poor academic organizational skills, such as always losing books or pens, or because of learning difficulties, such as an inability to express their thoughts in written form. Practitioners, in the spirit of SPS thinking, would do well to remain flexible in their solutions. They should consider ideas such as reading the academic self-responsibility worksheet questions to the student for discussion rather than stifling the student's expression of clear thinking with a rigid demand that he or she write down the responses.

School-Based Behavioral Problems

A variety of school detention and suspension categories and systems exist at the secondary school level. On one end of the continuum is a several-day suspension in which the student is not even permitted on school grounds; this consequence is designated for the most serious kinds of behavioral transgressions, such as physically assaulting another student. On the other end of the continuum is during-school or after-school detention given and supervised in the classroom by a content area teacher for minor transgressions such as talking during a test.

For the latter students, especially those who received SPS training during the elementary years, the use of problem-solving questioning by the adults who supervise the after-school and during-school detentions can prompt them to access some of the skills that they know but are not using. The following SPS questions have been taken by practitioners and put into worksheet form for use by students in detention. These questions also include the responses of a hypothetical seventh grader.

1. I got into trouble because . . . ("I cursed at Kevin.")
2. How did you feel before you did this? ("Angry. I'm sick of that kid.")
3. What were you trying to accomplish? ("To get him off my case.")
4. What happened after you did this? ("I got nailed by Mrs. Lake. She sent me to detention.")
5. Before you did what got you into trouble, what other solutions did you try? ("Nothing.")
6. Think of some other solutions that might have worked.
    "I know you want me to say ignore him."
    "I could have smacked him."
    "I could have yelled at him, not cursed."
7. Next to each solution, write down what you think could happen next.
    "I know you want me to say ignore him. I've tried that, and it doesn't work."

"I could have smacked him. More trouble for me with Mrs. Lake."

"I could have yelled at him, not cursed. It might have slowed him down and maybe I wouldn't have gotten detention."

8. Which is your best solution. ("The last one.")

9. What could happen that could keep your best solution from working? ("If I got too mad I might curse.") And how would you handle it? ("Next time I could just try to remember how awful detention is and that might stop me from cursing.")

10. What exactly would you say and do to keep out of trouble the next time? ("I'm getting mad, Kevin, so knock it off!")

11. If you hurt or damaged something, what can you do to make up for it? ("Say that I'm sorry.")

In one school in which such detention worksheets have been successfully used, the routine was established that the supervising teacher in detention would thoroughly explain to students how they are to use the worksheet. Once the students finished with the written responses, they were expected to review their worksheets with the supervising adult. The students were told that as soon as they had completed their worksheets, they could leave detention or suspension and thereby either leave earlier than they ordinarily would have or avoid having to stay longer to complete the task.

When students have gone through the effort of reviewing their transgressions and developing better alternative solutions, the school staff may want to keep copies of their responses to these questions. Within several days after the detention, a teacher, guidance counselor, mentor/adviser, or other involved staff member, in the true spirit of prevention, can review the plans with the students and deal with any obstacles. By meeting with the student within two or three days after the worksheet has been completed, the practitioner can more easily find opportunities to "catch the student being good" and appropriately compliment and support the student's improved behavior.

Working with students in special circumstances such as school detention challenges our energy, creativity, and thoughtfulness. Often, troubled young people are sent to practitioners without a moment's notice. The expectations of the referring persons may be quite high, and they may anticipate that effective solutions will be worked out rather quickly. The following section illustrates how social problem-solving can serve as a model to help a school practitioner reorganize in the midst of professional stress in order to use SPS to help an adolescent.

Using SPS in Multisession Counseling

Although this is not a book or even a full chapter on counseling, it is important to present at least a glimpse into a multisession, SPS-oriented counseling case, since so many school-based professionals also have roles as counselors and want to extend the benefits of SPS to young people who need this kind of special help in special circumstances. In this section, therefore, the thinking of an SPS-oriented practitioner is illustrated as she is confronted with a particularly troublesome call for help. In addition, the use of SPS as a counseling intervention to help a troubled adolescent and his family is presented. It is acknowledged that different counselors will have different ways of conceptualizing and handling such a case. Keep in mind that the purpose of the presentation is to show one example of how SPS can be a tool for self-organization by professionals and a way to plan and conduct counseling.

Professional Decision Making Using SPS

Karen, an experienced, licensed psychologist, had been in private practice for eight years. Answering her phone in late October, Karen listened as Denise, in a nonstop way, blurted out concerns regarding her son: "We're real worried about Jay. He's twelve years old and we think he's real depressed. He doesn't sleep well. At night, he goes to his room and I think he just rattles around until twelve o'clock. But then we hear him getting up and walking around at three or four in the morning! Jay says he hates school and sometimes he comes home with tears in his eyes. He says he has no friends and now he has started to say things that really scare us. He's asked us questions like, 'Would a person really die if he jumped out of a fast-moving car?' Last summer Jay had some serious surgery. It was a big success and we thought things were finally going to go so well for him. He's always been a depressed kind of kid, but before this he usually seemed to pull himself out of it. My husband is a good man but he's really not sure about getting help from a psychologist because it's expensive. He said that we could come but we could only see someone for two or three months and then that would be it."

Many counselors can relate to this kind of situation. In a brief, anxious conversation, a caller paints a scene of serious family anguish and presents the expectation of a "cure" occurring in a rapid fashion. What are our private feelings when we hear this kind of cry for help? Inside, we experience a wide array of feelings such as empathy for the family, self-doubt about what to do, and the realization that in this time of crisis the family needs to hear a tone of confidence and competence from the practitioner.

Karen's first decision was to obtain additional details over the phone regarding the family situation. It turned out that Denise is Jay's stepmother. Denise's husband, Frank, and Jay's natural mother (whose whereabouts had been unknown for several years) were divorced four years ago. Frank took on the responsibility of raising Jay, Jay's older sister, and Jay's two younger brothers. Frank and the family have not heard from Jay's natural mother since the divorce. Eighteen months ago, Frank married Denise. Five months ago, they had a new baby son, and four months ago they moved to a new community. The children, of course, changed school systems.

After questioning Denise further, Karen strongly suspected that Jay was significantly depressed. In addition to her private practice, Karen had been working for six years as a school psychologist doing psychological evaluations and helping special education teachers implement an SPS curriculum. Over the past six years, she had used the SPS approach to deal with her own professional and personal stress, as well as in her counseling work.

Karen told Denise that she was right to be concerned about Jay and that she would call her back in a short while with some advice. At this point, Karen took several deep calming breaths and, at this point of professional anxiety, she deliberately took herself through the eight social decision-making and problem-solving steps.

1. *Look for signs of different feelings.*

"I feel depressed just thinking about the pain that this mother, her stepson, and the entire family must be experiencing. I also feel quite tense and pressured myself to figure out a responsible way to help."

2. *Tell yourself what the problem is.*

"I feel pressured and somewhat angry because I have been presented here with a situation that is quite serious. This boy and his family probably should have been in counseling years ago! But the main problem now is that I need a plan regarding how to help them."

3. *Decide on your goal.*

"I need a plan that involves reducing the self-destructive risk that might be going on here."

4. *Stop and think of as many solutions to the problem as you can.*

a. "I could refer this family to the county child guidance clinic. There, at least, they will have related support services such as a twenty-four-hour, seven-day-a-week crisis unit. They might need that."
b. "I could see Jay in intensive, individual counseling because it sounds like he really needs a friend and confidant."
c. "I could get some additional information from Jay's school to help me determine the depth of his problem and then teach him some SPS skills as a way for him to take charge of his situation. I could include his parents in this as well."

5. *For each solution, think of all the things that might happen next.*

a. "I could refer the family to the county child guidance clinic."

a. They live 1½ hours from the county clinic and I'm afraid that they won't be able to consistently go to counseling on the weekly basis that seems to be a minimum need."

b. "I could see Jay in intensive, individual counseling."

b. "While I'm sure we'd be able to get close and that I could give him some support, I am concerned that this would be insufficient to sustain him when I'm not around."

c. "I could get some additional information from Jay's school to help me determine the depth of his problem and then teach him some SPS skills. I could include his parents in this as well."

c. "In this way I'd at least be on more solid ground about the seriousness of the problem I'm dealing with. And I think the skill-building approach of teaching social problem solving could make Jay feel that he is gradually taking charge of his life, which should help his depression."

6. *Choose your best solution.*

"I think I'll go with the last idea, of checking in with Jay's school and doing SPS training with Jay and his family."

7. *Plan it and make a final check.*

"I'll call Denise back and make an appointment to see them tomorrow night, and I'll explain my plan to her. I'll also ask her to monitor Jay carefully. She should know to call the local hospital emergency room if she thinks that Jay is at risk at any point. I'll do an intake interview with Jay and his parents at our first meeting and get written permission to contact Jay's school and the school he attended last year."

8. *Try it and rethink it.*

Karen was back on the phone to Denise within twenty minutes after the initial call. Denise validated Karen's concern that the county child guidance clinic was just too far for them. She seemed relieved that Karen would take the case. Denise also dutifully responded to Karen's advice regarding how to monitor Jay and how to handle an emergency, and she agreed with the plan of contacting the school for further information.

Assessment

As a result of interviewing Jay alone and then with his parents, Karen learned more about the many issues he was handling, including his surgery, the new school, the new neighborhood, his father's new marriage, and the birth of his new brother. But the one problem that gave him the most amount of stress was, surprisingly, his relationship with another student, Todd. Todd, who was from the new neighborhood, used to be Jay's best friend. For all of Jay's first summer in the neighborhood, he and Todd played together almost constantly. They hiked together in the woods, went to the shopping mall together, bought snacks and baseball cards, and generally had a good time. However, as soon as school began in September, things took an explosive and abrupt change for the worse. Quite simply, Todd completely turned on Jay. He would bully him unmercifully, shove him, and hit him, often in the presence of the other boys at school. After school, Todd would follow Jay home and taunt him by taking his hat from him and throwing it around. Jay was absolutely miserable about this. In his discussions with Karen, he stated that this was the problem he wanted to resolve. He confirmed with Karen and his parents that he had had some self-destructive thoughts that he felt were directly related to his trouble with Todd. He also said that he did not think that he would try to hurt himself at this time but that he was very upset about Todd's bullying.

Karen also contacted Jay's guidance counselor, who, along with his teachers, was just getting acquainted with Jay and his school records. The counselor was greatly concerned with Karen's description of Jay's state of mind and she assured Karen that she would be monitoring Jay. Jay was in regular education classes and his teachers reported that he was attentive and quiet in class. No referrals for counseling or special help had been made. The counselor at Jay's former school reported that Jay had always been an above-average student and had never been referred for counseling or remedial help. Accordingly, there were no psychological, psychiatric, social work, or counseling data to report to Karen. However, considering what Karen had learned from Jay directly and from his parents about his self-destructive thoughts, she was convinced that he was depressed and possibly at risk.

The next step for Karen was to communicate her impressions to Jay's parents. There were two SPS skills that were particularly useful to Karen in this difficult disclosure process. First, because she had identified her own anxieties about handling this sensitive meeting, she used Keep Calm several times before and during the meeting. Second, she remained goal focused; encounters such as these are so laden with emotion that the participants can drift into a variety of directions that may not directly relate to the matter at hand. Accordingly, before and during the meeting, Karen kept focusing on her goal of calmly validating the parents' concerns and winning their support of the intervention plan of teaching Jay the skills of clear thinking.

Using SPS in the Course of Treatment

Karen took care to speak with Jay and his parents at each session to make sure that he was safe and being monitored. Her focus then turned to giving Jay a working understanding of social problem solving. Jay was clearly motivated. He wanted very much to figure out how to deal with the painful feelings he received on a day-in, day-out basis from Todd. Karen photoduplicated four 8½-by-11-inch pages listing the SPS steps, kept one for herself, and gave a copy each to Jay and his parents. She took great care to explain the steps very carefully to Jay, making it clear to him that his knowledge and use of the eight steps would directly relate to how successful he would be at effectively dealing with Todd. Jay memorized all eight steps by the second session. Karen told Jay that she would role-play a person who had never heard of the SPS steps and he would "teach" these steps and their meanings to her. Much of this was done with an element of fun and play, including sessions in which Jay "taught" the eight steps to his parents in a family session. Jay and his parents were told that the purpose of these exercises was for Jay to "overlearn" SPS. The steps were also posted on the refrigerator at home.

Once Jay was conversant with the SPS steps, Karen used facilitative questioning to help him connect each step to his dilemma with Todd. The eight-step handout was used as a visual reminder and place saver throughout the counseling process and Jay wrote down his responses to each step in the following way.

1. *Look for signs of different feelings.*
"That's easy. I feel depressed and sad.'"

2. *Tell yourself what the problem is.*

"I used to be real good friends with Todd but now I'm not. He's mean to me and teases and picks on me every day."

3. *Decide on your goal.*

This is a tricky step that warranted a great deal of discussion between Karen and Jay. Jay was focusing on "ideal" outcomes that depended on significant changes in Todd's behavior: "I want Todd to be friends with me again" or "I want Todd to stop."

Part of Karen's concern was that if Jay had unrealistic and idealistic goals, the likelihood of his feeling depressed would increase, because the outcome of this kind of goal depends on another person's behavior. Sensitively and carefully, Karen discussed this with Jay.

A positive relationship was developing between them. Jay trusted Karen in part because she respected his ideas and let him explore goals and solutions in an unfettered way. This was probably one of the most important techniques that Karen used in the therapy. Jay was permitted to "try out" his goals in the session. When he explored alternative solutions, he discovered for himself that he could not be confident that his behavior would allow his goals to be reached. He began to see the value of selecting a realistic goal that involved a change in his own behavior and attitude, and his goal began to center on acting less like a victim. This goal was ultimately concretized by Jay: "I want to do something to make it harder for Todd to pick on me, and to try and take some of the fun out of it for Todd." The selection of this goal was soundly supported by his parents.

Jay was asked by Karen to take the lead in explaining to his parents what had been accomplished during each session. This approach encouraged Jay to take charge of the process. Again, it provided him with an opportunity to "overlearn" some of the problem-solving skills. It is important to note that Jay began to "look better" from the beginning of the time when his problem was identified and the counseling work began. His parents no longer heard self-destructive talk and Jay's fearfulness was subsiding.

4. *Stop and think of as many solutions to the problem as you can.*

a. "I could ignore Todd."
b. "I could just walk up to him the next time I see him and hit him."
c. "I could tell his mother about what's been happening. She likes me and I know she would straighten Todd right out."
d. "If he hits or pushes me, I'll hit him back."

   5. *For each solution, think of all the things that might happen next.*

a. "I could ignore Todd."

a. "Ignoring doesn't work. Believe me, I've tried it."

b. "I could just walk up to him the next time I see him and hit him."

b. "My parents would never agree to that. No way. They'd yell at me and then I'd have them on my back, too."

c. "I could tell his mother about what's been happening."

c. "Todd would make sure that everybody in school knew that I told his mother and then it would be worse than it ever was. Besides, he'd still find a way to tease and hit me and get away with it."

d. "If he hits or pushes me, I'll hit him back."

d. "This could be the best one yet. I'd be scared, but it might work. But I don't think my parents would go for it. They'd be afraid of me getting hurt and getting into trouble at school. No one in my family has ever really gotten into trouble at school."

   6. *Choose your best solution.*
   This was a very delicate point in the treatment. Jay chose the last solution, but had a real concern about his parents' support. At

this point, a rhythm had been set in the sessions of Jay bringing his parents up to date about his progress in problem solving. Jay felt that his Dad might support this solution but he was doubtful about Denise, especially because she was the person who seemed to worry the most about his health. He wanted very much to feel better but he did not want to upset Denise by surprising her some afternoon by coming home after a fight. So, emboldened by his role-playing practice and growing feeling of self-efficacy, he explained to his parents what he wanted to do. While Jay's father became quite supportive of this approach, Jay was right about Denise's reaction; she was very concerned about Jay's physical integrity, especially because of the surgery he had undergone the summer before.

Denise decided to talk with Jay's physician about the problem and about Jay's proposed solution. From the physician, she received full assurance that Jay was as able as any other twelve-year-old to handle himself physically. Still, more work needed to be done with Denise, and Jay's father was instrumental in normalizing for her the fact that young people, like it or not, may be placed in situations that are not of their own doing in which they have to physically defend themselves. He talked about his own boyhood experiences in that regard, and Denise was slowly brought around. She asked that Jay assure her that he would not *start* a fight with Todd, but would only fight as a reaction to Todd hitting him. Some detailed discussion also ensued about how, if there were a fight, Denise and the family needed to be prepared to see torn clothes or a scratched or bruised nose. The discussion centered on the fact that Jay might have torn clothes or a bruised nose in any case, since Todd evidently felt no hesitation about hitting Jay now. The family also discussed the fact that Jay had been depressed about this situation and that the repercussions of his staying passive and not taking charge of his life might be more serious.

7. *Plan it and make a final check.*

Jay began to set the scene for Karen by demonstrating in the office how Todd would begin to walk behind him, tease him, and then steal his books, take his hat, and shove or hit him. Karen was particularly struck with how upset Jay became when he talked about Todd taking his hat.

The time had come for Jay to plan and practice, through

role-playing, his solution, "If he hits or pushes me, I'll hit him back." Karen wanted to collaborate with Jay and his parents on a way to monitor and thus improve the quality of Jay's interpersonal presentation of his assertive behavior. Toward that end, Karen gave Jay a handout describing an adaptation of the four components of the SPS readiness skill: "Be Your BEST" (Elias and Clabby, 1989). She shared with Jay that the best way for him to prepare for Todd was to self-check whether his *Body* stance was steadfast, fully facing Todd, and erect; whether his *Eye* contact maintained itself in a steady manner; whether his *Speech* was characterized by clear, no-nonsense, and "to-the-point" language such as "Todd—Knock it off!"; and whether the *Tone* of his voice was steady, firm, and confident. Karen demonstrated a role-playing presentation herself showing how the absence of even one of these components significantly affected the impact of the solution. For example, she would have a steady body posture, a well-worded speech, and a firm tone of voice, but little eye contact; in such a way, she made it quite clear to Jay how critical self-monitoring his interpersonal presentation would be. Jay memorized the steps of BEST and once again over-learned this skill by explaining it and demonstrating it to his parents.

Denise was concerned that because Jay was developing greater self-confidence, he might actually initiate a fight, and she shared this concern with Jay. To deal with this possibility, they practiced a situation with Karen taking the role of Todd and "teasing" Jay. Jay's goal in this role-playing exercise was to experience verbal provocation and show physical self-control. Perhaps not surprisingly, he showed good skills in self-restraint. The major problem for him was moving from a timid voice tone and somewhat fidgety body stance to a presentation that was more assertive and that appeared strong.

This approach to counseling was an appealing one for Jay's parents. The process of narrowing Jay's unhappiness to the focal problem of dealing with Todd and the SPS steps that they were all learning had a practical appeal. The mystery and uncertainty were being taken out of counseling. The parents were included in the skill acquisition approach and were able to self-disclose occasions in their own lives in which their failure to use a problem-solving approach caused their ideas to backfire on them. They learned that part of planning a good solution was to role-play the scene ahead of time, so they were prepared to hear loud voices coming from Karen's office. At times, Jay's parents were brought in to help with a role-playing exercise in order to demystify the process for Denise as well as to obtain their advice and input.

Good problem solvers, of course, also begin to anticipate potential obstacles to their solutions. One of the chief obstacles that Jay anticipated was the possibility that Todd would get other boys to join him in physically attacking Jay. Jay discussed this with Karen and his parents and determined that while this was a possibility, it was probably unlikely for several reasons. One reason was that Jay knew most of Todd's friends and, on a number of occasions, they had tried to talk Todd out of his bullying. Also, Jay felt that Todd would not want to lose face by trying to pressure his friends into helping him. Following discussions of such obstacles, Jay, with his parents' approval, decided to stay with his solution of hitting Todd back if Todd hit him first.

8. *Try it and rethink it.*

During the course of counseling, Jay never had to physically defend himself. Karen had kept prominent in Jay's mind his goal "to do something to make it harder for Todd to pick on me, and to try and take some of the fun out of it for Todd." This did not necessarily imply that hitting Todd was the "something" to do, but that it was the solution of last resort if Todd started hitting Jay. Karen and Jay actively discussed how Jay's adoption of an assertive attitude, practiced by role-playing, was an important part of the plan.

As was mentioned earlier, Jay had begun to feel better and act differently. He carried himself more comfortably and with better confidence and would joke and relax much more frequently at home, as reported by his parents and in counseling. As the counseling progressed, Todd, interestingly enough, gradually began to back off from Jay, to the point where during the last few sessions, he was not bothering Jay at all. Indeed, a major explanation of Jay's for this positive development was that because he had changed to a more determined and assertive attitude, Todd's interest in teasing him had diminished.

Jay's father, although he was quite involved in the therapy, affirmed that he needed to keep to his initial contract that limited treatment to three months. Karen had been keeping an ongoing, active, and careful watch on whether Jay was at risk for acting self-destructively. What she learned from her varied ways of questioning Jay and his parents, combined with her own experience and judgment, indicated to all involved that he showed a significant absence of self-destructive talk and intent. As a result of the relationship she now had with Jay, Karen felt that he was no longer at risk. The family understood that they could contact Karen at any time if they felt the need, and counseling was concluded after eleven sessions.

Successful Use of SPS Techniques in Counseling

Thus far in this chapter practitioners have successfully used SPS as an overarching framework to flexibly help in a series of student problems. In the first case, Michelle wanted very much to have someone to sit with at lunchtime; in the second case, Frank wanted a summer job. The sixth grader with the academic organizational problem wanted to get his homework done, and the angry seventh grader worked through another way to deal with Kevin. Finally, Jay was able to use SPS to regain control of a situation that was seriously depressing him.

It is important to note that the successful use of SPS in counseling requires the practitioner to keep in mind basic principles and techniques of counseling, such as the avoidance of power struggles with students, as well as the other techniques, themes, and suggestions that are briefly discussed next.

Maintain Reasonable Expectations

Although SPS counseling approaches have been used successfully with students who have not had classroom instruction in social problem solving, they are most effective when the student has learned the eight SPS steps during calmer moments from his or her classroom teacher. A student who has experienced dealing with concepts such as generating alternative solutions by role-playing this situation with classmates using hypothetical detention examples will be better able to use SPS when she or he has to deal with real-life detention problems.

Avoid Power Struggles

With an early adolescent, for whom the issue of fairness is so important, a counselor may have to work through the student's feelings of being unjustly accused. In some cases, the student may be unwilling to "own" responsibility for what happened. Counselors in situations such as these may want to keep in mind that an important goal is to give the students an opportunity to think without the counselor becoming embroiled in a battle about blame.

Some counselors can become zealous in their belief that a student will benefit from a thorough problem-solving review and can fall into the trap of insisting that the student complete all of the items on an SPS worksheet even though the student is quite resistant or is adamant in denying his or her culpability. This, of course, is counterproductive and has the effect of changing the nature of the entire encounter. What was intended to be a supportive, thoughtful, problem-solving discussion now becomes a power struggle. Again, the counselor should remember that the goal is to get the student to think, and this can happen even if the student does not acknowledge responsibility.

Notice how Mrs. Gertrude uses reflective listening and works at minimizing an escalation of upset feelings:

Mrs. Gertrude: Okay, Ralph, let's go over the first question on the worksheet. "I got into trouble because. . . ."

Ralph: That's just it. I didn't do anything wrong, I never should have gotten detention!

Mrs. Gertrude: I know you're pretty upset about this whole thing, but Mr. Melone's referral note says that you cursed at Kevin.

Ralph: No way! Melone's a pain. He's always trying to get me in trouble. I didn't do anything and I shouldn't have been sent down here in the first place!

Mrs. Gertrude: This all feels pretty unfair to you.

Ralph: You bet!

Mrs. Gertrude: Ralph, is there anything that you did in that argument with Kevin that you think you shouldn't have done? I mean, I know you think Mr. Melone is acting unfairly but isn't there *something* you did?

Ralph: No! I'm always getting into trouble for something I didn't do.

Mrs. Gertrude: All right, tell you what, let's take a break for a few minutes, I think we both need to keep calm. I'm going to get a glass of water. Can I get you some?

At this point, let's assume that Mrs. Gertrude knows by Ralph's tone and her past experience with him that he is not going to budge on this issue. Staying with an SPS worksheet approach when the practitioner is running into such a level of resistance is not advisable. If Mrs. Gertrude is inflexible and chooses to relentlessly try to secure an admission of guilt from Ralph, then Ralph's and her own negative feelings will escalate. Most of all, she wants to keep an alliance going with Ralph because he will need counseling with her throughout the school year and she does not want to lose him. Consequently, Mrs. Gertrude stays with her goal of trying to get Ralph to think. Even if Ralph will not acknowledge any level of responsibility in such affairs (and because she does not have any first-hand knowledge of the Ralph-Kevin incident), Mrs. Gertrude decides to change the playing field by moving to the hypothetical.

Mrs. Gertrude: Okay, Ralph. Look, I know you're pretty upset. But we have to get you through detention and the way out is to do one of these worksheets. Humor me, and let's go through this as if it were not you but someone else who cursed at Kevin.

It is also important to note that students who want to escape conspicuous academic failure in a particular class may act up in order to be sent to the office. Others want a "red badge of courage" to demonstrate to their peers that they were willing to violate school rules and stand up for themselves to teachers and administrators. Insisting on the completion of written SPS worksheets may not be as appropriate as spending some time with the student in counseling to understand more fully the student's feelings and goals.

Remember Sensitivity and Timeliness

As with any such discussion with a student, talking about the student's problem requires sensitivity and timeliness. For example, holding an SPS review while a student is still angry and agitated would be counterproductive for everyone. It is when the student has calmed down that a problem-solving discussion may have its greatest impact, a technique that Mrs. Gertrude used in the most recent example.

Consider Being an SPS Journalist

In this adaptation, the counselor asks the student questions and then has the option of writing the answers down in a journalistic fashion. What is interesting about using this kind of format is that the mere act of writing down the answers validates to students the importance of their ideas and thoughts to adults.

Use SPS as an Approach, Not a Panacea

Despite preparation, good implementation, sensitivity, and communication, some students may still come to the attention of a counselor who are significantly emotionally disturbed, behaviorally disordered, or just very angry. They may scream at the counselor, rip up the worksheet, or even become violent. Again, staying with an SPS worksheet approach when the counselor encounters such a level of resistance is not advisable. The main focus for the counselor at this time should be to help students regain a sense of control by acknowledging their feelings; gradually, as they regain their composure, SPS dialoguing can assist them in rethinking their goals and anticipating the consequences of their solutions.

Conclusion

Using the SPS paradigm as a professional guide and source of counseling techniques can be a great help to practitioners. School-based counselors who want to explore further the use of the SPS model in the delivery of counseling services may consult several helpful resources.

George Spivack, Jerome Platt, and Myrna Shure have written *The Problem-Solving Approach to Adjustment* (1976), which, in addition to explaining interpersonal cognitive problem solving in terms of its research and theoretical base, also describes various programmatic applications of the approach, including, for example, the use of interpersonal cognitive problem solving with chronic aftercare clients.

Thomas D'Zurilla has researched and written about social problem solving extensively, as in his book entitled *Problem-Solving Therapy: A Social Competence Approach to Clinical Intervention* (D'Zurilla, 1986).

Arthur Nezu, Christine Nezu, and Michael Perri have also studied social problem solving and have written *Problem-Solving Therapy for Depression: Theory, Research, and Clinical Guidelines* (Nezu, Nezu, & Perri, 1989).

Freda Easton, as coauthor with W. J. Winters, wrote *The Practice of Social Work in the Schools* (Winters & Easton, 1983). Among the counseling approaches she has used are the use of an SPS skills approach in a nine-session group counseling program with K–5 children.

And, finally, those who wish to take a look at a sample of a more theoretically oriented article dealing with this topic can turn to a piece written by Frederick Kanfer and Jerome Busemeyer, entitled "The Use of Problem-Solving and Decision-Making in Behavior Therapy" (Kanfer & Busemeyer, 1982).

Today's school practitioner can be a visionary planner as well as a knowledgeable implementer in the effort to bring sound social-affective programming to as many children as possible. It is true that the practitioner should still be concerned with providing sensitive care directly to students who may have already been victimized by forces such as poverty, misunderstood learning styles, neglect, and physical health problems. However, today's school practitioner can affect many more children by looking at the school/community system as the client and by training teachers and parents to be the deliverers of research-validated programs such as social problem solving.

The long-term experiences of researchers and practitioners in programs such as the ISA-SPS Project can provide the blueprints for practitioners to follow in constructing and tailoring programs in their own communities to strengthen the psychosocial competence of their children.

The visionary planner in each of us must be convinced of the importance of all of the key elements of a psychosocial competence program if effective programming in this domain is to occur, particularly the key element of matching. A great deal is possible if the practitioner uses her or his talents in assessment to accurately read the needs of a community, judge what its resources are capable of sustaining, and match the community with an appropriate program.

This planning makes possible the successful execution of another key element: the acquisition of appropriate materials. The right match of community needs with appropriate program materials sets the stage for a well-regarded pilot program during the first year. This, in turn, encourages the community to open even more doors during the second year so that more children can benefit from programs such as SPS.

The knowledgeable implementer also realizes that one of the first real-life tests for the pilot program occurs when the training of teachers takes place. Well-planned, comprehensive, responsive, and enjoyable training leaves teachers confident and eager to begin their work with the children. And, when the practitioner is skilled in providing special help for special circumstances, he or she can extend the potency of the SPS program by bringing it to bear on those circumstances where students need something more than classroom training. What is the next port on this voyage for the visionary planner and the knowledgeable implementer? It is the area in which the leadership activities of monitoring, evaluation, and feedback are vital and ongoing, the next key element in our

MATS/MEF model. Part Five reviews practical ways for the SPS Committee or SPS-oriented practitioner to monitor overall service delivery and ensure that proper management and modification of SPS efforts are taking place. Examples are provided through case studies.

PART FIVE

Adapting the Social
Problem-Solving Approach
to Diverse
and Changing Settings

In Part Two, the way in which action research was used to develop the ISA-SPS Project was highlighted. In Parts Three and Four, key elements for practitioners to consider when carrying out SPS-related interventions were presented. In Chapter Eleven, the discussion is extended to show how the final set of key elements of action research—monitoring, evaluation, and feedback (MEF)—have been invaluable tools for the SPS Unit as it has brought the SPS approach into new, diverse, or changing settings. School-based professionals inevitably will find themselves engaged in similar activities, whether with SPS or another program. Therefore, Chapter Eleven reviews some available tools for carrying out MEF procedures and, most importantly, it features examples of how the action-research process presented in earlier chapters has been applied in response to environmental demand and the press of school-based needs. Throughout Chapter Eleven, practitioners' own accounts of their efforts at adaptation are used as source material, in order to show most clearly the ultimate dependence of successful program implementation on local conditions and human factors.

The concluding chapter offers a brief perspective on the challenges that await school-based professionals who attempt to enhance the SPS skills of children and adolescents. In this look ahead, training, program dissemination, and leadership considerations are seen as paramount and the research, action, and policy implications of these considerations are outlined.

Chapter Eleven

Using Action Research
to Generate Variations
on the Model

The expansion of any program brings with it the likelihood that demands for application will be made in contexts for which proven methods do not exist. This has happened with great regularity with the ISA-SPS Project. Our response to these occurrences is to move into an action-research cycle, because it is in the nature of action research to be generative. Our previous action-research history has always allowed us to begin in a new site with what appears to be the approach that most clearly fits the need of the setting. Following this largely conceptually based match of idea and need, the ISA-SPS team identifies key constituents in the setting and collaboratively develops a vehicle for conducting the program. While all facets of the action-research cycle then come into play, *matching the need and the idea, identifying constituencies,* and *creating a suitable vehicle* deserve special emphasis because of the way these processes exercise a formative influence on the course of the program's implementation.

The final aspect of MATS/MEF, the practitioner-oriented derivation of the facets of the action-research cycle, focuses on the implementation process. It may seem as if ensuring that implementation takes place as planned would be an unnecessary concern. However, many practitioners are aware of programs that are never implemented as planned, or that drift over time from the intended parameters of implementation. Some form of management system is advisable to track the overall operation of a program.

Exhibit 11.1 is used by the SPS Unit to document all aspects of program-related activity; it can easily be modified for use within the school district. For example, it can be completed on a regular basis by members of a district's SPS Committee, and additional questions can be appended on an attached page. The SPS Unit routinely asks which implementation issues required particular attention during the period of time covered by the sheets, which required follow-up investigation or further documentation, and which issues, projects, or activities should be brought to others' attention. A review of these summaries could easily constitute a major part of the agenda for SPS Committee meetings. Follow-up consultation, training, resource acquisition, and planning activities develop from such meetings.

Other important implementation monitoring techniques include the curriculum feedback sheets completed by teachers or other implementers (see Chapter Three) and observation of such indicators as the minutes of regularly held SPS Committee meetings, SPS lessons in teachers' lesson plans, regular discussion of SPS at faculty meetings and individual supervisory meetings with teachers, the presence of SPS posters and bulletin boards, SPS materials sent home to parents or conveyed formally or informally on report cards, or collected SPS classwork, such as worksheets, book reports, or projects. Tools presented in Chapter Four that can be used for monitoring teacher implementation strategies, evaluating student skill acquisition and improvement in behavioral skills, and capturing "consumer feedback" all have value as part of a management system (see Elias & Clabby, 1989, and Papke & Elias, in press, for specific SPS-focused assessment tools).

Adaptation of SPS to Varied School Settings, Contexts, and Needs

Using the approaches outlined in Parts One–Four and the action-research facets and tools just noted, the members of the SPS Unit have attempted to forge program adaptations that will meet the needs of diverse settings and populations. In the examples of adap-

Exhibit 11.1. SPS Weekly Summary of Services.

School District_____   Week Ending_____

School Serviced_____   SPS Committee Member_____

Part 1: Lessons	Grade Level	No. of Classes/ Classification	No. of Students	Total No. of Lessons Taught
Totals:				

Part 2: Direct Consultation (in person or on the phone)	Name of Consultees	Time	Preparation Time	Travel Time
Totals:				

Part 3: Formal workshops/ presentations	Type of Activity	Time	Preparation Time	Travel Time
Totals:				

Part 4: School system related writing Supervision Program evaluation	Type of Activity	Time
Totals:		

tations that follow, the action research facets of matching the need and the idea, identifying constituencies, and creating a suitable vehicle are highlighted. Throughout the adaptation process, the key elements of the SPS program are kept firmly in mind as a guide. Informal and, at times, formal MEF/MOD procedures are used to

gather information to create a viable adaptation. Given the three-
to five-year time span required to set up an adaptation capable of
receiving a formal summative evaluation (Elias & Clabby, 1984b),
the emphasis in the examples that follow will be on formative
MEF/MOD.

In reporting the examples, every attempt has been made to
draw from interviews with team members involved in the adaptations and publicly disseminated reports of their work as provided
in our *Problem Solving Connection* newsletter. The examples cover
five sets of circumstances in five New Jersey sites:

1. High school applications for self-contained special education
    students (South Plainfield)
2. Follow-up in the middle school for students who receive the
    program in elementary school (Middlesex Borough)
3. Development of a program structure that can operate effectively
    in a large district with many elementary schools (Woodbridge)
4. Applications for severely emotionally disturbed and behavior-
    disordered students in a regional special education secondary
    school (Central Valley)
5. Development of a K–12 approach flexible enough to be taught
    in a noncumulative manner that is appropriate for both regular
    and special education contexts (Ridgewood)

A Curriculum for High School Students
in Self-Contained Special Education Classes

The Match of Need and Idea

The school district of South Plainfield, New Jersey, was aware of
the success of the elementary-level social decision-making program
in neighboring Middlesex Borough, New Jersey. Around 1980,
South Plainfield formed classes for emotionally disturbed and per-
ceptually impaired high school students who previously had been
sent to out-of-district placements. The district lacked a structured
format for skill training, so administrators approached John
Clabby, the educator-clinician from the CMHC assigned to South

Plainfield, and asked if social decision making and problem solving could be applied at the high school level with their new classes.

Constituencies

South Plainfield was part of the CMHC's catchment area, and school liaison was a primary part of John Clabby's responsibilities, particularly liaison with special services. There were clear signals from the high school that the staff and students needed a framework from which to build skills. Although the ISA-SPS team focused primarily on elementary-level preventive intervention and related research and it was clear that South Plainfield would allow no formal research to take place, the needs of the other constituencies carried greater weight and a program was initiated.

The Vehicle

The intervention began with a pilot program consisting of lessons from the elementary curriculum. Teachers felt strongly that a curricular approach provided the greatest stability and continuity for students and staff. However, through MEF/MOD procedures, it quickly became clear that the content and mode of presentation of the lessons would have to be developmentally upgraded for high school students, while the basic instructional framework and skill base were kept.

Outcomes

The ASPIRE curriculum (described in Chapter Seven) was the outgrowth of John Clabby's work in South Plainfield. However, since then, South Plainfield has expanded its program to include the elementary level and currently is using the basic social decision-making curriculum (Elias & Clabby, 1989). At Riley School, in 1989, one teacher taught social decision-making skills to her class of students who were classified as emotionally disturbed. She also assisted the school nurse in integrating social decision-making activities and aerobics exercises at the weekly meetings of the nurse's after-school health club. The nurse started to plan the health club after she formulated a goal to help children learn about good nutrition and mental and social health. She had noticed a problem of weight gains during her annual recording of heights and weights. She talked to parents who also were concerned about their children's weight gains and they thought a health club would be a great idea.

The involvement of parents has been a particular emphasis of the ISA-SPS Project's work in South Plainfield. The SPS Unit's parent liaison specialist identified early the need for continuity from the school-based program to reinforcement and extension in the home. Parents of adolescent students who are learning decision-making skills are invited to monthly parents' meetings to learn the language and the steps that their children are learning in classes at school. The ultimate goal is to have parents prompt and cue their children to use decision making at home; a primary vehicle for accomplishing this goal is for teachers to send home "refrigerator notes" on the lessons the students are learning in class. These notes are posted on the refrigerator, where they will be in the company of other important family papers; they contain key words and phrases the parents can use to elicit their children's thoughts about what they learned in class. (We are fond of telling parents that anything of importance in a house can be found *on* the refrigerator—or *in* it!)

At the meeting, parents commiserated about how difficult it can be for them to get their adolescents to think clearly. They rallied to encourage each other and practice conversations designed to foster clearer thinking and decision making. By the end of the evening, a few parents said that their goal would be to try to use the decision-making steps to get themselves focused first, so that they could choose the best way to approach their adolescents. Subsequent meetings have continued and expanded this focus and increased the number of parents involved.

A "Survival Skills" Program to Bolster Social Decision Making in Middle School

The Match of Need and Idea

Two converging needs were apparent in Middlesex Borough after the fourth year of our work there. First, teachers and parents who were involved with social decision making in elementary school wanted to see the program followed up in middle school. Second, an analysis of discipline and detention records in the middle school revealed nearly two thousand documented incidents per year, creating considerable staff stress and instructional disruption. This disruption was also affecting scores on standardized academic tests. A primary reason for these incidents was behavior that resulted when students were not organized for class or aware of school rules, and when they were frustrated over school routines and academic task demands.

Nancy Asher-Shultz and Karen Haboush, two psychologists who at the time were doctoral students at the Graduate School of Applied and Professional Psychology at Rutgers University, were members of the ISA-SPS team. Their background research suggested that entrance into middle school is a developmental transition that can have a major impact on middle school students' ability to cope and adapt. The skills students need to adapt successfully to the middle school include (1) increased organizational abilities, (2) management skills to cope with the increased work, and (3) the skills necessary to negotiate the physical environment of the school. The way schools respond to these adaptation demands is embodied in the behavioral and programmatic regularities of middle schools. Some of these regularities may impede the development of flexible coping skills and, in doing so, may widen the gap between students who have developed these skills elsewhere and those who have not.

Asher-Shultz and Haboush began by scrutinizing the school's routines to find a place to intervene and to define the school's self-identified needs. Based on the available research, Asher-Shultz and Haboush designed a "survival package" to help students who are making the transition to middle school build up the flexible coping skills that increased adaptation demands require. One part of the package was the Organizational/Study Skills (O/S) Program. The second part was the reintroduction of the social decision-making framework into an academic content area: social studies. Both programs will be described later in this section (see Asher-Shultz, Haboush, & Elias, 1987).

Constituencies

The ISA-SPS team felt a very strong commitment to providing follow-up services to children who received the social decision-making program in elementary school. Elementary school teachers and parents felt similarly. At the middle school, low staff morale led to a generally unfavorable resiliency-resistances balance (Table 3.1). Therefore, it was clear that there was no broad-based constituency for such a program, despite the evident needs. However, key staff members identified themselves as both committed to excellence in instruction and willing to take a leadership role: the guidance counselor, Karen Welland, and the chair of middle school social studies, Barry Glickman.

The Vehicle: An O/S Program in Sixth Grade

After careful consideration of the alternatives, it was decided to focus on sixth graders—students who were first entering middle school. The existing class known as "study hall" was chosen as the intervention site and replaced with a study skills program. The program has three primary content areas: organizational skills, study skills, and test-taking skills. The teaching methods combine use of social decision-making and problem-solving skills with hands-on practice. Worksheets are used, as are role-playing exercises, pictures, a board game designed especially for O/S, and vignettes (hypothetical stories).

In the organizational skills part of the O/S Program, students are given the opportunity to learn how to organize their lockers, notebooks, assignment pads, and study environment. The students problem solve ways to determine efficient uses of their "Trapper Keepers" (a type of looseleaf binder required in this particular school) and then use half a class session to actually organize their own. From the basic organizational lessons, the students move on to the more familiar domains of study and test-taking skills. The emphasis is on encouraging the students to think about studying and test taking as problems to be worked out.

Classes meet once a week for three of the four marking periods. The first two units are skill based. The third unit is a review and makes use of an O/S board game, a student-developed study manual, role-playing, and vignettes; it elicits considerable creativity and spontaneity on the part of students. The O/S Program relies on the leadership of the school's guidance counselor, resources in the form of undergraduates from Rutgers University who serve as instructors, and an ongoing MEF/MOD process to make it responsive to the needs of the school and effective in building students' skills, as well as to keep it attuned to the changes in adaptation demands being made on newly entering middle school students.

The Vehicle: A Social Decision-Making Framework for Social Studies in the Seventh Grade

Most students at the middle school had received instruction in social decision-making and problem-solving skills during their last two years of elementary school and had experienced having their feelings and thoughts actively elicited and attended to. Haboush and Asher-Shultz set out to conceptualize and develop an empowering experience for these middle school students, in order to provide systematic opportunities for the maintenance, reinforcement, and generalization of social decision-making skills within an existing curriculum that was largely organized around the students' acquisition of factual knowledge.

Several factors determined the choice of an entry point in this particular setting. The content and logic of the social studies curriculum appeared to be well suited to the application of problem-solving skills: for example, the study of historical events clearly reflects the results of decision-making processes on the part of significant individuals. Additionally, the social studies curriculum included the study of current events, in which students often were exposed to controversial social issues and asked to form personal conclusions about them (the disposal of toxic waste and the abolition of the death penalty are two examples). It seemed reasonable that teaching students to apply social decision-making and problem-solving skills to social studies content would enable them to understand historical decision-making processes, as well as the manner in which their individual decisions contributed to the solution of social problems. In addition, attempts at teaching the application of social decision-making skills in social studies had proved successful at the elementary school level in this district. As a result, Haboush and Asher-Shultz knew that the nature of the content matter was well suited to this approach and that students actively participated in class when these lessons took place.

Another factor in finding a *flexible entry point* turned out to be related to the staff's concern about teaching critical thinking skills (based on recent district-wide achievement test profiles) and the presence of a content area chair who would facilitate the entrance of the program. Barry Glickman, a seventh-grade teacher and social studies chair, was identified as someone whose role definition would allow him to become involved with consultants from the ISA-SPS Project and whose personal values were recognized by the system to include a commitment to educational excellence and innovation. In this particular setting, then, the combination of factors favoring the importance of teaching critical thinking skills in the social studies curriculum and the presence of concerned, innovative leadership suggested that the social studies curriculum offered the needed entry point.

The consultative approach as initially conceived was to begin by training the social studies chair in the use of SPS skills in social studies lessons. The starting point and initial set of materials that was used was the social studies section of the application phase of the elementary grades' social decision-making curriculum (Elias & Clabby, 1989). The ISA-SPS consultants stressed that they did not approach the system or the social studies teachers with an offer to create an empowering experience for students. Instead, they approached the system with an offer to provide consultation in the instruction of critical thinking skills, which this middle school's curriculum guide identified as "the primary goal of social studies instruction."

There was an apparent paradox between the concern that existed among teachers regarding the instruction of critical thinking skills and the manner in which teachers attempted to achieve it. In this middle school, as in many others, social studies instruction was characterized by an emphasis on factual knowledge acquired through teachers' lectures, the prevailing use of textbooks, and specific styles of closed-ended questioning. This contrasted with the available research, which indicated that these instructional methods and materials actually reinforced students' use of rote memory and other lower-order cognitive skills, all of which are negatively related to academic achievement.

The consultants recognized that to intervene and suggest alternative teaching methods would require them to challenge many instructional regularities, and they would have to do this in a manner that would not create a great deal of resistance to their change efforts. Ultimately, they chose to offer consultation in critical thinking skills through the use of teacher-preferred instructional materials, such as textbooks, current events, and magazines.

Teachers were comfortable with paper-and-pencil instructional materials, so the consultants developed worksheets that provided systematic practice in the application of the social problem-solving framework to social studies textbooks. They then assisted teachers in rethinking the main theme of a chapter of the textbook as "a historical problem needing to be solved," and in discovering ways to apply the worksheets to the social studies textbook.

The teachers would ask the students to identify the historical event or problem, the groups of individuals involved, their goals, and the possible solutions to achieve the desired goals. Students would also be asked to generate their own solutions to historical problems. When these strategies were used at the end of the chapter, teachers viewed them as an effective means to review the chapter's content.

Furthermore, the opportunity presented students with practice in a very different cognitive and emotional process than merely engaging in factual recall aimed at reproducing "the" correct response. While use of the worksheets provided content review, it also built in skill maintenance and generalization, since the problem-solving framework could be repeatedly applied regardless of the specific content under study.

Finally, although it never explicitly challenged teacher-directed instructional methods such as lecturing, particularly when students were first learning to apply the framework, consultation also attempted to increase the teachers' comfort level with the use of small-group activities, which the consultants hypothesized might help to engage students in the learning process to a greater extent than lectures alone had been observed to do. The more recent popularity of instruction in cooperative learning dovetails nicely with and serves to reinforce the instructional approaches that are most compatible with SPS acquisition and application.

Outcomes

MEF/MOD procedures have highlighted the operation of both the O/S and social studies programs. Data have included class observation, curriculum feedback sheets, consumer satisfaction surveys, reviews of student products and direct measures of skill acquisition, and an analysis of relevant report card indices. Experimental and control groups also have been available at various times. As summarized in Smith (1989), the O/S program is well received, has led to skill gains, and has generated a positive impact on academic performance.

Some interesting findings on the social studies program are drawn from Haboush (1988). Student performance on seven report card variables was compared for both program students ($n = 172$) and nonprogram students ($n = 199$). Program students obtained significantly higher ($p < .05$) average levels of social studies achievement grades, language arts achievement grades, social studies effort grades, and social studies conduct grades during the marking periods in which the program was in effect. The students who were taught by the social studies chair demonstrated significantly greater knowledge ($p < .05$) of the eight-step social decision-making framework. Moreover, in this class, in which the greatest frequency of lessons was taught, a significant ($p < .05$) inverse relationship was found between students' knowledge of the social decision-making framework and the average number of areas of unsatisfactory progress noted on quarterly progress reports. In this case, the decision-making framework was applied in an ongoing manner at the classroom level to solve problems of academic preparedness and task completion. Students' use of the framework was then reflected in fewer areas of unsatisfactory progress. The finding of an inverse relationship was interpreted as providing support for the position that repeated instruction and application of the framework at the classroom level may help students (and teachers) to recognize this process as an integral part of their daily learning experience.

Haboush and Asher-Shultz designed the O/S and social studies programs with a view toward a complementary linkage between the two programs in addressing the environmental demands of middle school transition. They attempted to create a middle school survival package by combining a hands-on skill approach with reinforced use of social decision-making and problem-solving skills, thereby providing the environment with resources to empower its students. Both programs have been adapted into their settings' routines. Haboush and Asher-Shultz's work shows that a vehicle must be identified carefully and that we must not be fearful of challenging implicit regularities with a new paradigm for school-based intervention. Finally, their work stands out as an excellent longitudinal example of the role of action research and MEF/MOD in preventive and social competence promotion efforts in the schools (Haboush & Elias, in press; Welland & Elias, in press).

A Social Decision-Making Framework
for Elementary Guidance

The Match of Need and Idea

The town of Woodbridge, New Jersey, has the largest suburban school district in the state. Responding to district goals to promote responsible citizenship and to the availability of county funds, the district worked with the ISA-SPS team to set up a pilot curriculum-based program in three fifth-grade classrooms in one elementary school. The success of the pilot program led to two years of expansion in three other schools, focusing on grades 4–6.

The need was generated when the collaborative team attempted to find a model that would allow the program to spread to all elementary schools and all grades—in essence, a quadrupling of service delivery. Key school personnel believed that the process of training and consulting with teachers was too laborious and time consuming to serve as a viable model.

The idea emerged during a discussion between district staff and parents. Woodbridge had three guidance counselors who spent their time working in the fourteen elementary schools. The counselors spent forty-five minutes in each sixth-grade class once a week throughout the school year; they also spent forty-five minutes per month in each fifth-grade class. In the classrooms, the guidance counselors delivered a program consisting of lessons that were devoted to a series of topics; these topics included such things as self-esteem, peer relationships, careers, and transition to middle school. The counselors had worked extensively to develop this guidance program, but the director of guidance recognized that the program would benefit from having a framework that incorporated the social decision-making steps. He agreed with the ISA-SPS team that although the guidance lessons were individually interesting and valuable, they would derive greater strength from having the continuity that the social decision-making steps could provide.

Constituencies

Several administrators in the Woodbridge school district had come to develop a strong belief in the importance of the social decision-making program for the district's students. They believed that the program would complement the district's strong academic emphasis. Political issues that surrounded the implementation of the program in the elementary classrooms led to a mixed constituency among teachers. The key constituents for the program, of course, were the three elementary guidance counselors. Two of them had devoted considerable time to the development of the district's guidance program, and they were somewhat reluctant to engage in the process of creating yet another version of the program. However, a new guidance counselor, with no particular allegiance to the old program and with previous teaching experience in the Middlesex Borough schools, was favorably inclined to attempt something new with the guidance lessons.

Thus, several strong constituents propelled the program forward. Perhaps of greatest significance was the willingness of the new guidance counselor to conduct a pilot test for whatever vehicle was created by the ISA-SPS team and district personnel.

The Vehicle

A process was instituted by the director of guidance during which staff from the ISA-SPS team met in a series of workshops with the three guidance counselors. The goal of the workshops was to produce a set of new lessons that somehow wove together social decision making and the existing Woodbridge guidance activities. An initial decision was made to create seven lessons that would be added to the program in Woodbridge, with the purpose of teaching the social decision-making steps and key readiness skills such as VENT, Keep Calm, and listening position.

The lessons were piloted primarily by the new guidance counselor, under the observation of an ISA-SPS staff member. The staff member used MEF/MOD procedures to provide feedback to improve the lessons. Lesson revisions were developed with the entire team, and with the understanding that all three guidance counselors would soon be carrying out the lessons. In the subsequent year, the guidance counselors carried out the social decision-making lessons under the periodic observation of ISA-SPS team members. Once again the summer was used as a time for refinement of lesson activities.

The vehicle has progressed in three significant ways. First, the social decision-making steps and key readiness skills are being integrated into all guidance lessons, once they have been presented to the students in specific social decision-making lessons. Second, a series of teacher handouts has been developed to accompany the various lessons. Each handout is limited to one sheet of paper that contains a brief description of the highlight of the lesson. It also contains four or five suggestions for specific ways in which classroom teachers can integrate social decision-making skills into their lessons in a variety of areas. These reinforcing activities can be as simple as including new social decision-making terms as part of weekly spelling assignments, or as complex as using the social decision-making steps as a framework for analyzing current events. Finally, the Woodbridge schools have embarked on a program of training school aides in social decision making so that they can learn how to prompt the children's use of skills during the types of problematic situations that take place in the cafeteria and on the playground.

Through the vehicle of an elementary guidance–based program, social decision-making and problem-solving skills have been extended to include classroom reinforcement and reinforcement in other key social settings in which children have group interactions.

Outcomes

MEF/MOD procedures have been the main method of determining the outcome of the Woodbridge guidance program. Through direct class observation, curriculum feedback sheets, consumer satisfaction surveys, and a great deal of staff feedback, the ISA-SPS team and key Woodbridge administrators have derived a sense of the benefits of the program. The data reflect high levels of participation of students in the lessons and carryover into schoolyard and lunchroom contexts when the children are prompted to use the skills. Perhaps most relevant is the recognition by the building administrators that if they use facilitative questioning when the children come to them with difficulties, the children seem to be able to work through problems more easily and in a more satisfactory and sophisticated manner than they could previously. This result has had such a striking effect on the administrators that as of this writing, Woodbridge was undertaking a program to train all elementary principals in social decision making both to facilitate their ability to prompt the thinking of their students and to allow them to apply social decision making as a management tool for building planning and staff development and as a crisis-management and problem-solving technique. In addition, in the district's winter 1990–91 newsletter, an article described how parental request for the program was leading to a new adaptation context: the middle school guidance program.

A Video-Based Adaptation for Severely Disordered Secondary School Students

The Match of Need and Idea

Students are referred to Central Valley Regional School mainly because they need more intensive services than can be provided through special education classes in their home districts. The students are divided into three main communities: upper (ages sixteen through nineteen), middle (ages thirteen through fifteen), and junior (ages ten through twelve). Each class consists of approximately six to ten students, a teacher, a teacher's aide, and a counselor. The school has an elaborate behavior management program. Staff members were concerned that, although Central Valley provided a strong, positively structured environment, the generalization of gains to situations outside of school was not satisfactory. The staff recognized that the students needed a systematic, internal process that would help them deal more successfully with the problems and decisions they encountered when they were not in school.

The idea that the social decision-making and problem-solving approach might be the source of such an internal process came as a result of the input of two Central Valley staff members who attended summer workshops put on by the ISA-SPS team. Following their attendance at this workshop, the staff members shared what they had learned in an in-service program for the rest of the Central Valley personnel. At this point, the principal of the school, John Kazmark, who was himself trained in cognitive behavioral intervention approaches, took responsibility for seeing that the match of idea and need became actualized.

Constituencies

Central Valley Regional School is a part of the Middlesex County (N.J.) Educational Resources Commission. Its offices were located in Piscataway, New Jersey, very close to the offices of the UMDNJ-CMHC at Piscataway. Through informal contacts, the superintendent of the commission began talking with John Clabby about the possibility of bringing the program to Central Valley. While the school is not located within what was then seen as the catchment area of the CMHC, the location of the commission in Piscataway allowed the opportunity for the ISA-SPS team to work with the Central Valley Regional School.

From the perspective of the CMHC, Central Valley represented a primary constituency of severely disturbed, high-risk, high-need youth. Providing services to so many youngsters over a consistent period of time would be far easier through the ISA-SPS team than through either outpatient mental health services or the various short- and long-term hospital services for adolescents offered by the CMHC, all of which have limited capacities (particularly compared to the numbers of students who can be served through an ongoing school program). From the perspective of the university, initial conversations with John Kazmark suggested that he had considerable interest in research and would be an active participant in working with the ISA-SPS team's action-research procedures. Thus, there were a variety of constituencies whose convergent interests fostered the pursuit of a program with Central Valley Regional School.

The Vehicle: A Curriculum-Based, Video-Based Program

During the first year of the program, ASPIRE lessons were used in a pilot project with two classes in the upper community. The approach taken was to have teachers carry out ASPIRE lessons in the classroom while counselors used the corresponding ideas and principles in running their frequent group sessions with students. Evaluation of this pilot effort was highly informative. First, it was noticed that instructional continuity was compromised by the poor, or at least erratic, attendance of students. Among the reasons for this were the need for students to appear at police and court proceedings and students' occasional hospitalization. Further, observation of students suggested that at least half had significant drug involvements that severely impaired their ability to attend to, respond to, and retain the principles of the ASPIRE curriculum.

In the second year, a decision was made to shift the emphasis to children in the junior community. This reflected the staff's orientation toward prevention, particularly prevention of future substance abuse by the students. Further, it was felt that attendance would be more stable and that the social decision-making curricular approach would provide the strongest match to children in the ten- to twelve-year-old age range. It should be noted that an initial successful application of the social decision-making approach occurred with children at the Children's Village, a residential treatment center for students very much like those in the junior community at Central Valley (Elias, 1983). However, the teachers and ISA-SPS team consultants made a number of creative adaptations to the program based on action-research learnings subsequent to the Children's Village program. Among these was something called the "Keep Calm Rap." One of the teachers developed a rap song that expressed the rationale, importance, and wide applicability of Keep Calm. Written in the popular idiom of "rap," it engaged the students' attention so much that they made a video of it. This video was presented at an ISA-SPS workshop at the National Association of Social Workers' annual convention.

In the third year of the program, the entire school was revitalized and energized by the positive reception of the program in the junior community. The junior community continued to use the elementary curriculum with adaptations resulting from MEF/MOD. Teachers in the upper community began using sections of the ASPIRE curriculum in a flexible manner with their students, particularly the sections that focused on vocational applications. Some of the most exciting innovations occurred in the middle community. It was recognized that the medium of videotape had unique appeal to students. Therefore, ISA-SPS team members worked with Central Valley staff to make video a significant component of the middle community program. The impetus for this was drawn from students' experiences in the upper community viewing the videotapes that are part of the ASPIRE curriculum, and from the history of successful use of videotape at the Children's Village (Elias, 1983). The students felt that it would be beneficial for them to see fulllength, current films and to apply social decision-making skills to these films. The social decision-making lessons were modified so that students were able to view a film and then analyze it using a movie-viewing worksheet.

Teachers prepared students for viewing the film by dividing them into three groups and directing each group to focus on one of the main characters in the film. Each group was told that following the movie, they would be responsible for filling out the movieviewing worksheet. The worksheet provided the students with an opportunity to use the social decision-making and problem-solving steps and to study the decision-making skills of the characters in the movie; it also provided an in vivo opportunity for cooperative learning and group problem solving. The worksheet contained the following sequence of questions:

1. Identify the character that you are watching. What is this person feeling at the beginning of the movie? How can you tell?
2. What is the problem that he or she faces?
3. What is his or her goal?
4. What are the solutions that he or she tried and what were the consequences of each solution?
5. Were there any other solutions thought about that were not tried?
6. Based on what happened or what *could* have happened, what do you think would have been the best solution?
7. What obstacles did the characters not plan for in their solution?

After the movie was over, the group started talking about what they had written on the worksheets, and the teachers acted as recorders, charting the students' responses on the board. A follow-up lesson from the ASPIRE curriculum, "Using Social Problem Solving as a Critical Thinking Guide for the Media," took place within a week after the movie was shown. This lesson focused on the nature of the decision making and problem solving that goes into producing a film or video and gave the students a chance to put themselves in the role of movie makers. The introduction to this lesson also helped students to understand how the mass media attempts to create certain impressions and desires in audiences. The students at Central Valley quickly grasped the ways in which advertisers attempt to convince viewers to buy their products. In a similar way, they began to realize that the producers and directors of movies have their own goals and, along with their writers and actors, use decision-making strategies to get certain messages across.

Based on this initial experience, the middle community has embarked on a video-making unit that combines awareness of influence in mass media, viewing and analysis of different kinds of videotapes, and preparation of videotapes by the class.

Outcomes

The use of MEF/MOD once again allowed the buildup of curricular and instructional approaches that were well matched to the students' needs and learning styles. Given the nature of the Central

Valley population, engaging the students in the learning process was a very high priority. With the collaboration of John Kazmark, Michael Gara of the UMDNJ-CMHC at Piscataway, and two teams of Rutgers University undergraduates, formative research was conducted to investigate the relationship of self-control, social awareness, and social decision-making skills to the identity structures and behaviors of Central Valley students. The findings confirmed the existence of considerable variability among the Central Valley population and suggested that there were benefits in focusing on the instructional vehicles that would be most applicable to the students. Few students believed as part of their self-view that they had self-control, were part of a positive social milieu, or were skilled in solving their own problems. Instead, their identities were marked by reliance on questionable peer and family relationships and by considerable self-doubt. The nature of the social decision-making and problem-solving activities, which were involving, empowering, skill building, and competence enhancing, appeared to be a sound prescription for the identity and behavioral profiles of the Central Valley students.

A Flexible Approach to Teaching Social Decision Making in Regular and Special Education

The Match of Need and Idea

The Ridgewood, New Jersey, school district has a long tradition of focusing on innovation and of bringing together complementary programs. The school district had recognized that in addition to basic academic skills, intellectual enrichment could be attained through the use of such programs as Feuerstein's instrumental enrichment model (Feuerstein, 1980). Several staff members in Ridgewood heard about the social decision-making and problem-solving approach through contact with colleagues who had attended presentations by the ISA-SPS team. The director of Special Services requested further information from the team and concluded that there would be a great deal of compatibility between the instrumental enrichment approach and the social decision-making emphasis of the ISA-SPS Project. The director arranged a staff presentation and the staff was given an overview of the basic ideas and methods of the social decision-making approach. In essence, the staff of the Ridgewood school district created the match of need and idea largely through their own initiative and process of discovery.

Constituencies

The Ridgewood school district had a focus on academic excellence but also was concerned that many programs did not have clear extensions into special education. Thus, special education was the clear constituency for the efforts of the ISA-SPS team. From the perspective of the CMHC, Ridgewood was located in northern New Jersey, considerably outside CMHC's catchment area. At the time this work was initiated in 1983, the CMHC had yet to define for itself a broad mandate to establish social decision-making programs statewide. Thus, the decision was made that Ridgewood was not a sufficiently compelling constituency to warrant CMHC involvement. The responsibility for further development of the program fell to Maurice Elias, working in the capacity of an individual consultant, and a colleague he recruited to serve as a collaborator on the Ridgewood project, Steven Tobias, a school psychologist who was then a doctoral candidate at Rutgers University's Graduate School of Applied and Professional Psychology. For both Elias and Tobias, the prospect of providing a program for grades six through eight for children with a variety of handicaps (communication, learning, and emotional impairments) was a considerable challenge.

The Vehicle: A Curriculum-Based Social Decision-Making Program in Which All Steps Are Introduced to the Students and Used Simultaneously

From initial discussions with the teachers and observations of classes, it became apparent that the students in the special education classes in Benjamin Franklin Middle School would have a great deal of difficulty retaining social decision-making lessons presented to them in a cumulative manner (that is, one skill per week over an extended period of time). It was decided that the best solution would be an alternative route that would bring the entire decision-making strategy to the attention of the students at once, keep it visibly in the forefront, and yet allow for differential emphasis so that students could learn the skill associated with each of the decision-making steps. The program began with an emphasis on the readiness skills from the elementary curriculum, slightly upgraded and with examples that were appropriate for middle school students. The students were introduced to social decision making through FIG TESPN, a mnemonic for the eight social decision-making steps (Elias & Tobias, 1990):

1. *Feelings* are your cue to problem solve.
2. *Identify* the issue.
3. *Guide* yourself with a goal.
4. *Think* of many possible things to do.
5. *Envision* end results for each option.
6. *Select* your best solution.
7. *Plan* the procedure and anticipate roadblocks.
8. *Notice* what happened and remember it for next time.

FIG TESPN contains active, evocative language that the special education students found appealing. However, it was the FIG TESPN concept that they found most engaging. Appendix F contains sample FIG TESPN lessons drawn from the Ridgewood curriculum (Elias & Tobias, 1990; Tobias & Elias, 1991).

The use of FIG TESPN was supplemented by lessons in which a particular step was highlighted and activities relating to the appropriate skill were provided to students. Nevertheless, the entire FIG TESPN framework was featured as part of each instructional phase lesson throughout the three-year curricular program in the Benjamin Franklin Middle School. In summary, the vehicle used was a curriculum approach, featuring readiness, instructional, and application components; its most distinctive feature was the development of FIG TESPN as a way of bringing social decision making to students earlier and more frequently than had been the case in previous lesson structures, as well as in a way that could be prompted easily by teachers.

Outcomes

The development of the FIG TESPN curriculum was aided by the use of curriculum feedback sheets by both Ridgewood staff and Steven Tobias, who served as a consultant-observer to the teachers over a three-year period of time. In addition, key staff were trained to take over the supervisory role so that the consultation by Elias and Tobias could be phased out successfully while a consultative structure remained behind. The establishment of a group supervision model by the Ridgewood staff for the purposes of its own ongoing MEF/MOD procedures of the social decision-making curriculum is perhaps the most significant indicator of the long-term outcome of the program (Elias & Tobias, 1990).

Conclusion

Across all five examples, the basic elementary social decision-making curriculum and its ASPIRE variant serve as starting points to meet the diverse needs of school districts. In each case, an action-research process ensued that led to the development of other forms in which the social decision-making skills of students could be enhanced. It is noteworthy that across these examples, there is a relative paucity of outcome data reflecting specific skill acquisition or behavioral change (with the noteworthy exception of the Middlesex Borough Middle School programs). In each instance, this was the result of a decision by ISA-SPS team members that the available resources and the evaluation-related energies of the staff would be best used in focusing on formative evaluation. This reflects a strong belief that in the absence of sound formative evaluation data, the interpretation of summative evaluation data is highly unclear. Therefore, an emphasis was placed on MEF/MOD procedures that could be used by schools in an ongoing way, and particularly as they were used in Ridgewood, to serve as a sustaining force to carry on quality control of a program after involvement by ISA-SPS consultants was phased out.

If we accept that instituting a pilot program and launching a larger-scale program capable of gaining a solid foothold in a school is a process that takes a minimum of three years, then by extrapolation we should expect that serious attempts at gathering summative data and impact data would begin after that three-year period. Certainly, baseline data can be gathered in anticipation of the time when summative and impact evaluation information will be collected. However, the ultimate objective is to evaluate the impact of a well-formed program, and it is not until the program is established and operating with some regularity that conclusive summative evaluation can be obtained.

Chapter Twelve

Future Directions
for Social Problem-Solving
Research, Policy, and Practice

Enhancing the social problem-solving skills of children and adolescents is, ultimately, an effort requiring the work of researchers, practitioners, policy makers, and administrators. The schools have been the focus of increasing activity toward this end, but results have yet to be obtained in proportion to that activity. Among the streams of influence on the ISA-SPS Project (Figure 2.1), promising recent programs in prevention and social competence promotion were identified. There is reason to believe that widespread adoption of programs like these may have the desired impact on children's and adolescents' social competence, thereby propelling our schools toward meeting national educational goals relating to substance abuse prevention, responsible citizenship, and productive economic participation.

For these possibilities to become real, challenges must be addressed and met in the areas of coordination, training, program dissemination, and leadership. These areas, and their research, action, and policy implications, will be outlined next.

Coordination

We may legitimately ask what is involved in creating a place in the schools for social problem-solving and related competence-enhancing approaches. The coordinating impact of social problem solving depicted in Figure 1.2 is conceptual. What is not depicted is how the various mandates and programs will be organized and administered within school buildings and districts. The practical task of bringing diverse programs under common rubrics cannot be ignored, passed along to the next set of administrators, or addressed in a piecemeal manner. It seems plausible for SPS approaches and other approaches that promote school-based social competence to become linked with the kind of organization of services and programs advocated by the National Professional School Health Organizations (1984) and others (Connell, Turner, & Mason, 1985; Nader, 1989; Pentz et al., 1989; Perry & Jessor, 1985). The area of comprehensive school health education has made considerable strides toward unifying the disparate elements within the school and beyond the schoolyard walls that share the responsibility for the sound growth and development of children and adolescents. In one model (National Professional School Health Organizations, 1984), the key components are a community council, a schoolwide and parents' committee, health-related instruction, school health and mental health services, and a committee to focus on a healthful school environment. Health-related instruction is defined as including community, consumer, nutritional, and environmental health; personal, mental, and physical health care; family life; growth and development; prevention and control of diseases and disorders; safety and accident prevention; and substance use and abuse. Of critical importance is the delineation of a continuum of health and mental health services, including the classroom but extending to the school environment, food services, health of school personnel, basic health screening, follow-through, and liaison to community groups and resources, all facilitated by having a committee and council in place. Councils also are in a position to develop workplace and other community initiatives that serve to complement what goes on in the schools.

Weissberg, Caplan, and Harwood (in press) advocate calling such an array of coordinated resources "C-SCAHE" ("see-skay"), for Comprehensive Social Competence and Health Education. They feel that such a term most appropriately captures the goals of those calling for adoption of comprehensive health education programs in all schools (*Journal of School Health*, 1990). Specifically, it ensures that meaningful attention will be given to encouraging the growth of skills such as social problem solving, which underlie effective decision making in health, social, and academic domains (Elias & Tobias, 1990). Without the coordination that a C-SCAHE framework provides, Weissberg et al. (in press) argue, schools will continue to use their resources ineffectively, to the detriment of the students, families, and communities they serve and, especially, to those in greatest need.

Training

We must ask where the professional resources to carry out C-SCAHE and component health and social competence promotion programs will be found (Branden-Muller & Elias, 1991). Neither traditional school or clinical psychology training nor that given to educational administrators, teachers, health educators, guidance counselors, learning specialists, or policy makers provides an extensive background in the action-research approach, in prevention and social competence promotion models and programs, or in the kinds of interdisciplinary teaming and collaboration needed for these approaches and models to be effective. The lack of such a background inevitably limits advances in research, action, and policy making of the kind needed to enhance the social competence of children and adolescents nationwide. Action research is suited in unique ways to guide the development of preventive intervention, programs to promote social competence, and comprehensive service systems.

Most generally, it may be said that action research is conducted mainly within the *context of discovery*, while traditional research and intervention emerge primarily from the *context of justification*. In this distinction, made by Reichenbach in 1928, the context of discovery represents the cutting edge of a paradigm; it embodies a set of processes that leads to the generation of new ideas, predictions, and modes of inquiry and action. The context of justification resides primarily within an existing paradigm, and its emphases include formally documenting the validity of existing knowledge and action strategies, with the aim of weeding out weak explanatory concepts and intervention methods.

Table 12.1 outlines general features that should be made explicit in discussions of action research. Clearly, action researchers

Table 12.1. Dimensions for Comparing Action Research and Traditional Research and Intervention.

	Action Research	Traditional Research	Traditional Intervention
Settings involved	Schools, homes	Universities, labs	Agencies, offices
View of participants	Collaborators	Subjects	Patients, clients
Method of seeking participants	Active seeking	Variable	Passive waiting
Duration (typical unit)	Years	Months	Weeks
Frequency of personal contacts with participants	High	Low	Low
Affiliation with participants' settings	High	Low	Low
Feedback to participants	Extensive, two-way	Debriefing, one-way	Moderate
Accountability to participants	High	Low	High
Responsibility to host settings	High	Variable	High
Ethical dilemmas encountered	Constant	Episodic	Often
Control by professional	Low	High	Moderate
Risk for professional	High	Low	Moderate
Networking needed	Extensive	Infrequent	Occasional
Opportunities for new, unintended learning, directions	Extensive	Infrequent	Occasional

place themselves in a position of risk or vulnerability along several dimensions. Becoming enmeshed in the ecology of natural settings brings with it reduced control over influential events, as well as frequent distractions and barriers to objectivity. A premium is placed on proactive planning, crisis management, containment of budding problems, and maintenance of an active network of collaborators and system monitors. This seemingly inordinate attention to administration and organization is all in the service of preserving the knowledge-generating features of the action-research approach. These features are worth preserving, because the privilege of entry into others' settings is rewarded by a deepened understanding of the dynamic complexities of these settings and of the structures and skills needed to cope within them. So the risk of action research is, in a sense, the entry fee for the opportunity to pass through the gateway into the context of discovery.

Progress requires that members of all relevant fields whose collaboration is essential for school-based programs of all kinds have a basic and shared understanding of the realities of long-term program development. Without a commitment to add this component to a broad range of undergraduate, graduate, and professional development programs, it is difficult to see how substantial movement toward social competence goals can take place.

Program Dissemination

An additional way to build a critical mass of knowledge is to promote the sharing of local examples of successful, or even unsuccessful, program development efforts. The action-research cycle presented in Exhbit 3.1 provides a framework for conducting and documenting social problem solving and other social competence and health promotion interventions, or structures for coordinating services. It can be used to document and share action-research findings to allow a buildup of practical implementation and evaluation technology for school-based researchers, practitioners, and administrators (Elias & Branden, 1988). Indeed, too much valuable information is lost from the knowledge base because it does not fit the canons, or outlets, of traditional scientific research and professional journals.

Traditional methods are set up to test carefully existing knowledge and determine its range of accuracy. But, as Thomas Kuhn (1970) has pointed out, traditional research and action can accommodate only a limited range of phenomena, and these phenomena tend to be tangible, controllable, and simplifiable. The world of action research is quite different, as is the world in which most of us live. Research that is likely to contribute to valid SPS interventions, for example, requires an emphasis on both person and setting levels, because it is desirable to incorporate in a design not only individuals' competencies but also the ongoing capacity of settings to promote development of the competencies among setting inhabitants. Accordingly, both researchers and program developers and disseminators might wish to (1) study variations of the relevance of SPS skills in different environments and populations with different cultural and ethnic mixes, (2) conduct analyses of the differential impact of programs on subgroups of recipient populations, (3) specify and study the impact of implementation conditions and processes on outcomes, and (4) articulate the processes through which change is believed to be mediated in order to examine how well a program or service component follows the anticipated path. Outlets and forums that reflect realistic application contexts must be developed, used, and spread.

This book is an example of a program dissemination activity. It contains historical and research-based information, as well as an explication of a variety of interventions, procedures, and examples that can serve as an impetus to the enhancement of others' efforts. But other forms of dissemination are required, especially those that support interactive formats or types of on-line communication that are more current than books and journals. Some examples include newsletters, resource exchange directories, toll-free telephone numbers, teleconferencing, and electronic bulletin boards and computer-based mail systems. Regardless of the specific format, meeting the challenge of having a broad-based impact on social problem solving and related skills will require building propensities and capacities for sharing observations, adaptations, extensions, problems, and solutions encountered during the program development and implementation process.

Leadership

The kind of leadership that will be required if prevailing coordination, training, and program dissemination practices are to be changed can be characterized as bold, visionary, determined, and inspiring. Leadership of this kind will be needed in graduate education, professional training, supervision, and credentialing, as well as in educational administration and policy making. A weak link in any of these areas creates additional setbacks and places roadblocks in the path of achieving the goals noted earlier. We cannot afford the continuation of narrow, turf-protecting perspectives, because too many lives will be sacrificed as children "fall through the cracks." The leader who seeks to join disciplines and combine foci must keep a picture of the children to be helped in the forefront if the kind of wasteful disorganization shown in Figure 1.1 is to be diminished.

Thus, it must be emphasized that the commitment of leaders to addressing the content areas of social problem solving and other social and health competencies is not sufficient to ensure success. Approaches related to action research must be advanced in tandem with leadership in placing content related to children's social development on the agenda of schools and collaborating settings. The history of the ISA-SPS Project and related ones shows that it is the synergy of such collaborative models that holds out the promise of creating potent and enduring effects on schools and students (Combs, 1988; Comer, 1987; Schorr, 1988).

Conclusion

There can be no illusion of complacency as we confront the problems of children and adolescents and the challenges facing our educational system. The contribution of every school-based professional must be rethought, and sustained, innovative commitments must be made. Action research offers a methodology that can help to generate exciting discoveries and lead research, practice, and policy in directions that can have a significant positive impact on the social competence and psychoeducational functioning of children and adolescents. SPS skills are an important aspect of children's ability to function successfully, and they represent a promising launching pad and rallying point for school-based action-research efforts. The example of the ISA-SPS Project is intended to provide tangible and specific assistance to current and future leaders in a variety of fields who believe that new, well-coordinated, and comprehensive approaches are needed to resolve the problems of our schools and our youth.

Development of the ISA-SPS Elementary Curriculum Through Action Research

Time Period	Action Steps	Inputs for Subsequent Decision Making

Year 1 (Jan.–June 1980)	I. *Program Directions*
	1. *Curriculum*
	Implement selected lessons from AWARE book with SPS steps as framework
	2. *Training*
	Lessons coled by CMHC educator-clinician
	II. *Evaluation Design*
	2 *E*, 3 *C* fourth-grade classrooms
		I. *Research*
		1. *Formative*
		  a. More than 90 percent of children enjoy lessons
		  b. Positive reactions from teachers
		2. *Summative*
		  a. Ninety-five percent of children report improved coping
		  b. Eighty percent of children try to help others with problems
		  c. Self-report of SPS use in and out of school is high
		  d. Significant *E* vs. *C* improvement in interpersonal sensitivity, considering consequences
		  e. Significant *E* vs. *C* improvement in expected ability to resolve problems and use of prosocial, personally initiated strategies
		  f. Significant change in teachers' and consultants' ability to facilitate SPS
		  g. No significant shift in alternative thinking and planning
		  h. Observed carry-over of SPS is low
		II. *Environmental Press*
		1. *Schools*
		  a. Parents pressure superintendent to expand program to all four elementary schools
		  b. Concern with middle school adjustment; priority to continue program in fifth grade
		2. *CMHC*
		  a. Desire school program with wider impact
		  b. Mandate for visible, evaluated prevention
		3. *University*
		  a. Design possibilities enhanced by larger sample
		  b. More settings in which to train students in applied and community-based research and service delivery
		4. *Funding Sources*
		  a. School funding to partially support added CMHC consultant time
		  b. University Research Council to partially support experimental evaluation research

Year 2
1980–81

I. *Program Directions*
1. *Revised Curriculum*
   a. Instructional phase to teach all steps
   b. Application phase for carry-over
   c. Sequential presentation of SPS steps
   d. Separate fourth- and fifth-grade curricula
   e. Introduce "Inside/Out" videotapes, grade 5
   f. Retain role-playing, story vignettes
2. *Revised Training*
   In-service workshops and in-class predoctoral consultants to teachers

II. *Evaluation Design*
Two schools with instructional phase in fall, application phase in spring; two schools with no program in fall, instructional phase in spring

I. *Research*
1. *Formative*
   a. More than 90 percent of children enjoy lessons, especially videotapes and role-playing
   b. Positive reactions from teachers, administrators
   c. Schools with both phases more positive than schools with instructional phase only
   d. More structure requested for application phase
   e. Especially in larger groups, some children rarely participate
   f. Some groups appear immature—"not ready" for group format
   g. Special education teachers pilot lessons, find children highly responsive
2. *Summative*
   a. Seventy-five percent of children report improved coping
   b. Seventy-three percent of children try to help others with problems
   c. Nearly all children report using SPS in at least one out-of-class setting
   d. Significant E vs. C improvement in interpersonal sensitivity; other data not explored in detail
   e. Teachers shift significantly toward highly facilitative modes of problem solving as a function of training
   f. Observed carry-over good in some classes, poor in others

II. *Environmental Press*
1. *Schools*
   a. Meeting mandate for family life/health curriculum in schools
   b. Maintain quality control, ownership of program
   c. Encourage positive parent attitudes about, and involvement in, SPS activities
   d. Follow-up on how trained children adapt to middle school
   e. Low middle school faculty morale
2. *CMHC*
   a. Facilitate school ownership of program
   b. Balance quality control with expansion of involvement, parent contacts

Time Period	Action Steps	Inputs for Subsequent Decision Making
		c. Acquire funding to support continued effort
		d. Provide services to special education (at-risk, in-need) children
		3. *University*
		a. Follow-up of transition to middle school
		b. Continue assessment for longitudinal study
		c. Evaluate impact of SPS on special education children
		d. Provide training experiences for seminar students
		e. Acquire funding for continued involvement and analysis of data already collected
		4. *Funding Sources*
		a. Reduced availability of federal and foundation funds but some monies for prevention if research has clear relevance to mental health and understanding of psychopathology and coping with stress
		b. Cutbacks on school-based funding supporting CMHC consultation
		c. University Research Council partially supporting study of transition to middle school
Year 3 1981–82	I. *Program Directions* 1. *Revised Curriculum* a. Add lessons on group building b. Add inserts on "special teaching considerations" c. Structured, twelve-lesson application phase 2. *Revised Training* a. Series of workshops for master teachers, one in each elementary school and middle school b. "Parents' nights" fea-	I. *Research* 1. *Formative* a. Very strong, positive curriculum feedback from teachers, grades 4 and 5 b. Special education children require lessons on self-control skills and group cohesiveness, interpersonal trust c. Uneven use of application phase by teachers d. Teachers want more contact with project staff e. Administrators satisfied with project staff contacts f. Teachers request flexible format, indexing of curricula 2. *Summative* a. Middle school transition reported by teachers to be "smooth" b. Use of SPS by sixth-grade children steadily declined over the year in the assessment of follow-up programming

turing "Footsteps" videotapes

c. Contributions to Hazelwood P.T.O. newsletter

II. *Evaluation Design*

1. Monitor transition and adaptation of new sixth graders to middle school

2. Formative evaluation of special curriculum with elementary ED and PI classes

3. Continue baseline and monitoring of data collection, grades 4 and 5; vary instructional set in group assessment (explicit SPS set or general set to provide information about children their age)

4. Assess naturalistic family problem solving and relationship to children's school competence, sample in grades 2 and 5

c. Sixth-grade children use SPS in response to prompts, but not spontaneously

d. Normal and clinical fourth- and fifth-grade groups differentiated on SPS scores for interpersonal sensitivity, expectancies for outcome, and locus of control for problem resolution

e. Sixth graders identify five major middle school stressors: smoking and substance abuse, peer inclusion, dealing with authority, fears about peer pressure, logistics of new school

f. Girls and boys differ in prioritizing of problem areas

II. *Environmental Press*

1. *Schools*

a. Economic cutbacks impair teacher morale

b. Class size increased to thirty; increased use of mainstreaming, resource rooms for classified children

c. Some highly trained teachers are shifted out of grades 4 and 5

d. Parent concerns about middle school transition

e. School board requesting middle school follow-up

f. Failure to stabilize schedules, staffing until Sept. 1982

g. Meeting mandates for family life/health, talented and gifted; school board approved SPS as a way to meet family life mandate in grades K-5 and 7

2. *CMHC*

a. Pressure for direct clinical services

b. Concern for balancing quality control with expansion of coverage to more at-risk and identified children

c. Funding received from William T. Grant Foundation

3. *University*

a. Maintenance of quality control and researchable program

b. Need for special education and middle school comparison groups

c. Analysis of family research and data from years 2 and 3

d. Develop and evaluate middle school follow-up

e. Provide training opportunities for graduate and undergraduate students

f. Funding received from National Institute of Mental Health

Time Period	Action Steps	Inputs for Subsequent Decision Making
		4. *Funding Sources*
		a. Focus on action-research process
		b. Theme of "improving social awareness"
		c. Focus on special education children
		d. Microprocess studies
		e. Replication of elementary school training
		f. Study linkages between CMHC, parents, schools

Program Evaluation Plan for an SPS Unit

Program evaluation for the UMDNJ-CMHC at Piscataway Social Problem Solving Unit is the responsibility of the unit director, John F. Clabby, as per standard practice. Consultation to the SPS Unit concerning program evaluation is provided jointly by the ISA-SPS Project research office at Rutgers University, directed by Maurice J. Elias and Michael A. Gara of the UMDNJ-CMHC at Piscataway. (Hereafter, this collaboration will be referred to when the term "consultation team" is used.) The following procedures for program evaluation have been developed based on Joint Commission on the Accreditation of Hospital Organizations (JCAHO) guidelines for decentralized, unit-based quality assurance and are designed to bring the SPS Unit into a position of compliance with those guidelines and with others that can reasonably be expected to be applied to the work and mission of that program.

Procedures

1. All program evaluation activities of the SPS Unit will be drawn from the document *Tools for Action Research*. This document contains a compendium of approved, scientifically reliable instruments and procedures that can be used to provide quality assurance information for a wide variety of SPS Unit activities and services.

a. Use of instruments and procedures not presently in the *Tools for Action Research*, or modifications of the contents contained therein, will be acceptable only upon amendment of the document to include those additional instruments and procedures. To make such an amendment, an individual or team will present the proposed change to a scientific/review meeting, after which the *Tools for Action Research* document will be modified if the change is deemed appropriate.

2. The director of the SPS Unit will designate a staff member as having evaluation liaison responsibilities. This person will assist SPS Unit service and administrative staff in linking the quality assurance and information needs of the SPS Unit, school districts, and other service recipients with the procedures and instruments contained in the *Tools for Action Research*.

a. The evaluation liaison person will ensure that service delivery arrangements as described in letters of agreement include a contracted evaluation plan (CEP). The CEP will specify whether or not formal program evaluation is required or expected. If formal evaluation is to occur, the CEP will contain time-framed, measurable objectives linked to indices in the *Tools for Action Research*. CEPs also will specify the resources devoted to quality assurance activities needed to carry out the plan. (Note that the resources include the money, staff, and materials needed to carry out various assessments.)

b. The evaluation liaison person will gather all CEPs and meet with the consultation team to ensure that the CEPs that are submitted are methodologically feasible and appropriate for their slated goals. The review of CEPs should occur prior to finalization of service delivery arrangements and contracts.

c. The evaluation liaison person will work with SPS Unit site leaders and school consultants to coordinate the logistics of data gathering and the subsequent disposition of the data, working with the consultation team as necessary.

d. The evaluation liaison person, working with the SPS Unit director, will have the responsibility of developing a procedure for periodic review of the CEPs. This procedure will include monitoring the progress of the attainment of interim goals and bringing difficulties or discrepancies to the attention of relevant SPS Unit staff members; the consultation team also will be informed once problems are clarified and new directions are outlined. This procedure should be documented in writing with copies on file at the SPS Unit and with the consultation team.

3. The consultation team will provide consultation to the SPS Unit concerning data processing, analysis, and preparation, as well as the formation of CEPs submitted for review.

   a. In September of each year, the consultation team will conduct an in-service session for SPS Unit staff to review the *Tools for Action Research,* the overall procedures and plan for SPS Unit quality assurance, and the record of performance from the previous year's CEPs.

   b. The consultation team will conduct an additional in-service program for the evaluation liaison staff member and designated members of the SPS Unit administrative staff.

   c. The consultation team will initiate procedures with the SPS Unit to ensure compliance with the CEP; it also will have the option of requiring specific assessments, including those not previously included in the *Tools for Action Research,* which are required to meet external policy or funding mandates to the UMDNJ-CMHC at Piscataway or to Rutgers University.

   d. The consultation team will be available to assist the SPS Unit in the event of failure to meet interim goals as specified in the CEPs.

   e. The consultation team will work with the evaluation liaison person and the director of the SPS Unit to coordinate the action-research opportunities of the ISA-SPS Project with the program evaluation activities of the SPS Unit.

4. In June of each year, the CEP for the SPS Unit will be reviewed, amended as determined, and instituted for a subsequent year.

Using Social Problem Solving as a Critical Thinking Guide for the Media

Objectives

1. To provide practice in using the eight social problem-solving steps.
2. To encourage carry-over of the SPS approach to such real-life experiences as viewing videotapes, films, or advertising.
3. To illustrate that most successful endeavors, including the production of video programming, are the result of conscious problem-solving thinking.

Leader's Guide

If relevant, review any previous SPS lessons. It is important to take advantage of this opportunity to have the students overlearn key SPS skills.

State the goals of today's lesson. We need to deal with the fact that we are often in situations where someone is trying to persuade us to a certain point of view, so we need to be active listeners and viewers.

-   A newspaper ad for a television set may be designed to get us interested in going to a certain store so that we will buy not only that product but other products as well.

- Art designers for music tapes, discs, and videotapes are hired to create covers that will get us to purchase the product.
- Individuals who sell automobiles cultivate a particular sales approach to get us into an agreeable, pleasant mood, so that we are in a positive mindset to purchase.
- Producers of alcoholic beverages use ways of encouraging us to consume alcohol such as securing the services of professional athletes or musicians to endorse their product.
- Potential employers, recruiters from the armed forces, and potential co-workers may present a point of view about their organization that encourages us to join up.
- Makers of video and film programs also have the goal of trying to move us to laugh, or cry, or think, or feel about certain issues in a particular way.

Encourage the class to nominate examples in which producers of videos, films, and advertisements tried to influence us in a particular way.

Discuss with the class the differences between being an active or a passive viewer of these messages.

A *passive* viewer can be characterized as someone who does not do much thinking on his or her own but tends to accept what is being shown without much question. An *active* viewer is a person who evaluates and judges, and who appropriately challenges what is being shown. Active viewers have the advantage over passive viewers in that their impressions are the result of their own thinking and not just a result of what is shown.

At this point it is important to relate to the students that a completed video or film is usually the result of careful problem solving. The makers start out with the goal of trying to create a certain impression on their audience. A maker of a cigarette ad wants us to leave the ad experience with the feeling that having a cigarette will relax us or help us to appear sophisticated. The maker of a video or film to be shown in a guidance or health class may want to impress us with the importance of talking to someone when we have a problem.

This begins the video critique portion of the lesson. If this lesson guide is used a number of times with a variety of video

programs, you probably will not have to do the extensive preparation that was just outlined. Instead, you might just summarize,
review, or accent the major points. Show the students the video and
then lead them through the following questions, which essentially
follow the eight-step SPS strategy.

1. *Look for signs of different feelings.*

Remember, video programs and movies often try to reach
your mind and heart in order to change your opinion or persuade
you. Let's take a closer look at the kinds of feelings that this program generated in you.

- How did you feel? What was it about the program that influenced you to feel that way?
- Talk about how each character affected your feelings. Elicit
  these reactions in a discussion and use this identification of
  feelings as the first SPS step.

2. *Tell yourself what the problem is.*

There is usually one central, social problem that emerges in
interesting, successful dramatic programs. Often it involves two or
more people in some sort of conflict: a father and a son or daughter,
two best friends, a teacher and a student, a boyfriend and girlfriend
or an employee and employer.

- What is the central problem on which the writer has chosen to
  concentrate?
- What does the writer want us to focus on the most?

3. *Decide on your goal.*

Let's review again what we think is the main goal the producers of this video had in mind.

4. *Think of as many solutions to the problem as you can.*

Here you may need to remind the students that the problem
we are talking about is how to produce the goal the producer had
in mind. A good producer always thinks of many possible solutions
regarding how a program's components can be embellished, de-
leted, changed, and so on. This is the time to encourage the students

to think like video makers. How could the program be done differently to create the desired impression?

- Build up the argument between the friends to make it more intense and more real.
- Show more examples of how a character continued to be taken advantage of.
- Show more scenes of the teacher.
- Change the hair styles.

5. *For each solution, think of all the things that might happen next.*

What are the consequences of the choices that the producers made? How do you feel the audience reacted as a result of the solutions that the director chose?

6. *Choose your best solution.*

Is there one main change that you think the producer could have made that would have caused a real difference in creating the impression that you want? Explain.

7. *Plan it and make a final check.*

How well planned was the program? Would you have planned it differently? Do you think each of the actors planned all their words? If not, what scenes and individuals are you referring to? Would you have chosen a different setting? What are the factors that need to be considered in planning such a program?

- Find a site, such as a restaurant or school, in a good location.
- Keep within the budget.
- Select the right actors.
- Plan the wardrobe. Would you have done it differently? Why?
- Make sure that the video is not too short or too long for the allotted time.
- Plan the music. How important is the music? How would different kinds of music at different points affect the video?

What are some obstacles that might emerge during the process of putting together a program, for example, an actors' strike, a director becoming ill, or a disagreement between the director and the producer?

8. *Try it and rethink it.*

Ask the students to recall what they think the goal of the production was.

Ask the class to rate the work of the director with regard to how successful he or she was in creating the intended impression, on a scale of 1 to 10:

0   1   2   3   4   5   6   7   8   9   10

This production did not create   This production was very suc-
that impression in me.   cessful in creating that impres-
                                      sion in me.

Ask the class to rate particular actors on how successful they were. Remind the student that the rating should be based not on whether they liked the actor's character but whether the actor did a good job of reaching his or her goal of portraying an irritated high school senior, an optimistic job applicant, and so on:

0   1   2   3   4   5   6   7   8   9   10

The actor was absolutely unsuc-   The actor was really successful
cessful in portraying the   at portraying the character.
character.

As always, reinforce the appropriate contributions of the students with verbal compliments given now and throughout the lesson. Close with a summary of the major themes of critical thinking that emerged. Encourage the students to use their training in social problem solving in all areas of their lives.

ASPIRE Lesson Plans: "Decide on Your Goal"

ASPIRE Lesson 14: "Decide on Your Goal (A)"

Objectives

1. To facilitate a calming experience
2. To review the first two SPS steps, "look for signs of different feelings" and "tell yourself what the problem is"
3. To introduce the third SPS step, "decide on your goal"
4. To provide an active video viewing experience where the students can think in terms of goal setting

Materials

1. A poster showing the steps "look for signs of different feelings," "tell yourself what the problem is," and "decide on your goal"
2. Video players and a television monitor
3. The "On the Level" videotape program "Who Am I?"
4. SPS video worksheets 3: *What are the goals in "Who Am I?"*

Lesson Outline

1. Calming—Keep Calm (five minutes)
2. Review of the first two steps, "look for signs of different feelings" and "tell yourself what the problem is" (three minutes)

3. Introducing step 3, "decide on your goal" (five minutes)
4. Orienting the students as to what they can expect to see in "Who Am I?" and how to use SPS worksheet 3 (five minutes)
5. Active reviewing of "Who Am I?" (fifteen minutes)
6. Having students share worksheet responses (ten minutes)
7. Summary of the lesson (one minute)
8. Closing with the Keep Calm experience (one minute)

Leader's Guide

1. Facilitate an experience of Keep Calm
2. Review step 1, "look for signs of different feelings" and step 2, "tell yourself what the problem is." Emphasize the useful synthesis of these two steps as a first way to react to difficulty. Use an example like "I feel *rushed* because I'm late for class." Elicit an example from the class.
3. Introduce the new step, "decide on your goal." Many of us can recall situations in which we were energized or agitated by a problem and quickly moved into action without having a clear notion of where we wanted to go! We have problems when we don't take the time to choose a goal. We also may have difficulties if we try to pursue a number of goals simultaneously. For example: "I'd like to get a part-time job where I don't have to work on the weekends *and* I'd like to work with my friends." Generate a brief discussion with the class about how this last statement might be narrowed down.
4. Orient the students to the "Who Am I?" videotape and SPS worksheet 3. You might say, "The program we'll see is called 'Who Am I?' It's about a high school student, Tyrone, who is under a lot of pressure. It seems that everyone has a goal in mind with regard to what Tyrone should concentrate on. His parents want something for him, his boss wants something, and Tyrone has another goal in mind. It's rough for Tyrone to know which direction he should take because of all of these goals.'

    Let the class know that you want them to view the videotape in a certain way, and that you have a goal in mind for them. You'd like them to watch for the different goals that different people have for Tyrone.

Distribute copies of SPS worksheet 3, *"What are the Goals in 'Who Am I'?"* and go over it with the students. Ask them to write down the goals that might go there. Let them know that there may be differences among the class as to the answers and that this is fine.

5.   At this time, show the video.

Teacher's Tip—The following summary is provided for your convenience.

Story Summary

Tyrone works as a dishwasher at a local club. He works so late that it's hard for him to get out of bed the next day for school. His parents are concerned about his hours. At school his friends and a teacher increase the pressure. Tyrone cuts school, goes home, and runs into his father. They have a disagreement. Tyrone's Dad starts comparing Tyrone unfavorably to his older brother, who is deceased. Later on at work, Tyrone starts to daydream about being a star saxophone player at the club. The club owner seems to accept Tyrone's interest in the sax and "fires him for his own good." When he gets home, Tyrone sees that his parents are putting his brother's things away and they realize that it was wrong of them to compare the two of them.

6.   Students share their worksheet responses. Elicit from the class the various goals that Tyrone was trying to handle. It may be helpful to use the worksheet directly. You may want to duplicate the worksheet on the board with you or a student recording the class response.

7.   Summary of the lesson. Here we are looking for someone to be able to comment on the problems that might exist if too many or no goals are set.

8.   Facilitate a Keep Calm experience.

Teacher's Name:_____ Date:_____

SPS Video Worksheet

What are the Goals in "Who Am I?"

Name a goal that Tyrone's parents have for him.

Goal

_____
_____
_____

Name a goal that Tyrone's boss might have for him.

Goal

_____
_____
_____

Name a goal that Tyrone may have for himself.

Goal

_____
_____
_____

ASPIRE Lesson 15: "Decide on Your Goal (B)"

Objectives

1. To facilitate a calming experience
2. To review the first three SPS steps, "look for signs of different feelings," "tell yourself what the problem is," and "decide on your goal"
3. To have the students use these three steps to begin solving some hypothetical social problems

Materials

1. A poster showing the first three steps
2. A completed video worksheet 3: *"What are the goals in 'Who Am I?'"*
3. A steps worksheet: Help Mark rank-order his goals

Lesson Outline

1. Classwide use of Keep Calm
2. Reviewing the first three steps and in particular step 3, "decide on your goal"
3. Recalling with the class the main points of the video "Who Am I?"
4. Having the class use the first three steps and situations from "Who Am I?" to identify a goal after (a) looking for signs of different feelings and (b) telling themselves what the problem is
5. Additional activity: "Help Mark with his goals"
6. Summary of the lesson
7. Closing the Keep Calm experience

Leader's Guide

1. Focus the class on the task at hand by leading them through Keep Calm
2. Have one of the students read aloud the first three steps, "look for signs of different feelings," "tell yourself what the problem is," and "decide on your goal." Discuss how difficulties are handled much better when you pick a goal and can stick with it and not get distracted. You could offer an example, as you did during the last lesson, of what the experience is like when you are pursuing too many goals at the same time. This example, or others you may choose, may best be presented by diagramming the situation on the blackboard.
3. Using the last lesson's summary and SPS video worksheet 3— *What are the Goals in "Who Am I?"*—review with the students the events that took place in the Video "Who Am I?" Proceed to a more specific discussion of goals. It's best if you can elicit this material from the class. A good synopsis might look like this: "Last time, we saw a video program about a high school student named Tyrone. It seemed as if everybody had a goal for him! Discuss the pressure Tyrone may be having in trying not only to deal with his own goals but to achieve the goals others have for him.

    a.   Tyrone's parents' goal: that Tyrone finish high school
    b.   Tyrone's boss's goal: that Tyrone do a good job cleaning
         the dishes
    c.   Tyrone's own goal: to be a professional saxophone player
4. Have the students use the first three SPS steps to work through
    some of Tyrone's difficulties.

Situation 1 (Present this to the class). Tyrone is a high school student. He's also been working long hours as a dishwasher in a local
club, partly because he likes the live jazz music. Because he's been
so tired, he's been sleeping too late and coming to school very late.
His friends and his teachers have been giving him a real hard time
about it.
    a.   Aside from feeling tired, how else might Tyrone be *feeling?*
         (Have this written on the chalkboard.)
    b.   Have the class put his *problem* into words. "Tyrone feels
         ____ because _____." (Again, this should be written
         on the board.)
    c.   What do you think could be Tyrone's main *goal?* (Use of
         the blackboard is encouraged.)

Situation 2 (Read this with the class). Later on, at work, Tyrone
daydreams about becoming a star saxophone player. His boss learns
that *this is a goal* for Tyrone and talks to him about it. His boss
fires Tyrone because he believes that this is in Tyrone's best interest.
    a.   If you were Tyrone, how would you be *feeling?*
    b.   Complete this sentence to express what Tyrone's *problem*
         is: "Tyrone feels ____ because _____."
    c.   What is Tyrone's *goal?*

Situation 3 (Present and work on this situation). Imagine that it is
two years later and Tyrone has graduated from high school. He's
gotten his old job back as a dishwasher and every once in a while
he gets a great chance to practice the saxophone on stage with the
band. But he makes very little money and has been unable to buy
a car or even think about having his own apartment one day. His
father has just offered Tyrone a very good-paying job with his company but it's a job with hours that would not allow Tyrone to

practice the saxophone. Tyrone has to decide by tonight what he's going to do.

    a.   Imagine that you were Tyrone. How would you be *feeling* about this?

    b.   Finish this *problem* statement: "Tyrone feels ___ because _____."

    c.   Select a *goal* for Tyrone.

5.   *Additional Activity: "Help Mark with his goals"*

Imagine that it is late Friday evening. Mark is thinking about what he'd like to do on Saturday and he comes up with these goals:

> Get my hair cut
> Work at my regular restaurant job all day
> Buy some new clothes
> Make plans with some friends for Saturday night
> Finish the work I was supposed to do at home
> (Other goals the class might suggest)

See if the class can come up with other goals that Mark might have in mind. Our list only provides a few examples. If your students can come up with ideas of their own, all the better.

Generate a discussion of how Mark would feel or how they would feel if they tried to accomplish *all* of these things on Saturday.

Ask the students what *strategy* could be used to deal with the situation of having too many goals. Certainly a favorite strategy to start with would be to decide *what are the most important goals*. (Prioritize or rank order the goals).

Distribute SPS worksheet A, "Help Mark Rank Order His Goals," and/or SPS worksheet B, "Prioritizing My Goals," to the class. Worksheet A offers students a chance to prioritize a given set of goals, while worksheet B allows students to list and prioritize their own goals for Saturday.

Have the class complete the worksheets. Once everyone has finished, ask students to share how they reordered Mark's goals or prioritized their own goals.

SPS Worksheet A: Help Mark Rank Order His Goals

There are many goals that Mark has set for himself for this Saturday. Based upon your own experience, number these goals in the order of importance. The most important goal should get a ranking of "1."

_____ Get my hair cut
_____ Work at my regular restaurant job all day
_____ Buy some new clothes
_____ Make plans with some friends for Saturday night
_____ Finish the work I was supposed to do at home

SPS Worksheet B: Prioritizing My Goals

What could you do on a Saturday? First list all of the possibilities and then rank order these goals.

_____ _____
_____ _____
_____ _____
_____ _____

6. Summarize the main point of the lesson: the importance of being able to really identify what it is that you want to have happen: your *goal*.

7. Lead the class through a Keep Calm experience.

Appendix E

ASPIRE Vocational Application Lesson Plan: "Temper Control at Work"

ASPIRE Lesson 31: "Using Problem Solving to Control Your Temper At Work"

Objectives

1. To generate examples of situations that can trigger the students to lose their temper at work
2. To practice using social problem solving and quieting relaxation to maintain control

Materials

Additional materials are not needed.

Lesson Outline

1. Review the last lesson.
2. Discuss examples of situations and comments that others make that can trigger us to lose our temper.
3. Review Keep Calm as a way to maintain control in order to reach a goal.

4. Use social problem solving to work through examples of situations that would prompt an anger response.
5. Summarize.

Leader's Guide

1. Review the last lesson's major themes: the importance of accepting and profiting from employee evaluations and constructive criticisms.
2. Introduce the class to the main theme of today's lesson: that every one of us who works will have to deal with situations where someone angers us with a comment or behavior. In most cases, workers would like to control their tempers in order to keep their jobs and yet would like to be able to make sensible, appropriate responses. How can some of the SPS techniques that we have been learning help you to prevent your temper from controlling you? Ask the class to think about work difficulties and to offer examples of situations that have pushed them toward inappropriately losing their tempers. This is a delicate issue, because in a group session, a student may admit that he or she lost control, got into a fight, and subsequently lost a job, but may deny caring about it. Today's lesson rests on the premise that the student stands to lose a valued job by losing his or her temper. We *all* have situations where we need to express our anger; it is how we do so that makes the difference.
3. Elicit what strategies the students have used to control their tempers and list them on the board. If slow breathing emerges as an example, elaborate on its usefulness. If it has not emerged, nominate it as a technique.
4. Use the SPS approach to work through alternative ways of dealing with the problem situations that the class has nominated. Here are some additional work situations that you can use to promote the discussion.

Situation 1. You are carrying a case of motor oil out to the gas island at your uncle's service station where you work on weekends. As you walk out of the door, the box breaks and the cans of oil go rolling all over the ground. Tom, the person who just joined you on the shift, says, "What a jerk. No wonder the only place you could get a job was with your uncle."

    a.   How do you feel?_____
    b.   What is your goal?_____
    c.   Generate alternative ways of handling this:_____

_____

Situation 2. You've been working as a cashier at the supermarket for about a year now and you're doing very well. This evening, however, you gave someone more money than they should have gotten and you came up short at the end of the night. Mark, one of your supervisors, says, "Hey, stupid, what are you trying to do, give money away?!" Everyone else in the room seems to be looking at you.

    a.   How do you feel?_____
    b.   What is the problem?_____
    c.   What is your goal?_____
    d.   Generate alternative solutions:_____

Situation 3. You're new at the job of being a busboy at a restaurant in town. You work on weekend nights clearing away the dirty dishes from customers' tables. Your customers seem to enjoy talking to you as you clear their dishes. You go back into the kitchen and Andrew, the headwaiter, who is your supervisor, says to you, "Hey, won't you ever learn to shut up and stop talking to the customers?!"

    a.   How do you feel?_____
    b.   What is the problem?_____
    c.   Name your goal._____
    d.   Generate alternative solutions:_____

Situation 4. For about six months, you've been working at a day-care center helping young children after school, from 3:30 P.M. to 6:00 P.M., with your friend Janet. You were sick yesterday and had called in to your supervisor. Today, Sandra, one of your co-workers, tells you in a loud, sarcastic voice, "Too bad you came in today. We got so much more accomplished with you not being here yesterday." Your friend Janet comes over to you and says, "I can't believe you. You let her get away with comments like that all the time. If you're going to be such a baby I don't want to have anything to do with you!"

    a.   Who are you upset with most?_____

    b.   Why?_____

    c.   How do you feel?_____

    d.   Describe the main problem that you want to work on:____

                _____

    e.   What is your goal?_____

    f.   Generate as many solutions to the problem as you can:____

                _____

5.   Propose the following question to the class: "If someone gave you a hard time at work, what kind of difference would it make to your solution if the following people were there?"

    a.   Your girlfriend or boyfriend? Discuss.

    b.   Your father? Discuss.

    c.   Your mother? Discuss.

    d.   Friends from school? Discuss.

6.   Summarize the main theme of today's lesson:

    a.   All workers feel pressure to get angry and even lose tempers.

    b.   A situation that may push one person to get quite angry may not push another person to get angry, and vice versa.

    c.   We all experience situations where letting our tempers control us puts a job that we really like at risk.

Talk about some of the techniques that the class mentioned as having been useful in anger control.

Close the lesson by complimenting the class for their participation.

A Lesson Plan
to Introduce "FIG-TESPN"
to Middle School Students

The objectives of the FIG TESPN lesson are:

1. To introduce students to the social decision-making and social problem-solving steps
2. To provide students with a centralizing concept so that the SPS steps can be remembered as a whole rather than as discrete steps
3. To provide students and teachers with a prompt for problem solving

Procedure

1. Have handouts of FIG TESPN and a large poster of the FIG TESPN steps written out fully.
2. Review the readiness skills and how students have used them.
3. Tell the students: "The purpose of today's lesson is to introduce FIG TESPN, but I am not really sure who or what FIG TESPN is. FIG TESPN helps you solve problems and figure out how to do things in the best way possible. FIG lets you use your own resources and abilities rather than doing it for you. It helps you to think before acting and to decide the best thing to do to get what you want. FIG comes on the scene when feelings become strong and people have difficulty deciding what to do." (FIG TESPN = social decision making.)

4. Generate from the students examples of who FIG TESPN might be like. If the students are having difficulty, discuss who provides guidance and helps others succeed without acting directly for them. If students cannot generate examples, prompt them with examples such as sports coaches, managers, movie characters, or rock concert producers.
5. Encourage students to develop their own image of who FIG TESPN is like. Have them discuss this with the class.
6. Distribute FIG TESPN handouts. Explain that FIG can help them solve problems by reminding them to picture these ideas to themselves. Have students read the FIG TESPN steps and review the relevant vocabulary and concepts.
7. Model a problem-solving situation using FIG's steps. Provide a semipersonal situation in which you had to solve a problem, make a decision, or resolve a conflict with someone.
8. Assign students to think about situations in which FIG TESPN's steps could be helpful to them. Review these situations at the beginning of the next lesson.

Activities

NOTE: It is important for students to be actively involved with FIG TESPN; the following activities strongly reinforce the concept and personalize it.

1. Have students draw pictures or computer-generated images of FIG TESPN.
2. Have students write stories about FIG TESPN: how FIG came to be, how FIG helped solve someone's problem, and so on.
3. Have a poster of different images of FIG TESPN and the eight steps in the room for the students to refer to in subsequent lessons and/or have them make their own copies of the steps in the handout.
4. Have students draw problem-solving comic strips involving FIG TESPN.
5. Show the Walt Disney version of the film *Pinocchio* and discuss comparisons between FIG TESPN and Jiminy Cricket; the

same can be done with excerpts from *Star Wars,* comparing FIG with Obi-wan Kenobe.

6. Give a writing assignment with a beginning (feeling and problem) and an end. Have the students fill in the middle of the story using FIG TESPN (that is, connecting the beginning and end through use of the social decision-making steps).

Tips for Teachers

1. Encourage students to be imaginative in their conception of FIG. Try to avoid priming them with preconceived images in order to ensure that they develop their own images. This will enhance their use of FIG.

2. Avoid referring to FIG as "he" or "she" because FIG should be universal.

3. Gradually move toward using FIG as a prompt for decision making and problem solving. For example, "How could FIG help you with this?"

References

Achenbach, T., & Edelbrock, C. (1987). *Manual for the Youth Self-Report and Profile.* Burlington, VT: University of Vermont Department of Psychiatry.

Agency for Instructional Technology. (1990). *On the Level.* Bloomington, IN: Agency for Instructional Technology.

Allen, G. J., Chinsky, J. M., Larcen, S. W., Lochman, J. E., & Selinger, H. V. (1976). *Community psychology and the schools: A behaviorally oriented multi-level preventive approach.* Hillsdale, NJ: Erlbaum.

Asher-Shultz, N., Haboush, K., & Elias, M. J. (1987, October). *Preventive interventions in the middle school: A social-ecological perspective.* Paper presented at the annual Northeast Community Psychology Conference, Yale University, New Haven, CT.

Battistich, V., Elias, M. J., & Branden-Muller, L. (in press). Two school-based approaches to promoting children's social competence. In G. Albee, L. Bond, & T. Monsey (Eds.), *Improving children's lives: Global approaches to prevention.* Newbury Park, CA: Sage.

Baumrind, D. (1987). A developmental perspective on adolescent risk taking in contemporary America. In C. E. Irwin, Jr. (Ed.), *Adolescent social behavior and health: New directions for child development* (No. 37, pp. 93–126). San Francisco: Jossey-Bass.

Belsky, J. (1980). Child maltreatment: An ecological integration. *American Psychologist, 35,* 320–335.

Benard, B., Fafoglia, G., & Perone, J. (1987, February). Knowing what to do—and not to do—reinvigorates drug education. *Association for Supervision and Curriculum Development Curriculum Update,* pp. 1–12.

Bergmann, S., & Rudman, G. J. (1985). *Decision making skills for middle school students.* Washington, DC: National Education Association.

Billington, R. J., Washington, L. A., & Trickett, E. J. (1981). The research relationship in community research: An inside view from public school principals. *American Journal of Community Psychology, 9,* 461–480.

Bower, E. M. (1972). Education as a humanizing process and its relationship to other humanizing processes. In S. E. Golann & C. Eisdorfer (Eds.), *Handbook of community mental health.* New York: Appleton-Century-Crofts.

Branden-Muller, L. R., & Elias, M. J. (1991). Catalyzing the primary prevention revolution in the schools: The role of school psychologists. *Journal of Educational & Psychological Consultation, 2,* 73–88.

Bransford, J., Sherwood, R., Vye, N., & Rieser, J. (1986). Teaching thinking and problem solving: Research foundations. *American Psychologist, 41,* 1078–1089.

Brion-Meisels, S., & Selman, R. (1982). *Adolescent Issues Project— Adolescent Decisions Curriculum: Program manual, Decisions About Work, Decisions About Drug Use, Adolescent Development and Sexuality, People and Government, and Juvenile Law.* Boston, MA: Judge Baker Guidance Center.

Bronfenbrenner, U. (1979). Contexts of child rearing: Problems and prospects. *American Psychologist, 34,* 844–850.

Bronowski, J. (1973). *The ascent of man.* Boston: Little, Brown.

Camp, B. W., & Bash, M. S. (1985a). *Think aloud: Increasing social and cognitive skills—A problem-solving program for children. Classroom program grades 1–2.* Champaign, IL: Research Press.

Camp, B. W., & Bash, M. S. (1985b). *Think aloud: Increasing social and cognitive skills—A problem-solving program for children. Classroom program grades 3–4.* Champaign, IL: Research Press.

Camp, B. W., & Bash, M. S. (1985c). *Think aloud: Increasing social and cognitive skills—A problem-solving program for children. Classroom program grades 5-6.* Champaign, IL: Research Press.

Caplan, M. Z., Jacoby, C., Weissberg, R., & Grady, K. (1988). *The Positive Youth Development Program: A substance abuse prevention program for young adolescents.* New Haven, CT: Consultation Center of the Community Consultation Board; Connecticut Mental Health Center; Department of Psychiatry, Yale University School of Medicine, and Department of Psychology, Yale University.

Carnegie Council on Adolescent Development. (1989). *Turning points: Preparing American youth for the 21st century.* Washington, DC: Carnegie Corporation of New York.

Cartledge, G., & Milburn, J. (1980). *Teaching social skills to children.* Elmsford, NY: Pergamon Press.

Cartledge, G., & Milburn, J. (1986). *Teaching social skills to children* (2nd ed.). Elmsford, NY: Pergamon Press.

Center for Early Adolescence. (1988). *Before it's too late: Dropout prevention in the middle grades.* Carrboro, NC: Center for Early Adolescence.

Centers for Disease Control. (1988). *Guidelines for effective school health education to prevent the spread of AIDS* (DHHS Pub. No. CDC 88-8017). Atlanta: Centers for Disease Control.

Clabby, J. (1992). *ASPIRE: Adolescent Problem-Solving Interventions with Relaxation Exercises.* (Available from the University of Medicine and Dentistry of New Jersey, Community Mental Health Center at Piscataway, Social Problem-Solving Program, 240 Stelton Rd., Piscataway, NJ 08854)

Clabby, J. F., & Elias, M. J. (1986). *Teach your child decision making,* New York: Doubleday.

Clabby, J. F., & Elias, M. J. (1987–88). Your child can learn to make decisions. *PTA Today, 13,* 14–15.

Cohen, J. A., Brennan, C. D., & Sexton, B. (1984). *A social-cognitive approach to the prevention of adolescent substance abuse, intervention I: Sixth grade student curriculum: Project New Directions.* New Haven, CT: Consultation Center of the Connecticut Mental Health Center, Department of Psychiatry–Yale University School of Medicine and Community Consultation Board.

Combs, A. W. (1988). New assumptions for education reform. *Educational Leadership, 45*(5), 38–41.

Comer, J. (1987, March). New Haven's school-community connection. *Educational Leadership, 44*, 13–16.

Commins, W. W., & Elias, M. J. (in press). Institutionalization of mental health programs in organizational contexts: The case of elementary schools. *Journal of Community Psychology.*

Commission on the Prevention of Mental-Emotional Disabilities (1986). *The prevention of mental-emotional disabilities.* Alexandria, VA: National Mental Health Association.

Connell, D. B., Turner, R. R., & Mason, E. F. (1985). Summary of the findings of the School Health Education Evaluation: Health promotion effectiveness, implementation, and costs. *Journal of School Health, 55*, 316–323.

Consortium on the School-Based Promotion of Social Competence (in press). A guide to selecting prevention and social competence promotion programs for the schools. In J. Hawkins (Ed.), *Community-wide approaches to prevention of delinquency.* Washington, DC: Office of Juvenile Justice and Delinquency Prevention.

Consultation Center of the Connecticut Mental Health Center, Department of Psychiatry–Yale University School of Medicine and Community Consultation Board (1989). *Decision-making infusion: A supplement to a social-cognitive approach to the prevention of adolescent substance abuse, intervention I: Sixth grade.* New Haven, CT: The Consultation Center and the Westchester County Department of Community Mental Health.

Copple, C., Sigel, I., & Saunders, R. (1979). *Educating the young thinker.* New York: Van Nostrand Reinhold.

Cowen, E. L. (1980). The wooing of primary prevention. *American Journal of Community Psychology, 8*, 258–284.

Crabbe, A. (1989). The future problem solving program. *Educational Leadership, 46*, 27–29.

Davis, H. T., & Salasin, S. E. (1975). The utilization of evaluation. In E. L. Struening & M. Guttentag (Eds.), *Handbook of evaluation research* (Vol. 1). Newbury Park, CA: Sage.

Denham, S., & Almeida, M. C. (1987). Children's social problem-solving skills, behavioral adjustment, and interventions: A meta-analysis evaluating theory and practice. *Journal of Applied Developmental Psychology, 8,* 391-410.

Dewey, J. (1933). *How we think.* Lexington, MA: Heath.

Dodge, K. A., Pettit, G. S., McClaskey, C. L., & Brown, M. M. (1986). Social competence in children. *Monographs of the Society for Research in Child Development, 51.*

Dorman, G., Geldof, D., & Scarborough, B. (1984). *Living with 10-to-15-year-olds: A parent education curriculum.* Carrboro, NC: Center for Early Adolescence, University of North Carolina at Chapel Hill.

Duncker, K. (1945). On problem solving. *Psychological Monographs, 58*(5, Whole No. 270), 1-113.

D'Zurilla, T. (1986). *Problem-solving therapy: A social competence approach to clinical intervention.* New York: Springer.

D'Zurilla, T. J., & Goldfried, M. R. (1971). Problem solving and behavior modification. *Journal of Abnormal Psychology, 78,* 107-126.

Educational Leadership. (1988). Youth at risk. *45*(6), entire issue.

Elardo, P., & Cooper, M. (1977). *AWARE: Activities for social development.* Reading, MA: Addison-Wesley.

Elias, M. J. (1980). *Evaluation report for Project AWARE pilot study: January 1980–June 1980.* Middlesex, NJ: Middlesex Public Schools.

Elias, M. J. (1981). *Project AWARE: A curriculum program for teaching interpersonal problem prevention skills—Initial evaluation report for 1980-1981.* New Brunswick, NJ: Rutgers University.

Elias, M. J. (1983). Improving coping skills of emotionally disturbed boys through television-based social problem solving. *American Journal of Orthopsychiatry, 53,* 61-72.

Elias, M. J. (1987). Establishing enduring prevention programs: Advancing the legacy of Swampscott. *American Journal of Community Psychology, 15,* 539-553.

Elias, M. J. (1988). Living the good life under the decision tree. *Creative Living, 18,* 8-12.

Elias, M. J. (1989). Schools as a source of stress to children: An analysis of causal and ameliorative factors. *Journal of School Psychology, 27,* 393-407.

Elias, M. J. (1990a). Promoting social competence: Protective factors that promote positive life trajectories. In M. Green & R. Haggerty (Eds.), *Ambulatory Pediatrics* (4th ed.). Philadelphia: Saunders.

Elias, M. J. (1990b). The role of affect and social relationships in health behavior and school health curriculum and instruction. *Journal of School Health, 60,* 157–163.

Elias, M. J. (1991). A multi-level action research perspective on stress-related interventions. In M. Colten & S. Gore (Eds.), *Adolescent stress: Causes and consequences.* Hawthorne, NY: Aldine.

Elias, M. J., Beier, J. J., & Gara, M. A. (1989). Children's responses to interpersonal obstacles as a predictor of social competence. *Journal of Youth and Adolescence, 18,* 451–465.

Elias, M. J., & Branden, L. (1988). Primary prevention of behavioral and emotional problems in school-aged populations. *School Psychology Review, 17,* 581–592.

Elias, M. J., Branden-Muller, L., & Sayette, M. (1990, April). The Improving Social Awareness–Social Problem Solving Project: A school-based preventive program reaching beyond the school yard walls. In M. Greenberg (Chair), *Systems issues in the implementation of school-based mental health and prevention programs.* Symposium at the annual meeting of the American Education Research Association, Boston, MA.

Elias, M. J., Branden-Muller, L., & Sayette, M. (1991). Teaching the foundations of social decision making and problem solving in the elementary school: A curriculum-based approach which integrates emotional and cognitive processes. In J. Baron & R. Brown (Eds.), *Adolescent decision making.* Hillsdale, NJ: Erlbaum.

Elias, M. J., & Clabby, J. F. (1984a, August). *Action research and primary preventive services: An essential linkage.* Paper presented at the meeting of the American Psychological Association, Toronto, Canada.

Elias, M. J., & Clabby, J. F. (1984b). Integrating social and affective education into public school curriculum and instruction. In C. Maher, R. Illback, & J. Zins, (Eds.), *Organizational psychology in the schools: A handbook for professionals* (pp. 143–172). Springfield, IL: Thomas.

Elias, M. J., & Clabby, J. F. (1988). Teaching social decision making. *Educational Leadership, 45(6),* 52–55.

Elias, M. J., & Clabby, J. F. (1989). *Social decision-making skills: A curriculum guide for the elementary grades.* Rockville, MD: Aspen.

Elias, M. J., Clabby, J. F., & Hett, C. A. (in preparation). *Parenting with pride: Raising your children with thoughtfulness and self-respect.*

Elias, M. J., Gara, M., & Ubriaco, M. (1985). Sources of stress and support in children's transition to middle school: An empirical analysis. *Journal of Clinical Child Psychology, 14,* 112–118.

Elias, M. J., Gara, M., Ubriaco, M., Rothbaum, P., Clabby, J., & Schuyler, T. (1986). Impact of a preventive school problem-solving intervention on children's coping with middle-school stressors. *American Journal of Community Psychology, 14(3),* 259–275.

Elias, M. J., Rothbaum, P., & Gara, M. (1986). Social-cognitive problem solving in children: Assessing the knowledge and application of skills. *Journal of Applied Developmental Psychology, 7,* 77–94.

Elias, M. J., & Tobias, S. (1990). *Problem solving/decision making for social and academic success: A school-based approach.* Washington, DC: National Education Assocation.

Elias, M. J., & Weissberg, R. P. (1990). School-based social competence promotion as a primary prevention strategy: A tale of two projects. In R. Lorion (Ed.), *Protecting the children: Strategies for optimizing emotional and behavioral development.* (pp. 177–200). New York: Haworth.

Elkind, D. (1981). *The hurried child.* Reading, MA: Addison-Wesley.

Elliot, D., Ageton, S., Huizinga, D., Knowles, B., & Canter, R. (1983). *The prevalence and incidence of delinquent behavior: The National Youth Survey, Report No. 26.* Boulder, CO: Behavioral Research Institute.

Erikson, E. H. (1954). *Childhood and society.* New York: W. W. Norton.

Feldhusen, J. (1975). Problem solving and the concrete-abstract dimension. *Gifted Child Quarterly, 19,* 122–129.

Felner, R. D., Farber, S., & Primavera, J. (1983). Transitions and stressful life events: A model for primary prevention. In R. Felner, L. Jason, J. Moritsugu, & S. Farber (Eds.), *Prevention psychology: Theory, research and practice.* Elmsford, NY: Pergamon Press.

Feuerstein, R. (1980). *Instrumental enrichment.* Baltimore, MD: University Park Press.

Flavell, J. H. (1979). Metacognition and cognitive monitoring: A new area of cognitive-developmental inquiry. *American Psychologist, 34,* 906–911.

Ford, M. E. (1982). Social cognition and social competence in adolescence. *Developmental Psychology, 18,* 323–340.

Francescani, C. (1983). *A resource manual for the development and evaluation of special programs for exceptional students—Volume V-C: Affective curriculum for secondary emotionally handicapped students.* Tallahassee, FL: State of Florida Department of Education, Bureau of Education for Exceptional Students.

Gagne, R. M. (1975). *Essentials of learning for instruction.* Hillsdale, IL: Dryden Press.

George, P., & Oldaker, L. (1986). A national survey of middle school effectiveness. *Educational Leadership, 43,* 15–18.

Gibbs, J. T., Huang, L. N., and Associates (Eds.). (1989). *Children of color: Psychological interventions with minority youth.* San Francisco: Jossey-Bass.

Gilligan, C. (1987). Adolescent development reconsidered. In C. E. Irwin, Jr. (Ed.), *Adolescent social behavior and health: New Directions for Child Development* (No. 37, pp. 63–92). San Francisco: Jossey-Bass.

Godin, S., Carr-Kaffashan, L., & Moore-Hines, P. (1990). The development and management of prevention services within a comprehensive medical school–based, community mental health center. *Prevention in Human Services, 7*(2), 1–48.

Goldfried, M. R., & Davison, G. C. (1976). *Clinical behavior therapy.* Troy, MO: Holt, Rinehart, & Winston.

Goldfried, M. R., & D'Zurilla, T. J. (1969). A behavioral-analytic model for assessing competence. In C. D. Spielberger (Ed.), *Current topics in clinical and community psychology* (Vol. 1). San Diego, CA: Academic Press.

Greeno, J. G. (1980). Psychology of learning, 1960–1980: One participant's observations. *American Psychologist, 35,* 713–728.

Haboush, K. (1988). *An evaluation of student learning outcomes under a critical thinking social studies program.* Unpublished doctoral dissertation, Graduate School of Applied and Professional Psychology, Rutgers University, New Brunswick, NJ.

Haboush, K., & Elias, M. J. (in press). Infusing social decision making and problem solving into social studies and other academic areas in the middle school. In M. Elias (Ed.), *Social decision making in the middle school: Models for excellence.* Gaithersburg, MD: Aspen.

Harre, R. (1974). Some remarks on "rule" as a scientific concept. In T. Mischel (Ed.), *Understanding other persons.* Totowa, NJ: Rowman & Littlefield.

Higgins, J., & Thies, A. (1981). Problem-solving and social position among emotionally disturbed boys. *American Journal of Orthopsychiatry, 51,* 356–358.

Hord, S. M., Rutherford, W. L., Huling-Austin, L., & Hall, G. E. (1987). *Taking charge of change.* Alexandria, VA: Association for Supervision and Curriculum Development.

Houtz, J. C., & Feldhusen, J. F. (1975). Problem solving ability of disadvantaged elementary school children under four testing formats: A replicated experiment. *Psychology in the Schools, 12,* 26–33.

Huberman, M., & Miles, M. (1984). *Innovation up close: How school improvement works.* New York: Plenum.

Irwin, C. D., Jr. (Ed.). (1987). *Adolescent social behavior and health: New Directions for Child Development* (No. 37). San Francisco: Jossey-Bass.

Jones, B. F. (1986). Quality and equality through cognitive instruction. *Educational Leadership, 43,* 4–11.

Journal of School Health. (1990). Comprehensive school health programs: Their current status and future prospects. *60*(4), entire issue.

Kanfer, F., & Busemeyer, J. (1982). The use of problem-solving and decision-making in behavior therapy. *Clinical Psychology Review, 2,* 239–266.

Kaplan, S. (1975). Adaptation, structure and knowledge. In G. T.

Moore & R. G. Golledge (Eds.), *Environmental knowing: Theories, perspectives, and methods.* Stroudsburg, Pa.: Dowden, Hutchinson, & Ross.

Kelly, J. G. (1979). 'Tain't what you do, it's the way that you do it. *American Journal of Community Psychology, 7,* 244–261.

King, D. (1986, June). Broad-based support pushes health education beyond what the coach does between sessions. *Association for Supervision and Curriculum Development Curriculum Update,* pp. 1–8.

Kuhn, T. S. (1970). *The structure of scientific revolutions* (2nd ed.). Chicago: University of Chicago Press.

Ladd, G. W., & Mize, J. (1983). A cognitive social learning model of social skills training. *Psychological Review, 90,* 127–157.

Lazarus, R. S., & Folkman, S. (1984). *Stress, appraisal, and coping.* New York: Springer.

Levine, D. (1988). Teaching thinking to at-risk students. Generalizations and speculation. In B. Presseisen (Ed.), *At-risk students and thinking: Perspectives from research* (pp. 117–137). Washington, DC: National Education Association/Research for Better Schools.

Lewin, K. (1951). *Field theory in social science.* New York: Harper & Row.

Lewis, M., & Saarni, C. (Eds.). (1984). *The socialization of affect.* New York: Plenum.

Lipsitz, J. (1977). *Growing up forgotten: A review of research and programs concerning early adolescence.* Lexington, MA: Lexington Books.

Lipsitz, J. (1980, March). *Sexual development of young adolescents.* Speech given before the American Association of Sex Education, Counselors, and Therapists. Carrboro, NC: The Center for Early Adolescence, University of North Carolina at Chapel Hill.

London, P. (1987). Character education and clinical intervention: A paradigm shift for U.S. schools. *Phi Delta Kappan, 68,* 667–673.

Loper, A. (1980). Metacognitive development: Implications for cognitive training. *Exceptional Education Quarterly, 1,* 1–8.

McLaughlin, S. D., Brennan, C., Jacoby, C., Wayne, S., Grady, K., & Snow, D. (1984). *A social-cognitive approach to the prevention of adolescent substance abuse intervention II: Eighth/ninth grade student curriculum: Decision-making.* New Haven: Consultation Center of the Connecticut Mental Health Center, Department of Psychiatry–Yale University School of Medicine and Community Consultation Board.

McLaughlin, S. D., Jacoby, C., Grady, K., & Snow, D. (1986). *A social-cognitive approach to the prevention of adolescent substance abuse, intervention III: Tenth/eleventh grade student curriculum: Decision-making and stress.* New Haven: Consultation Center of the Connecticut Mental Health Center, Department of Psychiatry–Yale University School of Medicine and Community Consultation Board.

Maher, C., & Bennett, R. (1984). *Planning and evaluating special education services.* Englewood Cliffs, NJ: Prentice-Hall.

Maier, N.R.S. (Ed.). (1970). *Problem solving and creativity in individuals and groups.* Belmont, CA: Brooks-Cole.

Mercer, J., Gomez-Palacio, M., & Padilla, E. (1986). The development of practical intelligence in cross-cultural perspective. In R. Sternberg & R. Wagner (Eds.), *Practical intelligence: Nature and origins of competence in the everyday world* (pp. 307–337). New York: Cambridge University Press.

Miller, G. A., Galanter, E., & Pribam, K. H. (1960). *Plans and the structure of behavior.* Troy, MO: Holt, Rinehart & Winston.

Mirman, J., Swartz, R., & Barell, J. (1988). Strategies to help teachers empower at-risk students. In B. Presseisen (Ed.), *At-risk students and thinking: Perspectives from research* (pp. 138–156). Washington, DC: National Education Association/Research for Better Schools.

Mischel, W. (1979). On the interface of cognition and personality: Beyond the person-situation debate. *American Psychologist, 34,* 740–754.

Muñoz, R. F., Snowden, L. R., & Kelly, J. G. (1979). *Social and psychological research in community settings.* San Francisco: Jossey-Bass.

Nader, P. (1989, June). *The concept of "comprehensiveness" in the design and implementation of school health programs.* Paper presented at the National Invitational Conference on Comprehensive School Health Programs, The Carter Center, Atlanta, GA.

National Commission on Excellence in Education. (1983). *A nation at risk: The imperative for educational reform.* Washington, DC: U.S. Government Printing Office.

National Professional School Health Organizations. (1984). Comprehensive school health education. *The Journal of School Health, 54,* 312–315.

Nezu, A. C., Nezu, C., & Perri, M. (1989). *Problem-solving therapy for depression: Theory, research, and clinical guidelines.* New York: Wiley.

Office of Educational Research and Improvement. (1987). *Dealing with dropouts: The urban superintendents' call to action.* Washington, DC: U.S. Government Printing Office.

Osborn, A. F. (1963). *Applied imagination: Principles and procedures of creative problem solving* (3rd ed.). New York: Charles Scribner's Sons.

Papke, M., & Elias, M. J. (in press). Tools for monitoring and evaluating middle school programs. In M. Elias (Ed.), *Social decision making in the middle school: Models for excellence.* Gaithersburg, MD: Aspen.

Parnes, S. J. (1962). Do you really understand brainstorming? In S. J. Parnes & H. F. Harding (Eds.), *A source book for creative thinking.* New York: Charles Scribner's Sons.

Pentz, M. A., Dwyer, J. H., MacKinnon, D. P., Flay, B. R., Hansen, W. B., Wang, E.Y.I., & Johnson, C. A. (1989). A multicommunity trial for primary prevention of adolescent drug abuse: Effects on drug use prevalence. *Journal of the American Medical Association, 261,* 3259–3266.

Perkins, D. N. (1986). Thinking frames. *Educational Leadership, 43*(8), 4–11.

Perry, C. (1991). *The social world of adolescents: Family, peers, school, and culture.* Minneapolis, MN: University of Minnesota Division of Epidemiology.

Perry, C., & Jessor, R. (1985). The concept of health promotion and the prevention of adolescent drug abuse. *Health Education Quarterly, 12,* 169–184.

Price, R., Cowen, E., Lorion, R., & Ramos-McKay, J. (Eds.). (1988). *Fourteen ounces of prevention: A casebook for practitioners.* Washington, DC: American Psychological Association.

Price, R., & Smith, S. (1985). *A guide to evaluating prevention programs in mental health* (DHHS Publication No. ADM 85-144). Washington, DC: U.S. Government Printing Office.

Putallaz, M., & Gottman, J. (1982). Conceptualizing social competence in children. In P. Karoly & J. Steffan (Eds.), *Improving children's competence—Advances in child behavioral analysis and therapy* (Vol. 1). Lexington, MA: Lexington Books.

Ralph, J., & Dwyer, M. C. (1988). *Making the case: Evidence of program effectiveness in schools and classrooms.* Washington, DC: U.S. Department of Education, Office of Educational Research and Improvement.

Ramsey, E., & Patterson, G. R. (1989). Coping with antisocial children. *Principal, 69*(2), 34–47.

Reichenbach, H. (1928). *Experience and prediction.* Chicago: University of Chicago Press.

Robinson, B., & Elias, M. J. (in preparation). Contribution of nonverbal skills to the social competence and treatment of emotionally disturbed children.

Rotter, J. B. (1954). *Social learning and clinical psychology.* Englewood Cliffs, NJ: Prentice-Hall.

Rotter, J. B. (1978). Generalized expectancies for problem solving and psychotherapy. *Cognitive Research and Therapy, 2,* 1–10.

Rutter, M. (1975). *Helping troubled children.* New York: Plenum.

Rutter, M. (1987). Psychosocial resilience and protective mechanisms. *American Journal of Orthopsychiatry, 57,* 316–331.

Sanford, N. (1970). Whatever happened to action research? *Journal of Social Issues, 26,* 3–23.

Sarason, S. B. (1978). The nature of problem solving in social action. *American Psychologist, 33,* 370–380.

Sarason, S. (1982). *The culture of the school and the problem of change* (2nd ed.). Needham Heights, MA: Allyn & Bacon.

Schank, P., & Abelson, R. P. (1977). *Scripts, plans, goals, and understanding: An inquiry into human knowledge structures.* Hillsdale, NJ: Erlbaum.

Schorr, L. (1988). *Within our reach: Breaking the cycle of disadvantage.* New York: Doubleday.

Shure, M. B., & Spivack, G. (1974). *ICPS: A mental health program for kindergarten and first-grade children.* Philadelphia: Hahnemann University, Department of Mental Health Services.

Shure, M. B., & Spivack, G. (1978). *Problem solving techniques in childrearing.* San Francisco: Jossey-Bass.

Shure, M. B., & Spivack, G. (1982). *ICPS: A mental health program for intermediate elementary grades.* Philadelphia: Hahnemann University, Department of Mental Health Services.

Sigel, I. (Ed.) (1985). *Parental belief systems: The psychological consequences for children.* Hillsdale, NJ: Erlbaum.

Smith, C. E. (1989). *Assessing student improvement in study skills: The role of O/S.* New Brunswick, NJ: Rutgers University.

Spivack, G., Platt, J. J., & Shure, M. B. (1976). *The problem-solving approach to adjustment.* San Francisco: Jossey-Bass.

Spivack, G., & Shure, M. (1974). *Social adjustment of young children.* San Francisco: Jossey-Bass.

Stephens, T. (1980). Foreword. In G. Cartledge & J. Milburn (Eds.), *Teaching social skills to children.* Elmsford, NY: Pergamon Press.

Sternberg, R., & Wagner, R. (Eds.). (1986). *Practical intelligence: Nature and organization of competence in the everyday world.* Cambridge: Cambridge University Press.

Stolz, S. (1984). Preventive models: Implications for a technology of practice. In M. Roberts & L. Peterson (Eds.), *Prevention of problems in childhood* (pp. 391–413). New York: Wiley.

Stone, G. L., Hinds, W. C., & Schmidt, G. W. (1975). Teaching mental health behaviors to elementary children. *Professional Psychology, 6,* 34–40.

Tobias, S., & Elias, M. J. (1991). *FIG TESPN goes to middle school: A social decision making program for regular and special education.* New Brunswick, NJ: Rutgers University.

Toepfer, C., & Marani, J. (1980). School based research. In M. Johnson (Ed.), *Toward adolescence: The middle school years. Seventy-ninth yearbook of the National Society for the Study of education.* Chicago: University of Chicago Press.

Urbain, E. S. (1985). *The friendship group manual for social skills development (elementary grades—Interpersonal problem-solving training for friendship-making).* St. Paul, MN: Wilder Child Guidance Center.

Urbain, E. S., & Kendall, P. C. (1980). Review of social-cognitive problem-solving interventions with children. *Psychological Bulletin, 88,* 109–143.

Walberg, H. J. (1986). What works in a nation still at risk. *Educational Leadership, 44,* 7–11.

Waters, E., & Sroufe, L. A. (1983). Social competence as a developmental construct. *Developmental Review, 3,* 79–97.

Weick, K. E. (1984). Small wins: Redefining the scale of social problems. *American Psychologist, 39,* 40–49.

Weissberg, R. P., Caplan, M. Z., & Harwood, R. L. (in press). Promoting competent young people in competence-enhancing environments. *Journal of Consulting and Clinical Psychology, 59.*

Weissberg, R. P., Caplan, M. Z., & Sivo, P. J. (1989). A new conceptual framework for establishing school-based social competence promotion programs. In L. A. Bond & B. E. Compas (Eds.), *Primary prevention and promotion in the schools* (pp. 255–296). Newbury Park, CA: Sage.

Weissberg, R. P., Gesten, E. K., Liebenstein, N. L., Schmid, K. D., & Hutton, H. (1980). *The Rochester social problem-solving program (SPS): A training manual for teachers of 2nd–4th grade children.* Rochester, NY: Primary Mental Health Project, Center for Community Study.

Welland, K., & Elias, M. J. (in press). Self-organization/study skills modules for students entering middle school. In M. Elias (Ed.), *Social decision making in the middle school: Models for excellence.* Gaithersburg, MD: Aspen.

Westchester County Social Competence in the Schools Task Force. (1990). *Promoting social development in elementary school children: A task force report.* Westchester County, NY: Department of Community Mental Health.

White, B. (1988). *Educating the infant and toddler.* Lexington, MA: Lexington Books.

William T. Grant Commission on Work, Family, & Citizenship (1988). *The forgotten half: Pathways to success for America's youth and young families.* New York: William T. Grant foundation.

Winters, W. G., & Easton, F. (1983). *The practice of social work in the schools.* New York: Free Press.

Zins, J., & Forman, S. (1988). Mini-series on primary prevention in the schools: From theory to practice. *School Psychology Review*, *17*(4), 539–634.

Zins, J. E., & Ponti, C. R. (1990). Best practices in school-based consultation. In A. Thomas & J. Grimes (Eds.), *Best practices in school psychology—II* (pp. 673–694). Washington, DC: National Association of School Psychologists.

Index

A

A-VICTORY framework, for matching and planning, 101–108

Abelson, R. P., 23

Ability, of school, in matching and planning, 102–104

Absence and tardiness, and program effectiveness, 82

Academic organizational problems: counseling for, 206–209; middle school program for, 240–241

Academic performance, and program effectiveness, 84–85

Achenbach, T., 88

Action research: applies to program development, 45–69; aspects of, 43–91; background on, 45–51; case history of, 51–69; and community need, 52–53; concept of, 45; conclusions on, 68–69, 256–257; context for, 260–262; critical indicators for, 48–49; and curriculum development, 267–272; decision points in, 47, 49; evaluation in, 59–60; facets in cycle of, 46–47; formulation and

setting for, 55–56; idea and need coinciding for, 54–61; and implications for school interventions, 62–63; negotiation and reformulation of, 57–59; procedures in, 65–66, 91; on program effectiveness, 70–91; and service delivery system, 63–68; on variations, 233–257; vehicles for, 60–62, 237, 240–244, 247–248, 250–252, 254–255

Activity-Mood-Learning, 86

Adjustment: and scripts, 24; social competence distinct from, 12–13

Adolescents: addressing needs of, 136–157; cognitive/intellectual changes for, 139; developmental characteristics of, 138–140; older, 148–149; physiological/sexual changes for, 138–139; social/emotional changes for, 139–140; sociological change for, 141. *See also* Children; Secondary level; Students

Agency for Instructional Technology, 154

Ageton, S., 88

Allen, G. J., 21